Collins
CANADIAN
WORLDATLAS

bringing the world to life

contents

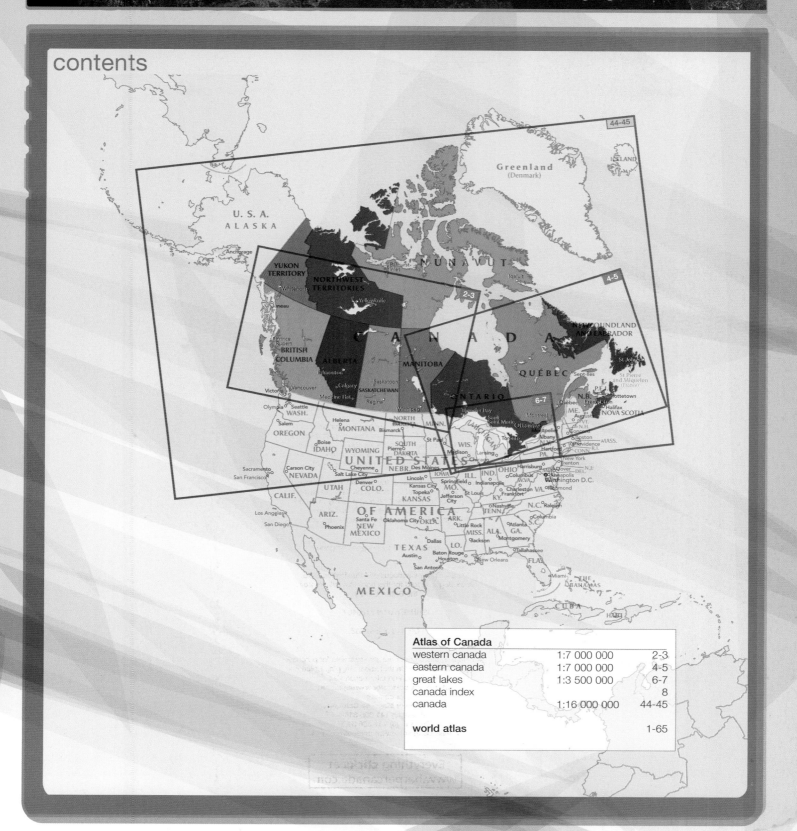

Atlas of Canada		
western canada	1:7 000 000	2-3
eastern canada	1:7 000 000	4-5
great lakes	1:3 500 000	6-7
canada index		8
canada	1:16 000 000	44-45
world atlas		1-65

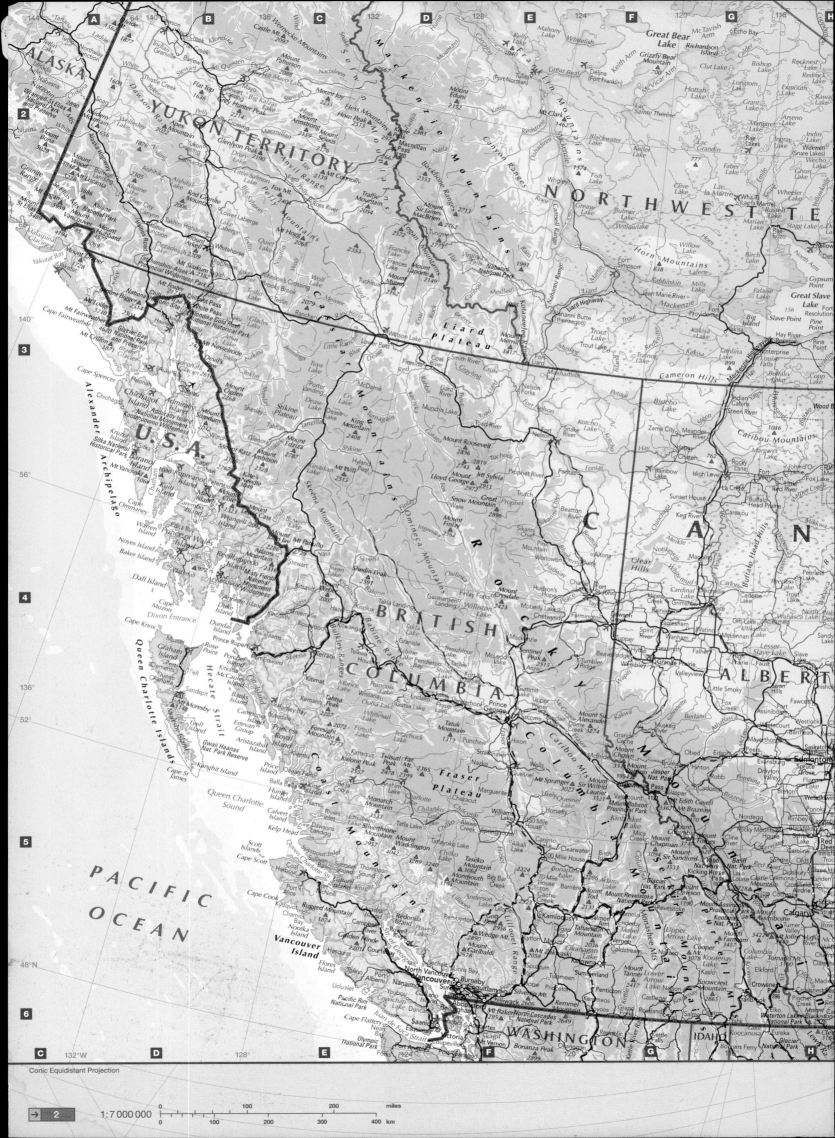

canada
western canada

3

This index includes the names of the most significant places and physical features in Canada. Names are indexed to the Canadian regional maps in the Atlas of Canada section, and to the map of Canada on pages 44-45 in the World Atlas section. For an explanation of any abbreviations used in this index, refer to page 57 of the main index to the world atlas.

2F5 100 Mile House
3I5 Abbey
2F5 Abbotsford
3L1 Aberdeen Lake
7G1 Abitibi r.
7G1 Abitibi, Lake
7G4 Acton
7K3 Acton Vale
5K3 Adlavik Islands
6E2 Agawa r.
5J4 Aguanus r.
7G4 Ailsa Craig
2H5 Airdrie
7H4 Ajax
4E3 Akimiski Island
44E3 Aklavik
5I1 Akpatok Island
4E3 Albany r.
2H4 Alberta prov.
5K3 Alexis r.
2F4 Alexis Creek
7H3 Algonquin Park
5I5 Allardville
5H4 Alma
45K3 Amadjuak Lake
2D3 Ambition, Mount
5I5 Amherst
6F4 Amherstburg
7I3 Amherst Island
7H1 Amos
45I2 Amund Ringnes Island
44F2 Amundsen Gulf
6E1 Amyot
44F3 Anderson r.
3H4 Andrew
7H3 Angus
7G1 Ansonville
5J4 Anticosti, Île d' i.
5J5 Antigonish
3L5 Arborg
45J2 Arctic Bay
44C2 Arctic Ocean
44E3 Arctic Red r.
5I6 Argyle
7G4 Arkona
3J5 Arm r.
5H2 Arnaud r.
7I3 Arnprior
6C1 Arrow r.
7G4 Arthur
3I2 Artillery Lake
3M2 Arviat
6D1 Ashburton Bay
4D3 Asheweig r.
5I3 Ashuanipi r.
7K1 Ashuapmushuan r.
3J5 Assiniboia
3L5 Assiniboine r.
2H5 Assiniboine, Mount
3I3 Athabasca r.
3I3 Athabasca, Lake
7J3 Athens
4E3 Atikameg r.
4E3 Attawapiskat
4E3 Attawapiskat r.
6F2 Aubinadong r.
7G4 Auburn
4D4 Auden
7J2 Augustines, Lac des l.
5L5 Avalon Peninsula
45I2 Axel Heiberg Island
7G4 Aylmer
3I1 Aylmer Lake
2E4 Babine r.
3M1 Back r.
2D2 Backbone Ranges mts
45L2 Baffin Bay sea
45L3 Baffin Island
5H4 Baie-Comeau
5H5 Baie-St-Paul
3J1 Baillie r.
3M1 Baker Lake
3M1 Baker Lake l.
3K5 Baldy Mountain hill
7I3 Bancroft
2H5 Banff
2D4 Banks Island
44F2 Banks Island
3M2 Barbour Bay
7I1 Barraute
2H4 Barrhead
7H3 Barrie
5I6 Barrington
45I2 Barrow Strait
7I3 Barrys Bay
7J2 Baskatong, Réservoir
6E2 Batchawana r.
5I5 Bath
7I3 Bath
5I5 Bathurst
44F2 Bathurst, Cape
44H3 Bathurst Inlet
44H3 Bathurst Inlet inlet
45I2 Bathurst Island
3I4 Battle r.
3I4 Battleford
5L4 Bauld, Cape
7G4 Bayfield
7J2 Bazin r.
4E3 Bear Island
2F3 Beatton r.
7I1 Beattyville
44D2 Beaufort Sea
3H2 Beaulieu r.
3L5 Beauséjour
2E3 Beaver r.
3J4 Beaver r.
4D3 Beaver r.
2G4 Beaverlodge
5J5 Bedford
7K3 Bedford
4F2 Belcher Islands
7I1 Bell r.
2D4 Bella Bella
5L4 Belle Isle i.
5K4 Belle Isle, Strait of
7I3 Belleville
44F3 Belot, Lac l.
3L4 Berens r.
3L4 Berens River
2G4 Berland r.
5H4 Betsiamites r.
5K3 Big r.
3J4 Biggar
2C2 Big Salmon r.
3J4 Big Sandy Lake
3N4 Big Trout Lake
3H4 Big Valley
3H3 Birch r.
3M5 Birch Lake
2H3 Birch Mountains
2G3 Bistcho Lake
3L5 Black r.
6D1 Black r.
7G1 Black r.
3L5 Black Island
3J3 Black Lake
6C1 Black Sturgeon r.
7G4 Blenheim
3L5 Bloodvein r.
7I4 Bloomfield
2D3 Blue r.
2F3 Blueberry r.
7H3 Bobcaygeon
3K5 Boissevain
7H4 Bolton
5L4 Bonavista
3I4 Bonnyville
45J3 Boothia, Gulf of
45I2 Boothia Peninsula
45G2 Borden Island
45J2 Borden Peninsula
5H2 Borel r.
7G4 Bothwell
5L4 Botwood
7K3 Boucherville
7G1 Bourkes
3I5 Bow r.
7H3 Bracebridge
7H3 Bradford
7H4 Brampton
3L5 Brandon
7G4 Brantford
5J5 Bras d'Or Lake
2H4 Brazeau r.
5I5 Bridgetown
5I5 Bridgewater
7I3 Brighton
2F5 British Columbia prov.
4F4 Broadback r.
7J3 Brockville
45J2 Brodeur Peninsula
3L5 Brokenhead r.
3I5 Brooks
7G3 Bruce Peninsula
3J4 Bruno
5H1 Buet r.
2H2 Buffalo r.
2G3 Buffalo Head Hills
3I4 Buffalo Narrows
3K1 Bullen r.
5K5 Burgeo
5L5 Burin
5L5 Burin Peninsula
7H4 Burlington
2F5 Burnaby
44H3 Burnside r.
2E4 Burns Lake
3L4 Burntwood r.
5H2 Buron r.
45K2 Bylot Island
5H5 Cabano
7G3 Cabot Head
5J5 Cabot Strait
2G3 Cadotte r.
2G1 Calder r.
7H4 Caledonia
2H5 Calgary
7I2 Camachigama r.
7G4 Cambridge
45H3 Cambridge Bay
2G3 Cameron Hills
45H2 Cameron Island
7I3 Campbellford
3J2 Campbell Lake
2E5 Campbell River
7I3 Campbells Bay
5I5 Campbellton
3H4 Camrose
5I5 Canaan r.
5H3 Caniapiscau
5H2 Caniapiscau r.
5H3 Caniapiscau, Lac l.
3K5 Canora
2E2 Canyon Ranges mts
5J5 Cap-aux-Meules
7K2 Cap-de-la-Madeleine
5J5 Cape Breton Island
5J5 Cape George
5I5 Caraquet
2D1 Carcajou r.
2H5 Cardston
2F4 Cariboo Mountains
2E2 Caribou r.
3M3 Caribou r.
45J4 Caribou Lake
2H3 Caribou Mountains
3K5 Carlyle
3L5 Carman
3K4 Carrot r.
7G2 Cartier
44F5 Cascade Range mts
2D2 Cassiar Mountains
2G5 Castlegar
4F3 Castor, Rivière du r.
5J2 Caubvick, Mount
5I4 Causapscal
7H4 Cayuga
3K4 Cedar Lake
5I4 Chaleur Bay inlet
5H3 Chambeaux, Lac l.
7K1 Chambord
7K3 Champlain, Lake
5I4 Chandler
5K5 Channel-Port-aux-Basques
6F2 Chapleau
3J5 Chaplin
5H5 Charlesbourg
3I3 Charles Lake
5J5 Charlottetown
3M4 Charron Lake
2G5 Chase
7K3 Châteauguay
5H2 Châteauguay r.
7F4 Chatham
7G3 Chatsworth
5I5 Chester
3N2 Chesterfield Inlet
3M2 Chesterfield Inlet inlet
7J3 Chesterville
2F4 Chetwynd
4G3 Chevreulx r.
4G4 Chibougamau
5H4 Chicoutimi
45L3 Chidley, Cape
2F4 Chilanko r.
2F5 Chilcotin r.
2F4 Chilko r.
2C3 Chilkoot Pass
2F5 Chilliwack
2G3 Chinchaga r.
5I5 Chipman
4F3 Chisasibi
45L2 Christian, Cape
3I3 Christina r.
3M3 Churchill
3M3 Churchill r.
5J3 Churchill r.
3M3 Churchill, Cape
3H3 Claire, Lake
5L4 Clarenville
2H5 Claresholm
2G3 Clear Hills
2H4 Clearwater r.
3I3 Clearwater r.
3J1 Clinton-Colden Lake
6C1 Cloud Bay
45L2 Clyde River
2E3 Coal r.
2E4 Coast Mountains
5H5 Coaticook
45J3 Coats Island
7I3 Cobden
3M4 Cobham r.
45K2 Coburg Island
2H5 Cochrane
7G1 Cochrane
3K3 Cochrane r.
5J2 Cod Island
7I4 Colborne
3I4 Cold Lake
2G5 Coldstream
3I5 Coleville
7G3 Collingwood
45H2 Collinson Peninsula
2G4 Columbia, Mount
2F4 Columbia Mountains
45J3 Committee Bay
4F3 Conn r.
3I4 Consort
7K3 Contrecoeur
3I1 Contwoyto Lake
7G2 Copper Cliff
2H1 Coppermine r.
2F5 Coquitlam
5K4 Corner Brook
7J3 Cornwall
45I2 Cornwallis Island
45I2 Cornwall Island
44G3 Coronation Gulf
7I3 Coulonge r.
2E5 Courtenay
6F2 Cow r.
7K3 Cowansville
2H5 Cranbrook
3J3 Cree r.
3J3 Cree Lake
7G3 Creemore
3K4 Creighton
2G5 Creston
7G3 Croker, Cape
3L4 Cross Lake
2H5 Crowsnest Pass
2H5 Crowsnest Pass pass
45L3 Cumberland Peninsula
45L3 Cumberland Sound sea chan.
3I5 Cypress Hills
3M4 Dafoe r.
5I4 Dalhousie
3J4 Dalmeny
5J5 Dartmouth
3K5 Dauphin
3J5 Davidson
5J3 Davis Inlet
45M3 Davis Strait
2B1 Dawson
2F4 Dawson Creek
2D3 Dease r.
44H3 Dease Strait
3J4 Debden
7I2 Deep River
3M4 Deer Lake
5H2 Delay r.
2F1 Délįne
3K5 Deloraine
7I3 Denbigh
4F3 Denys r.
6F2 Devon
45I2 Devon Island
2H5 Didsbury
3I5 Diefenbaker, Lake
5I5 Digby
3I4 Dillon r.
5H5 Disraëli
2C4 Dixon Entrance sea chan.
6C1 Dog r.
6C1 Dog Lake
7K1 Dolbeau
2H4 Drayton Valley
7F4 Dresden
3H5 Drumheller
5G5 Drummondville
7K3 Drummondville
2C2 Drury Lake
3M5 Dryden
3L2 Dubawnt r.
3K2 Dubawnt Lake
4F2 Dufferin, Cape
7I2 Dumoine r.
2F5 Duncan
4F3 Duncan, Lac l.
7H4 Dundas
7H4 Dunnville
7G3 Durham
45L3 Dyer, Cape
5K3 Eagle r.
3J4 Eagle Creek r.
6C1 Eaglehead Lake
2G4 Eaglesham
4F3 Eastmain r.
5J5 East Point
7H4 East York
2G1 Echo Bay
6E2 Echo Bay
3M4 Echoing r.
2G4 Edith Cavell, Mount
2H4 Edmonton
5H5 Edmundston
2G4 Edson
2D3 Edziza, Mount
4E3 Ekwan r.
5J2 Eliot, Mount
2H5 Elk r.
2H5 Elkford
3I4 Elk Point
45H2 Ellef Ringnes Island
45J2 Ellesmere Island
3K1 Ellice r.
6F2 Elliot Lake
5J5 Elmira
7G4 Elmira
7J3 Embrun
2G2 Emile r.
7H3 Emsdale
2G5 Enderby
3M5 English r.
7G4 Erie, Lake
7G4 Erin
44E3 Eskimo Lakes
7G2 Espanola
2F5 Esquimalt
6F4 Essex
3K5 Estevan
7H4 Etobicoke
45J2 Eureka Sound sea chan.
2H4 Evansburg
3P2 Evans Strait
6F3 Evansville
7G4 Exeter
5L4 Exploits r.
2G3 Fairview
2B3 Fairweather, Mount
5H2 False r.
2G5 Farnham, Mount
3N4 Fawn r.
7G4 Fergus
5H2 Feuilles, Rivière aux r.
2E3 Finlay r.
2E3 Finlay, Mount
2F4 Finlay Forks
45J3 Fisher Strait
3M4 Flanagan r.
2E2 Flat r.
3K4 Flin Flon
6E1 Flint Lake
3K5 Foam Lake
3J3 Fond du Lac r.
2F3 Fontas r.
2G4 Forbes, Mount
2E4 Foresight Mountain
7G4 Forest
5H4 Forestville
4E3 Fort Albany
2H4 Fort Assiniboine
2F2 Fort Liard
2H5 Fort Macleod
3I3 Fort McMurray
2F3 Fort Nelson
2F3 Fort Nelson r.
2H4 Fort Saskatchewan
4D2 Fort Severn
2F2 Fort Simpson
3H2 Fort Smith
2E4 Fort St James
2F3 Fort St John
5L5 Fortune Bay
2E3 Fox r.
3M3 Fox r.
2G4 Fox Creek
45K3 Foxe Basin g.
45J3 Foxe Channel
45K3 Foxe Peninsula
7I3 Frankford
2F2 Franklin Mountains
45I2 Franklin Strait
2F5 Fraser r.
5J2 Fraser r.
7G1 Fraserdale
2E4 Fraser Lake
2E4 Fraser Plateau
7G1 Frederick House r.
5I5 Fredericton
45L3 Frobisher Bay
3N2 Fullerton, Cape
5I5 Fundy, Bay of g.
5L4 Gambo
7I3 Gananoque
5L4 Gander
7G1 Gardiner
6E2 Gargantua, Cape
2F5 Garibaldi, Mount
5I4 Gaspé
5I4 Gaspé, Cap c.
5I4 Gaspé, Péninsule de pen.
2E3 Gataga r.
7J3 Gatineau
7J3 Gatineau r.
3L3 Gauer Lake
3K3 Geikie r.
5I2 George r.
7G3 Georgian Bay
6D1 Geraldton
45J2 Gifford r.
3M3 Gillam
4G3 Gipouloux r.
5K5 Glace Bay
3L5 Glenboro
7G4 Glencoe
6E2 Glendale
5L4 Glovertown
7G4 Goderich
3M3 Gods r.
3O1 Gordon r.
7J1 Gouin, Réservoir
6B1 Graham
2C4 Graham Island
45I2 Graham Island
7K3 Granby
5L5 Grand Bank
5I5 Grand Bay
7G4 Grand Bend
2G4 Grande Cache
2G4 Grande Prairie
5I5 Grand Falls
5L4 Grand Falls
2G5 Grand Forks
5G5 Grand-Mère
7K2 Grand-Mère
3L4 Grand Rapids
3L3 Grass r.
7H3 Gravenhurst
2E3 Grayling r.
2E1 Great Bear r.
2G1 Great Bear Lake
3I5 Great Sand Hills
2H2 Great Slave Lake
2E3 Great Snow Mountain
2D4 Greenville
3K5 Grenfell
5L4 Grey Islands
2G3 Grimshaw
7G1 Groundhog r.
5H2 Guè, Rivière du r.
7G4 Guelph
3L4 Gunisao r.
2F3 Halfway r.
7H3 Haliburton
7H3 Haliburton Highlands hills
5J5 Halifax
45L3 Hall Peninsula
7H3 Halls Lake
7H4 Hamilton
5K3 Hamilton Inlet
3I5 Hanna
7G3 Hanover
5J3 Happy Valley - Goose Bay
2H3 Harper Creek r.
7H1 Harricanaw r.
5K3 Harrison, Cape
44E3 Hart r.
7I3 Hastings
3J4 Haultain r.
7I3 Havelock
5J4 Havre-St-Pierre
5K4 Hawkes Bay
7J3 Hawkesbury
2H2 Hay r.
3M3 Hayes r.
45I3 Hayes r.
44G3 Hay River
45G2 Hazen Strait
6F1 Hearst
5J2 Hebron
2D4 Hecate Strait
7K3 Hemmingford
4E3 Henrietta Maria, Cape
7G4 Hensall
2C2 Hess r.
2C2 Hess Mountains
2G3 High Level
2G4 High Prairie
2H5 High River
2G4 Hinton
45L3 Home Bay
5I4 Honguedo, Détroit d' sea chan.
2F5 Hope
4F2 Hopewell Islands
2G2 Horn r.
6E1 Hornepayne
2F2 Horn Mountains
2D2 Horn Peak
5L4 Horse Islands
44F3 Horton r.
2G1 Hottah Lake
2E4 Houston
7K3 Howick
5I2 Hubbard, Pointe pt
3K4 Hudson Bay
45J4 Hudson Bay sea
45K3 Hudson Strait
3K3 Hughes r.
7J3 Hull
3J4 Humboldt
2D1 Hume r.
7J3 Huntingdon
7H3 Huntsville
7G3 Hurd, Cape
6F3 Huron, Lake
5G3 Iberville, Lac d' l.
6B1 Ignace
2B2 Indian r.
3K5 Indian Head
2E3 Ingenika r.
7G4 Ingersoll
2C3 Inklin r.
2H4 Innisfail
4F2 Inukjuak
44E3 Inuvik
5J5 Inverness
45L3 Iqaluit
6F2 Iron Bridge
7G1 Iroquois Falls
2F2 Island r.
3M4 Island Lake
45K3 Ivujivik
5I4 Jacques-Cartier, Détroit de sea chan.
5I4 Jacques Cartier, Mont mt.
4E3 James Bay
45I3 James Ross Strait
2G4 Jasper
6D1 Jellicoe
2C3 Jennings r.
7K2 Joliette
45J2 Jones Sound sea chan.
5H4 Jonquière
44F5 Juan de Fuca Strait
6E1 Kabinakagami r.
6E1 Kabinakagami Lake
2G4 Kakwa r.
7I3 Kaladar
2E4 Kalone Peak
2F5 Kamloops
3K5 Kamsack
4F3 Karaaupscow r.
5K3 Karairiktok r.
5I2 Kangiqsualujjuaq
5H1 Kangirsuk
4E3 Kapiskau r.
6F1 Kapuskasing
3K2 Kasba Lake
3K3 Kasmere Lake
3M2 Kazan r.
2E3 Kechika r.
5I5 Kedgwick
2E1 Keele r.
2D2 Keele Peak
3M5 Keewatin
2F1 Keith Arm b.
2G5 Kelowna
3K4 Kelvington
7H2 Kerabeek
45J3 Kendall, Cape
4D4 Kenogami r.
3M5 Kenora
44H3 Kent Peninsula
3I5 Kerrobert
7H3 Keswick
2G5 Kettle r.
7G3 Key Harbour
2G5 Kicking Horse Pass
7G3 Killarney
2G4 Kinbasket Lake
3J5 Kincaid
7G3 Kincardine
3I5 Kindersley
4F2 King George Islands
2E4 King Island
7I3 Kingston
45I3 King William Island
4E3 Kinushseo r.
7H3 Kirkfield
7G1 Kirkland Lake
7G4 Kitchener
2D4 Kitimat
2C4 Knox, Cape
2G5 Kootenay r.
2G5 Kootenay Lake
44G3 Kugluktuk
5H2 Kuujjuaq
4F3 Kuujjuarapik
5H4 La Baie
5I2 La Baleine, Rivière à r.
7J2 Labelle
5J3 Labrador reg.
5I3 Labrador City
45M3 Labrador Sea
7K2 Lac-aux-Sables
7K1 Lac Bouchette
3L5 Lac du Bonnet
7J3 Lachute
3I4 Lac La Biche
2H4 Lacombe
2G2 Laferte r.
5G3 Laforge r.
4F3 La Grande 2, Réservoir
4G3 La Grande 3, Réservoir
5G3 La Grande 4, Réservoir
45K4 La Grande 4, Réservoir
7H3 Lakefield
5J5 La Madeleine, Îles de is
5H5 La Malbaie
2G2 La Martre, Lac l.
7G4 Lambeth
7I3 Lanark
7J3 Lancaster
45J2 Lancaster Sound strait
3K5 Langenburg
2F5 Langley
3J5 Lanigan
5G2 La Potherie, Lac l.
7G2 Larchwood
7H1 Larder Lake
3J4 La Ronge
3J4 La Ronge, Lac l.
7K3 La Salle
7H1 La Sarre
5L4 La Scie
7K2 La Tuque
7K3 Laval
2D4 Lax Kw'alaams
6F4 Leamington
4G2 L'Eau Claire, Lac à l.
7I1 Lebel-sur-Quévillon
2H4 Leduc
5H2 Lefroy r.
4D4 Legarde r.
45L3 Lemieux Islands
5H1 Lepellé r.
5I5 Lepreau, Point
2H4 Lesser Slave Lake
3H5 Lethbridge
5H5 Lévis
2E2 Liard Plateau
7J3 Limoges
7H3 Lindsay
7K2 Linton
2F5 Lions Bay
7G4 Listowel
3M3 Little Churchill r.
7G3 Little Current
4D4 Little Current r.
5I5 Liverpool
3I4 Lloydminster
6E1 Lochalsh
2A2 Logan, Mount
2F5 Logan Lake
2D2 Logan Mountains
7G4 London
6D1 Longlac
7G4 Long Point
3L4 Long Point pt
7G4 Long Point pt
7G4 Long Point Bay
5K4 Long Range Mountains
5K5 Long Range Mountains
7K3 Longueuil
2H3 Loon r.
4F3 Louis-XIV, Pointe pt
45J3 Low, Cape
2G5 Lower Arrow Lake
7G4 Lucknow
3J5 Lumsden
3M1 Lunan Lake
7G4 Luther Lake
3I2 Łutselk'e
2D4 Lyell Island
3J2 Lynx Lake
3I3 MacKay r.
3I2 MacKay Lake
2F4 Mackenzie
2F2 Mackenzie r.
44E3 Mackenzie Bay
45G2 Mackenzie King Island
2C1 Mackenzie Mountains
2C2 Macmillan r.
7I3 Madawaska r.
7I3 Madoc
3K4 Mafeking
5G5 Magog
5I4 Magpie r.
6E2 Magpie r.
4F4 Maicasagi r.
45L5 Maine, Gulf of
5H4 Manicouagan
5H4 Manicouagan r.
5H4 Manicouagan, Réservoir
3L4 Manitoba prov.
3L5 Manitoba, Lake
7F3 Manitoulin Island
7J2 Maniwaki
2G3 Manning
5H4 Manouane r.
45K3 Mansel Island
3I5 Maple Creek
3I1 Mara r.
6D1 Marathon
4F2 Marcopeet Islands
4F2 Mariet r.
7G3 Markdale
7H4 Markham
2F2 Martin r.
5L3 Mary's Harbour
7K3 Mascouche
7F2 Massey
4F4 Matagami
4F4 Matagami, Lac l.
5I4 Matane
7K2 Matawin r.
7G1 Mattagami r.
7H2 Mattawa
7I3 Maynooth
5I5 McAdam
45H2 McClintock Channel
44G2 McClure Strait
2H2 McCrea r.
2F4 McGregor r.
7G2 McGregor Bay
2G4 McLennan
2H4 McLeod r.
2F4 McLeod Lake
2B2 McQuesten r.
2G1 McTavish Arm b.
2F1 McVicar Arm b.
3I4 Meadow Lake
7G3 Meaford
5K3 Mealy Mountains
3I5 Medicine Hat
2G3 Meikle r.
2E2 Meilleur r.
2D2 Meister r.
6F3 Meldrum Bay
3J4 Melfort
3K5 Melita
3K5 Melville
45H2 Melville Island
45J3 Melville Peninsula
45L3 Mercy, Cape
2F5 Merritt
7I2 Messines
5H4 Métabetchouan
6E2 Michipicoten Bay
7K1 Micosas r.
5I5 Middleton
7H3 Midland
2H3 Mikkwa r.
7K2 Milieu r.
7H3 Millbrook
6B1 Mille Lacs, Lac des l.
2H4 Millet
3L5 Minnedosa
44G2 Minto Inlet
5I5 Miramichi
4E4 Missinaibi r.
4D3 Missisa r.
4F4 Missisicabi r.
6F2 Mississagi r.
7H4 Mississauga
7I3 Mississippi r.
5J4 Mistanipisipou r.
45K5 Mistassibi r.
7K1 Mistassini
5G4 Mistassini r.
4G4 Mistassini, Lac l.
7G4 Mitchell
5I4 Moisie r.
2G5 Monashee Mountains
5I5 Moncton
7J3 Montebello
5H4 Mont-Joli
7J2 Mont-Laurier
5H5 Montmagny
7K3 Montréal
6E2 Montreal r.
7H2 Montreal r.
3J4 Montreal Lake
6E2 Montreal River
4E4 Moose r.
3J5 Moose Jaw
3J5 Moose Jaw r.
3K5 Moose Mountain Creek r.
4E4 Moosonee
3L5 Morden
2C4 Moresby Island
7G4 Morpeth
3L5 Morris
3K4 Mossy r.
3I4 Mostoos Hills
2D1 Mountain r.
7G4 Mount Forest
5L5 Mount Pearl
5I2 Mucalic r.
3J3 Mudjatik r.
4D3 Muketei r.
3L4 Mukutawa r.
5L4 Musgrave Harbour
2F2 Muskeg r.
2C2 Nadaleen r.
6E1 Nagagami r.
2F2 Nahanni Range mts
2C3 Nakina r.
2G5 Nakusp
2F5 Nanaimo
45I1 Nansen Sound sea chan.
7G4 Nanticoke
3H1 Napaktulik Lake
7K3 Napierville
45K2 Nares Strait
5J3 Naskaupi r.
2D4 Nass r.
4F2 Nastapoca r.
4F2 Nastapoka Islands
5J4 Natashquan r.
2D2 Natla r.
3L5 Neepawa
2G5 Nelson
3M3 Nelson r.
2F3 Nelson Forks
4F4 Némiscau r.
7J3 Nepean
5I5 Nepisiguit r.
45K3 Nettilling Lake
7I3 Newboro
5I5 New Brunswick prov.
5I4 New Carlisle
7H4 Newcastle
5K4 Newfoundland i.
5K3 Newfoundland and Labrador prov.
5J5 New Glasgow
7H2 New Liskeard
7H3 Newmarket
7H4 Niagara Falls
7H4 Niagara-on-the-Lake
6F2 Nicholson
7K2 Nicolet
7G1 Nighthawk Lake
3J4 Nipawin
6C1 Nipigon
6C1 Nipigon r.
6C1 Nipigon, Lake
7H2 Nipissing, Lake
3N3 Niskibi r.
2B2 Nisling r.
2C2 Nisutlin r.
7I3 Noire r.
3I2 Nonacho Lake
7H1 Noranda
7K1 Normandin
3I4 North Battleford
7H2 North Bay
5I5 North Cape
6F2 North Channel lake channel
4E4 North French r.
3M3 North Knife r.
3J4 North Saskatchewan r.
3L3 North Seal r.
5I5 Northumberland Strait
2F5 North Vancouver
44F3 Northwest Territories admin. div.
7H4 North York
7I3 Norway Bay
45I2 Norwegian Bay
7G4 Norwich
5J2 Notakwanon r.
2G3 Notikewin r.
5H5 Notre Dame, Monts mts
5L4 Notre Dame Bay
7J3 Notre-Dame-de-la-Salette
7H2 Notre-Dame-du-Nord
7G3 Nottawasaga Bay
4F4 Nottaway r.
3J5 Notukeu Creek r.
5I6 Nova Scotia prov.
3L2 Nueltin Lake
4G1 Nunavik reg.
45I3 Nunavut admin. div.
2H2 Nyarling r.
7H4 Oakville
3L3 Odei r.
6E2 Ogidaki
44E3 Ogilvie r.
44D3 Ogilvie Mountains
4D4 Ogoki r.
2G5 Okanagan Lake
2I5 Oldman r.
2H5 Olds
4F4 Olga, Lac l.
5J4 Olomane r.
4D4 Ontario prov.
7I4 Ontario, Lake
6F1 Opasatika r.
4F3 Opinaca r.
4E3 Opinnagau r.
5H3 Opiscotéo, Lac l.
7G4 Orangeville
6C1 Orient Bay
7H3 Orillia
7K3 Ormstown
5I5 Oromocto
6E1 Osawin r.
7J3 Osgoode
7H4 Oshawa
2E3 Osilinka r.
2G5 Osoyoos
5I3 Ossokmanuan Lake
3N5 Otoskwin r.
7J3 Ottawa
4E2 Ottawa Islands
7J3 Outaouais, Rivière des r.
5H4 Outardes r.
3J5 Outlook
7G3 Owen Sound
3M3 Owl r.
3K5 Oxbow
3I5 Oyen
6E1 Pagwachuan r.
7G4 Palmerston
45L3 Pangnirtung
7J3 Papineauville
7I1 Paradis
5K3 Paradise r.
3I4 Paradise Hill
7J2 Parent
7G4 Paris
6F2 Parkinson
45G2 Parry Channel
45G2 Parry Islands
7G3 Parry Sound
4E4 Partridge r.
7J1 Pascagama r.
3K4 Pasquia Hills
2I3 Peace r.
2G3 Peace River
45I2 Peary Channel
44E3 Peel r.
6F5 Pelee Island
7F5 Pelee Point
2C2 Pelly r.
2C2 Pelly Mountains
6F2 Pemache r.
2F5 Pemberton
2H4 Pembina r.
7I3 Pembroke
7H3 Penetanguishene
2G5 Penticton
5I4 Percé
7I3 Perth
5I5 Perth-Andover
7I3 Petawawa
7H3 Peterborough
5K4 Petit Mécatina r.
2F2 Petitot r.
7I4 Petre, Point
7F4 Petrolia
4F3 Piagochioui r.
6D1 Pic r.
7H4 Pickering
7I4 Picton
5J5 Pictou
7G3 Pike Bay
2H5 Pincher Creek
3L5 Pine Falls
3N4 Pineimuta r.
3N4 Pipestone r.
5H4 Pipmuacan, Réservoir
5I3 Pitaga
2D4 Pitt Island
4E4 Pivabiska r.
5L5 Placentia
5L5 Placentia Bay
5I5 Plaster Rock
7G2 Pogamasing
7K1 Pointe-Bleue
2H1 Point Lake
2H4 Ponoka
5H2 Pons r.
4F4 Pontax r.
3L4 Poplar r.
5K3 Porcupine, Cape
3K4 Porcupine Hills
3L5 Portage la Prairie
2E5 Port Alberni
2E5 Port Alice
5K4 Port aux Choix
7H3 Port Bolster
5I4 Port-Cartier
7G3 Port Elgin
7H4 Port Hope
2E5 Port McNeill
5H4 Portneuf r.
7H3 Port Perry
7H3 Port Severn
5L5 Pouch Cove
2E5 Powell River
3K4 Prairie River
3K5 Preeceville
3J4 Prince Albert
44G2 Prince Albert Peninsula
44F2 Prince Alfred, Cape
45K3 Prince Charles Island
5J5 Prince Edward Island prov.
2F4 Prince George
45I2 Prince of Wales Island
44G2 Prince of Wales Strait
44G2 Prince Patrick Island
45I2 Prince Regent Inlet sea chan.
2D4 Prince Rupert
2D4 Princess Royal Island
2F5 Princeton
2F3 Prophet r.
6E1 Pukaskwa r.
2G5 Purcell Mountains
4F1 Puvurnituq
45L3 Qikiqtarjuaq
3K5 Qu'Appelle r.
45L3 Quaqtaq
5H5 Québec
45K4 Québec prov.
2C4 Queen Charlotte
2C4 Queen Charlotte Islands
2D5 Queen Charlotte Sound sea chan.
2E5 Queen Charlotte Strait
45H2 Queen Elizabeth Islands
45H3 Queen Maud Gulf
2F4 Quesnel
3M1 Quoich r.
7I3 Quyon
2E3 Rabbit r.
2F2 Rabbitskin r.
5L5 Race, Cape
2G2 Rae-Edzo
5H4 Ragueneau
2G3 Rainbow Lake
6C1 Raith
2F2 Ram r.
6F2 Ramsey
2D2 Rancheria
2D2 Rancheria r.
7H2 Rapide-Deux
7K2 Rawdon
5K5 Ray, Cape
2E3 Red r.
5K4 Red Bay
2H4 Red Deer
3I5 Red Deer r.
3K4 Red Deer r.
2G2 Redknife r.
3M5 Red Lake
2E5 Redonda Island
6C1 Red Rock
2E1 Redstone r.
7G1 Redstone r.
2H4 Redwater
3J5 Regina
3K4 Reindeer r.
3L4 Reindeer Island
3K3 Reindeer Lake
3I2 Reliance
7I3 Renfrew
45J3 Repulse Bay
45L3 Resolution Island
5I5 Restigouche r.
2G5 Revelstoke
44E3 Richards Island
3I3 Richardson r.
44E3 Richardson Mountains
7J3 Richmond
7J3 Rideau r.
7I3 Rideau Lakes
4D4 Ridge r.
7G4 Ridgetown
7J3 Rigaud
2H4 Rimbey
5H4 Rimouski
3J5 Riverhurst
5I5 Riverview
7K2 Rivière-à-Pierre
7K2 Rivière-aux-Rats
5H5 Rivière-du-Loup
7K1 Roberval
2C2 Robinson
3K5 Roblin
2G4 Robson, Mount
2E2 Rock r.
7J3 Rockland
5K4 Rocky Harbour
2H4 Rocky Mountain House
44H5 Rocky Mountains
45J3 Roes Welcome Sound sea chan.
4F3 Roggan r.
5J4 Romaine r.
2E3 Roosevelt, Mount
2F2 Root r.
2H5 Rosebud r.
2D4 Rose Point
3J5 Rosetown
2G5 Rossland
7H1 Rouyn
4F4 Rupert r.
3K5 Russell
7J3 Russell
7H2 Rutherglen
2F5 Saanich
5I6 Sable, Cape
5K6 Sable Island
7F2 Sables, River aux r.
44F2 Sachs Harbour
5I5 Sackville
5H4 Saguenay r.
2H4 St Albert
7K2 St-Alexis-des-Monts
7J3 St-André-Avellin
5L4 St Anthony
5K4 St-Augustin
5K4 St Augustin r.
7H4 St Catharines
7K3 St-Césaire
6F4 St Clair, Lake
7J3 Ste-Adèle
7J2 Ste-Agathe-des-Monts
3L5 Sainte Anne
7J2 Ste-Anne-du-Lac
7K2 Ste-Émélie-de-l'Énergie
7K3 Ste-Julienne
2A2 St Elias Mountains
5I4 Ste-Marguerite r.
3L5 Sainte Rose du Lac
7K3 Ste-Thérèse
7K3 St-Eustache
7J2 Ste-Véronique
5H4 St-Fabien
7K1 St-Félicien
7K2 St-Félix-de-Valois
7K2 St-François r.
7K2 St-Gabriel
5H5 St-Georges
5K4 St George's Bay
7K3 St-Hyacinthe
7K2 St-Ignace-du-Lac
7H1 St-Jacques-de-Dupuy
5I4 St-Jean r.
7K1 St-Jean, Lac l.
7K3 St-Jean-sur-Richelieu
4G5 St-Jérôme
7J3 St-Jérôme
5I5 Saint John
5L5 St John's
3N5 St Joseph, Lake
7J2 St-Jovité
5L5 St Lawrence
7K3 St Lawrence inlet
5J4 St Lawrence, Gulf of
7J3 St Lawrence Seaway sea chan.
7K2 St-Léonard
5K3 St Lewis r.
7K2 St-Louis-de-France
7G4 St Mary's
7H1 St-Mathieu
7K2 St-Maurice r.
7K2 St-Michel-des-Saints
5H5 St-Pacôme
5H5 St Pascal
5K4 St Paul r.
7K3 St-Pie
7K3 St-Rémi
7J3 St-Sauveur-des-Monts
5H5 St Siméon
7G4 St Thomas
7G4 St Williams
4F3 Sakami r.
4F3 Sakami Lake
7J3 Salaberry-de-Valleyfield
2G5 Salmon Arm
6E2 Sand Lake
3M4 Sandy Lake
4F2 Sanikiluaq
7F4 Sarnia
3J4 Saskatchewan prov.
3K4 Saskatchewan r.
3J4 Saskatoon
2H2 Sass r.
6E2 Sault Sainte Marie
5H4 Savane r.
7H4 Scarborough
5I3 Schefferville
6D1 Schreiber
2D5 Scott, Cape
7G4 Seaforth
3M3 Seal r.
2F5 Sechelt
6B1 Seine r.
3L5 Selkirk
2G4 Selkirk Mountains
2C2 Selous, Mount
3J2 Selwyn Lake
2D1 Selwyn Mountains
7I1 Senneterre
2F4 Sentinel Peak
5I4 Sept-Îles
5H3 Sérigny r.
3M5 Seul, Lac l.
4D3 Severn r.
4D3 Shagamu r.
7K2 Shawinigan
5I5 Shediac
6E1 Shekak r.
5I6 Shelburne
7G3 Shelburne
3J4 Shellbrook
5H5 Sherbrooke
2C3 Sheslay r.
2G5 Sicamous
6C1 Silver Islet
7G4 Simcoe
7H3 Simcoe, Lake
2G4 Simonette r.
7G3 Singhampton
3N5 Sioux Lookout
2E2 Sir James MacBrien, Mount
2G5 Sir Sandford, Mount
2G4 Sir Wilfrid Laurier, Mount
2D4 Skeena r.
2D3 Skeena Mountains
3H2 Slave r.
2H4 Slave Lake
2H2 Slave Point
4F2 Sleeper Islands
5I3 Smallwood Reservoir
7I3 Smiths Falls
7G1 Smooth Rock Falls
2C1 Snake r.
2G2 Snare r.
3I2 Snowdrift r.
3K4 Snow Lake
5L3 Snug Harbour
45I2 Somerset Island
7K2 Sorel
3K5 Souris
3L5 Souris r.
7G3 Southampton
45J3 Southampton Island
7F3 South Baymouth
3L3 Southern Indian Lake
7H3 South River
3J4 South Saskatchewan r.
3L3 South Seal r.
6F2 Spanish
7F2 Spanish r.
2G4 Spirit River
7F3 Spring Bay
5L4 Springdale
5I5 Springhill
2H4 Spruce Grove
7G3 Stayner
6D1 Steel r.
2G3 Steen r.
45H2 Stefansson Island
3L5 Steinbach
3H4 Stettler
2B2 Stewart r.
2C3 Stikine r.
2D3 Stikine Plateau
7I3 Stirling
3L5 Stonewall
4E3 Stooping r.
7G4 Stratford
2H5 Strathmore
7G4 Strathroy
3M4 Stupart r.
3J4 Sturgeon r.
7H2 Sturgeon r.
7H2 Sturgeon Falls
7G2 Sudbury
6F2 Sultan
5L4 Summerford
2H5 Sundre
7H3 Sundridge
6D2 Superior, Lake
2F5 Surrey
7K3 Sutton
4E3 Sutton r.
45I2 Sverdrup Islands
5H2 Swampy r.
3K4 Swan r.
4E3 Swan r.
2H4 Swan Hills
3K4 Swan River
3J5 Swift Current
3J5 Swiftcurrent Creek r.
5J5 Sydney
5J5 Sydney Mines
2H4 Sylvan Lake
3H5 Taber
3L3 Tadoule Lake
2C2 Tagish
2E4 Tahtsa Peak
2C3 Taku
3H2 Taltson r.
3K1 Tammarvi r.
2D3 Tanzilla r.
5H2 Tasiujaq
2E4 Tatuk Mountain
2C2 Tay r.
2F3 Taylor
3I2 Tazin r.
7G3 Teeswater
7H2 Temagami Lake
5G4 Témiscamie r.
6F2 Tenby Bay
2D4 Terrace
6D1 Terrace Bay
2C2 Teslin r.
3M2 Tha-anne r.
7F4 Thames r.
3L1 Thelon r.
3K4 The Pas
6F2 Thessalon
5H5 Thetford Mines
3M2 Thlewiaza r.
3I2 Thoa r.
3L4 Thompson
2F5 Thompson r.
2E5 Thompson Sound
7I3 Thousand Islands
2H5 Three Hills
6C1 Thunder Bay
6C1 Thunder Bay b.
3J5 Thunder Creek r.
5G4 Tichégami r.
6F4 Tilbury
7G4 Tillsonburg
7G1 Timmins
7F1 Tionaga
2E3 Toad r.
7G3 Tobermory
3K4 Tobin Lake
2E5 Tofino
7H2 Tomiko
3K4 Torch r.
2H5 Tornado Mountain
5I2 Torngat Mountains
7H4 Toronto
7K2 Tracy
4C4 Trading r.
2G5 Trail
7J2 Tremblant, Mont hill
2E4 Trembleur Lake
7K2 Trenche r.
7I3 Trenton
5L5 Trepassey
5L5 Trinity Bay
7K2 Trois-Rivières
2E3 Trout r.
2G2 Trout r.
7H3 Trout Creek
2F2 Trout Lake
2F2 Trout Lake l.
3M5 Trout Lake l.
5J5 Truro
2F4 Tumbler Ridge
2D2 Tungsten
7G1 Tunis
5I2 Tunulic r.
7H1 Turgeon r.
2E3 Turnagain r.
2H5 Turner Valley
7I3 Tweed
5I3 Twin Falls
4F2 Umiujaq
4G1 Ungava, Péninsule d' pen.
5I2 Ungava Bay
3I4 Unity
2G5 Upper Arrow Lake
3I3 Uranium City
7H3 Uxbridge
7I1 Val-d'Or
5H5 Vallée-Jonction
2F5 Vancouver
2E5 Vancouver Island
2E4 Vanderhoof
4F3 Vauquelin r.
3H5 Vauxhall
3H4 Vegreville
3I4 Vermilion
7K2 Vermillon r.
7G2 Verner
2G5 Vernon
5H4 Vert, Île i.
2F5 Victoria
44H2 Victoria Island
5H5 Victoriaville
7H2 Ville-Marie
3K5 Virden
45G2 Viscount Melville Sound sea chan.
4C4 Wabakimi Lake
2H3 Wabasca r.
4D4 Wabassi r.
5I3 Wabush
2E5 Waddington, Mount
3K5 Wadena
3I4 Wainwright
3J4 Wakaw
7J3 Wakefield
3L4 Walker Lake
7G3 Walkerton
7F4 Wallaceburg
3I2 Walmsley Lake
2G4 Wapiti r.
3J4 Warman
7G3 Wasaga Beach
4F4 Waskaganish
4F4 Waswanipi r.
7G4 Waterloo
7K3 Waterloo
7G4 Watford
3K3 Wathaman r.
3J5 Watrous
3J4 Watson
2D2 Watson Lake
6E2 Wawa
7H1 Wawagosic r.
4D3 Webequie
7J3 Weir
7H4 Welland
7G4 Wellesley
7I4 Wellington
5K3 West Bay
2H4 Westlock
7G4 West Lorne
2H4 Wetaskiwin
3K5 Weyburn
7H4 Whitby
7H4 Whitchurch-Stouffville
6D1 White r.
5K4 White Bay
2H4 Whitecourt
2E1 Whitefish r.
3J2 Whitefish Lake
2C2 Whitehorse
2G3 Whitemud r.
2C3 White Pass
2H2 Whitesand r.
3K5 Whitewood
3J2 Wholdaia Lake
7G3 Wiarton
6C1 Wild Goose
3I4 Wilkie
2D3 Will, Mount
2F4 Williams Lake
2F4 Williston Lake
2F2 Willowlake r.
7J3 Winchester
2C1 Wind r.
7K2 Windigo r.
5I5 Windsor
6F4 Windsor
7G4 Wingham
4D3 Winisk r.
3L5 Winnipeg
3L5 Winnipeg r.
3L5 Winnipeg, Lake
3K4 Winnipegosis, Lake
2C2 Wolf r.
5I5 Wolfville
3K3 Wollaston Lake
44G3 Wollaston Peninsula
3L5 Woodridge
45I5 Woods, Lake of the
5I5 Woodstock
7G4 Woodstock
7H3 Woodville
3J5 Wynyard
2F5 Yale
5I6 Yarmouth
2H2 Yates r.
2H2 Yellowknife
2H2 Yellowknife r.
7H4 York
3K5 Yorkton
2B2 Yukon r.
2C2 Yukon Territory admin. div.

Collins WORLDATLAS

bringing the world to life

contents

map symbols and time zones		2
national statistics		3–5
world		
world countries	1:83 000 000	6–7
world physical features	1:83 000 000	8–9
europe		
scandinavia and the baltic states	1:5 000 000	10–11
inset: iceland	1:6 000 000	
inset: faroe islands	1:5 000 000	
northwest europe	1:5 000 000	12–13
england and wales	1:2 000 000	14–15
scotland	1:2 000 000	16
inset: shetland	1:2 000 000	
ireland	1:2 000 000	17
france	1:5 000 000	18
spain and portugal	1:5 000 000	19
italy and the balkans	1:5 000 000	20–21
western russian federation	1:7 500 000	22–23
asia		
northern asia	1:20 000 000	24–25
central and southern asia	1:20 000 000	26–27
eastern and southeast asia	1:20 000 000	28–29
japan, north korea and south korea	1:7 000 000	30–31
africa		
northern africa	1:16 000 000	32–33
inset: cape verde	1:16 000 000	
central and southern africa	1:16 000 000	34–35
republic of south africa	1:5 000 000	36–37
oceania		
australia, new zealand and southwest pacific	1:20 000 000	38–39
australia	1:13 000 000	40–41
southeast australia	1:5 000 000	42
new zealand	1:5 250 000	43
north america		
canada	1:16 000 000	44–45
united states of america	1:12 000 000	46–47
inset: hawaiian islands	1:12 000 000	
northeast united states	1:3 500 000	48
southwest united states	1:3 500 000	49
central america and the caribbean	1:14 000 000	50–51
south america		
northern south america	1:14 000 000	52–53
inset: galapagos islands	1:14 000 000	
southern south america	1:14 000 000	54
southeast brazil	1:7 000 000	55
the poles		
arctic ocean and antarctica	1:35 000 000	56
index		57–65

SETTLEMENTS

Population	National Capital	Administrative Capital	Other City or Town
over 10 million	**BEIJING** ✴	**Karachi** ◉	**New York** ◉
over 5 million	**JAKARTA** ✴	**Tianjin** ◉	**Nova Iguaçu** ◉
1 million to 5 million	**KĀBUL** ✴	**Sydney** ◉	**Kaohsiung** ◉
500 000 to 1 million	**BANGUI** ✴	**Trujillo** ◉	**Jeddah** ◉
100 000 to 500 000	WELLINGTON ✴	Mansa ◉	Apucarana ◉
50 000 to 100 000	PORT OF SPAIN ✴	Potenza ○	Arecibo ◉
10 000 to 50 000	MALABO ✴	Chinhoyi ○	Ceres ◉
under 10 000	VALLETTA ✴	Ati ○	Venta ◉

    ▒ Built-up area

BOUNDARIES

▭▭▭	International boundary
▪▪▪▪	Disputed international boundary or alignment unconfirmed
────	Administrative boundary
•••••	Ceasefire line

MISCELLANEOUS

-----	National park
-----	Reserve or Regional park
✴	Site of specific interest
▭▭▭	Wall

LAND AND SEA FEATURES

	Desert
	Oasis
	Lava field
1234 △	Volcano *height in metres*
	Marsh
	Ice cap or Glacier
	Escarpment
	Coral reef
1234	Pass *height in metres*

LAKES AND RIVERS

	Lake
	Impermanent lake
	Salt lake or lagoon
	Impermanent salt lake
	Dry salt lake or salt pan
123	Lake height *surface height above sea level, in metres*
────	River
────	Impermanent river or watercourse
‖	Waterfall
─	Dam
‖	Barrage

RELIEF

Contour intervals and layer colours

metres

6000
5000
4000
3000
2000
1000
500
200
0
below sea level
0
200
2000
4000
6000

1234 ▲	Summit *height in metres*
-123	Spot height *height in metres*
123	Ocean deep *depth in metres*

TRANSPORT

──▶ ┄┄┄	Motorway (tunnel; under construction)
──── ┄┄┄	Main road (tunnel; under construction)
──── ┄┄┄	Secondary road (tunnel; under construction)
········	Track
▪▪▪▪ ┄┄┄	Main railway (tunnel; under construction)
──── ┄┄┄	Secondary railway (tunnel; under construction)
──── ┄┄┄	Other railway (tunnel; under construction)
────	Canal
✈	Main airport
✈	Regional airport

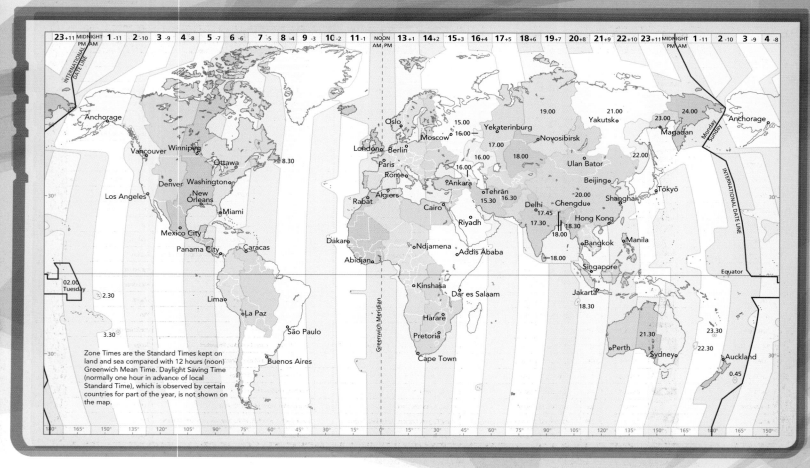

Zone Times are the Standard Times kept on land and sea compared with 12 hours (noon) Greenwich Mean Time. Daylight Saving Time (normally one hour in advance of local Standard Time), which is observed by certain countries for part of the year, is not shown on the map.

map symbols and time zones

EUROPE		area sq km	area sq miles	population	capital	languages	religions	currency
ALBANIA		28 748	11 100	3 164 000	Tirana	Albanian, Greek	Sunni Muslim, Albanian Orthodox, Roman Catholic	Lek
ANDORRA		465	180	94 000	Andorra la Vella	Spanish, Catalan, French	Roman Catholic	Euro
AUSTRIA		83 855	32 377	8 069 000	Vienna	German, Croatian, Turkish	Roman Catholic, Protestant	Euro
BELARUS		207 600	80 155	10 106 000	Minsk	Belorussian, Russian	Belorussian Orthodox, Roman Catholic	Belarus rouble
BELGIUM		30 520	11 784	10 276 000	Brussels	Dutch (Flemish), French (Walloon), German	Roman Catholic, Protestant	Euro
BOSNIA-HERZEGOVINA		51 130	19 741	4 126 000	Sarajevo	Bosnian, Serbian, Croatian	Sunni Muslim, Serbian Orthodox, Roman Catholic, Protestant	Marka
BULGARIA		110 994	42 855	7 790 000	Sofia	Bulgarian, Turkish, Romany, Macedonian	Bulgarian Orthodox, Sunni Muslim	Lev
CROATIA		56 538	21 829	4 657 000	Zagreb	Croatian, Serbian	Roman Catholic, Serbian Orthodox, Sunni Muslim	Kuna
CZECH REPUBLIC		78 864	30 450	10 250 000	Prague	Czech, Moravian, Slovak	Roman Catholic, Protestant	Czech koruna
DENMARK		43 075	16 631	5 343 000	Copenhagen	Danish	Protestant	Danish krone
ESTONIA		45 200	17 452	1 361 000	Tallinn	Estonian, Russian	Protestant, Estonian and Russian Orthodox	Kroon
FINLAND		338 145	130 559	5 183 000	Helsinki	Finnish, Swedish	Protestant, Greek Orthodox	Euro
FRANCE		543 965	210 026	59 670 000	Paris	French, Arabic	Roman Catholic, Protestant, Sunni Muslim	Euro
GERMANY		357 028	137 849	81 990 000	Berlin	German, Turkish	Protestant, Roman Catholic	Euro
GREECE		131 957	50 949	10 631 000	Athens	Greek	Greek Orthodox, Sunni Muslim	Euro
HUNGARY		93 030	35 919	9 867 000	Budapest	Hungarian	Roman Catholic, Protestant	Forint
ICELAND		102 820	39 699	283 000	Reykjavik	Icelandic	Protestant	Icelandic króna
IRELAND, REPUBLIC OF		70 282	27 136	3 878 000	Dublin	English, Irish	Roman Catholic, Protestant	Euro
ITALY		301 245	116 311	57 449 000	Rome	Italian	Roman Catholic	Euro
LATVIA		63 700	24 595	2 392 000	Riga	Latvian, Russian	Protestant, Roman Catholic, Russian Orthodox	Lats
LIECHTENSTEIN		160	62	33 000	Vaduz	German	Roman Catholic, Protestant	Swiss franc
LITHUANIA		65 200	25 174	3 682 000	Vilnius	Lithuanian, Russian, Polish	Roman Catholic, Protestant, Russian Orthodox	Litas
LUXEMBOURG		2 586	998	448 000	Luxembourg	Letzeburgish, German, French	Roman Catholic	Euro
MACEDONIA (F.Y.R.O.M.)		25 713	9 928	2 051 000	Skopje	Macedonian, Albanian, Turkish	Macedonian Orthodox, Sunni Muslim	Macedonian denar
MALTA		316	122	393 000	Valletta	Maltese, English	Roman Catholic	Maltese lira
MOLDOVA		33 700	13 012	4 273 000	Chişinău	Romanian, Ukrainian, Gagauz, Russian	Romanian Orthodox, Russian Orthodox	Moldovan leu
MONACO		2	1	34 000	Monaco-Ville	French, Monegasque, Italian	Roman Catholic	Euro
NETHERLANDS		41 526	16 033	15 990 000	Amsterdam/The Hague	Dutch, Frisian	Roman Catholic, Protestant, Sunni Muslim	Euro
NORWAY		323 878	125 050	4 505 000	Oslo	Norwegian	Protestant, Roman Catholic	Norwegian krone
POLAND		312 683	120 728	38 542 000	Warsaw	Polish, German	Roman Catholic, Polish Orthodox	Zloty
PORTUGAL		88 940	34 340	10 049 000	Lisbon	Portuguese	Roman Catholic, Protestant	Euro
ROMANIA		237 500	91 699	22 332 000	Bucharest	Romanian, Hungarian	Romanian Orthodox, Protestant, Roman Catholic	Romanian leu
RUSSIAN FEDERATION		17 075 400	6 592 849	143 752 000	Moscow	Russian, Tatar, Ukrainian, local languages	Russian Orthodox, Sunni Muslim, Protestant	Russian rouble
SAN MARINO		61	24	27 000	San Marino	Italian	Roman Catholic	Euro
SERBIA AND MONTENEGRO		102 173	39 449	10 522 000	Belgrade	Serbian, Albanian, Hungarian	Serbian Orthodox, Montenegrin Orthodox, Sunni Muslim	Dinar, Euro
SLOVAKIA		49 035	18 933	5 408 000	Bratislava	Slovak, Hungarian, Czech	Roman Catholic, Protestant, Orthodox	Slovakian koruna
SLOVENIA		20 251	7 819	1 983 000	Ljubljana	Slovene, Croatian, Serbian	Roman Catholic, Protestant	Tólar
SPAIN		504 782	194 897	39 924 000	Madrid	Castilian, Catalan, Galician, Basque	Roman Catholic	Euro
SWEDEN		449 964	173 732	8 823 000	Stockholm	Swedish	Protestant, Roman Catholic	Swedish krona
SWITZERLAND		41 293	15 943	7 167 000	Bern	German, French, Italian, Romansch	Roman Catholic, Protestant	Swiss franc
UKRAINE		603 700	233 090	48 652 000	Kiev	Ukrainian, Russian	Ukrainian Orthodox, Ukrainian Catholic, Roman Catholic	Hryvnia
UNITED KINGDOM		244 082	94 241	59 657 000	London	English, Welsh, Gaelic	Protestant, Roman Catholic, Muslim	Pound sterling
VATICAN CITY		0.5	0.2	472	Vatican City	Italian	Roman Catholic	Euro

ASIA		area sq km	area sq miles	population	capital	languages	religions	currency
AFGHANISTAN		652 225	251 825	23 294 000	Kābul	Dari, Pushtu, Uzbek, Turkmen	Sunni Muslim, Shi'a Muslim	Afghani
ARMENIA		29 800	11 506	3 790 000	Yerevan	Armenian, Azeri	Armenian Orthodox	Dram
AZERBAIJAN		86 600	33 436	8 147 000	Baku	Azeri, Armenian, Russian, Lezgian	Shi'a Muslim, Sunni Muslim, Russian and Armenian Orthodox	Azerbaijani manat
BAHRAIN		691	267	663 000	Manama	Arabic, English	Shi'a Muslim, Sunni Muslim, Christian	Bahrain dinar
BANGLADESH		143 998	55 598	143 364 000	Dhaka	Bengali, English	Sunni Muslim, Hindu	Taka
BHUTAN		46 620	18 000	2 198 000	Thimphu	Dzongkha, Nepali, Assamese	Buddhist, Hindu	Ngultrum, Indian rupee
BRUNEI		5 765	2 226	341 000	Bandar Seri Begawan	Malay, English, Chinese	Sunni Muslim, Buddhist, Christian	Brunei dollar
CAMBODIA		181 000	69 884	13 776 000	Phnom Penh	Khmer, Vietnamese	Buddhist, Roman Catholic, Sunni Muslim	Riel
CHINA		9 584 492	3 700 593	1 279 557 000	Beijing	Mandarin, Wu, Cantonese, Hsiang, regional languages	Confucian, Taoist, Buddhist, Christian, Sunni Muslim	Yuan, HK dollar*, Macau pataca
CYPRUS		9 251	3 572	797 000	Nicosia	Greek, Turkish, English	Greek Orthodox, Sunni Muslim	Cyprus pound
EAST TIMOR		14 874	5 743	779 000	Dili	Portuguese, Tetun, English	Roman Catholic	United States dollar
GEORGIA		69 700	26 911	5 213 000	T'bilisi	Georgian, Russian, Armenian, Azeri, Ossetian, Abkhaz	Georgian Orthodox, Russian Orthodox, Sunni Muslim	Lari
INDIA		3 065 027	1 183 414	1 041 144 000	New Delhi	Hindi, English, many regional languages	Hindu, Sunni Muslim, Shi'a Muslim, Sikh, Christian	Indian rupee
INDONESIA		1 919 445	741 102	217 534 000	Jakarta	Indonesian, local languages	Sunni Muslim, Protestant, Roman Catholic, Hindu, Buddhist	Rupiah
IRAN		1 648 000	636 296	72 376 000	Tehrān	Farsi, Azeri, Kurdish, regional languages	Shi'a Muslim, Sunni Muslim	Iranian rial
IRAQ		438 317	169 235	24 246 000	Baghdād	Arabic, Kurdish, Turkmen	Shi'a Muslim, Sunni Muslim, Christian	Iraqi dinar
ISRAEL		20 770	8 019	6 303 000	Jerusalem	Hebrew, Arabic	Jewish, Sunni Muslim, Christian, Druze	Shekel
JAPAN		377 727	145 841	127 538 000	Tōkyō	Japanese	Shintoist, Buddhist, Christian	Yen
JORDAN		89 206	34 443	5 196 000	'Ammān	Arabic	Sunni Muslim, Christian	Jordanian dinar
KAZAKHSTAN		2 717 300	1 049 155	16 027 000	Astana	Kazakh, Russian, Ukrainian, German, Uzbek, Tatar	Sunni Muslim, Russian Orthodox, Protestant	Tenge
KUWAIT		17 818	6 880	2 023 000	Kuwait	Arabic	Sunni Muslim, Shi'a Muslim, Christian, Hindu	Kuwaiti dinar
KYRGYZSTAN		198 500	76 641	5 047 000	Bishkek	Kyrgyz, Russian, Uzbek	Sunni Muslim, Russian Orthodox	Kyrgyz som
LAOS		236 800	91 429	5 530 000	Vientiane	Lao, local languages	Buddhist, traditional beliefs	Kip
LEBANON		10 452	4 036	3 614 000	Beirut	Arabic, Armenian, French	Shi'a Muslim, Sunni Muslim, Christian	Lebanese pound
MALAYSIA		332 965	128 559	23 036 000	Kuala Lumpur/Putrajaya	Malay, English, Chinese, Tamil, local languages	Sunni Muslim, Buddhist, Hindu, Christian, traditional beliefs	Ringgit
MALDIVES		298	115	309 000	Male	Divehi (Maldivian)	Sunni Muslim	Rufiyaa

*Hong Kong dollar

		area sq km	area sq miles	population	capital	languages	religions	currency
MONGOLIA		1 565 000	604 250	2 587 000	Ulan Bator	Khalka (Mongolian), Kazakh, local languages	Buddhist, Sunni Muslim	Tugrik (tögrög)
MYANMAR		676 577	261 228	48 956 000	Rangoon	Burmese, Shan, Karen, local languages	Buddhist, Christian, Sunni Muslim	Kyat
NEPAL		147 181	56 827	24 153 000	Kathmandu	Nepali, Maithili, Bhojpuri, English, local languages	Hindu, Buddhist, Sunni Muslim	Nepalese rupee
NORTH KOREA		120 538	46 540	22 586 000	P'yŏngyang	Korean	Traditional beliefs, Chondoist, Buddhist	North Korean won
OMAN		309 500	119 499	2 709 000	Muscat	Arabic, Baluchi, Indian languages	Ibadhi Muslim, Sunni Muslim	Omani riyal
PAKISTAN		803 940	310 403	148 721 000	Islamabad	Urdu, Punjabi, Sindhi, Pushtu, English	Sunni Muslim, Shi'a Muslim, Christian, Hindu	Pakistani rupee
PALAU		497	192	20 000	Koror	Palauan, English	Roman Catholic, Protestant, traditional beliefs	United States dollar
PHILIPPINES		300 000	115 831	78 611 000	Manila	English, Pilipino, Cebuano, local languages	Roman Catholic, Protestant, Sunni Muslim, Aglipayan	Philippine peso
QATAR		11 437	4 416	584 000	Doha	Arabic	Sunni Muslim	Qatari riyal
RUSSIAN FEDERATION		17 075 400	6 592 849	143 752 000	Moscow	Russian, Tatar, Ukrainian, local languages	Russian Orthodox, Sunni Muslim, Protestant	Russian rouble
SAUDI ARABIA		2 200 000	849 425	21 701 000	Riyadh	Arabic	Sunni Muslim, Shi'a Muslim	Saudi Arabian riyal
SINGAPORE		639	247	4 188 000	Singapore	Chinese, English, Malay, Tamil	Buddhist, Taoist, Sunni Muslim, Christian, Hindu	Singapore dollar
SOUTH KOREA		99 274	38 330	47 389 000	Seoul	Korean	Buddhist, Protestant, Roman Catholic	South Korean won
SRI LANKA		65 610	25 332	19 287 000	Sri Jayewardenepura Kotte	Sinhalese, Tamil, English	Buddhist, Hindu, Sunni Muslim, Roman Catholic	Sri Lankan rupee
SYRIA		185 180	71 498	17 040 000	Damascus	Arabic, Kurdish, Armenian	Sunni Muslim, Shi'a Muslim, Christian	Syrian pound
TAIWAN		36 179	13 969	22 548 000	T'aipei	Mandarin, Min, Hakka, local languages	Buddhist, Taoist, Confucian, Christian	Taiwan dollar
TAJIKISTAN		143 100	55 251	6 177 000	Dushanbe	Tajik, Uzbek, Russian	Sunni Muslim	Somoni
THAILAND		513 115	198 115	64 344 000	Bangkok	Thai, Lao, Chinese, Malay, Mon–Khmer languages	Buddhist, Sunni Muslim	Baht
TURKEY		779 452	300 948	68 569 000	Ankara	Turkish, Kurdish	Sunni Muslim, Shi'a Muslim	Turkish lira
TURKMENISTAN		488 100	188 456	4 930 000	Ashgabat	Turkmen, Uzbek, Russian	Sunni Muslim, Russian Orthodox	Turkmen manat
UNITED ARAB EMIRATES		83 600	32 278	2 701 000	Abu Dhabi	Arabic, English	Sunni Muslim, Shi'a Muslim	United Arab Emirates dirham
UZBEKISTAN		447 400	172 742	25 618 000	Tashkent	Uzbek, Russian, Tajik, Kazakh	Sunni Muslim, Russian Orthodox	Uzbek som
VIETNAM		329 565	127 246	80 226 000	Ha Nôi	Vietnamese, Thai, Khmer, Chinese, local languages	Buddhist, Taoist, Roman Catholic, Cao Dai, Hoa Hao	Dong
YEMEN		527 968	203 850	19 912 000	Şan'ä'	Arabic	Sunni Muslim, Shi'a Muslim	Yemeni rial

AFRICA

		area sq km	area sq miles	population	capital	languages	religions	currency
ALGERIA		2 381 741	919 595	31 403 000	Algiers	Arabic, French, Berber	Sunni Muslim	Algerian dinar
ANGOLA		1 246 700	481 354	13 936 000	Luanda	Portuguese, Bantu, local languages	Roman Catholic, Protestant, traditional beliefs	Kwanza
BENIN		112 620	43 483	6 629 000	Porto-Novo	French, Fon, Yoruba, Adja, local languages	Traditional beliefs, Roman Catholic, Sunni Muslim	CFA franc*
BOTSWANA		581 370	224 468	1 564 000	Gaborone	English, Setswana, Shona, local languages	Traditional beliefs, Protestant, Roman Catholic	Pula
BURKINA		274 200	105 869	12 207 000	Ouagadougou	French, Moore (Mossi), Fulani, local languages	Sunni Muslim, traditional beliefs, Roman Catholic	CFA franc*
BURUNDI		27 835	10 747	6 688 000	Bujumbura	Kirundi (Hutu, Tutsi), French	Roman Catholic, traditional beliefs, Protestant	Burundian franc
CAMEROON		475 442	183 569	15 535 000	Yaoundé	French, English, Fang, Bamileke, local languages	Roman Catholic, traditional beliefs, Sunni Muslim, Protestant	CFA franc*
CAPE VERDE		4 033	1 557	446 000	Praia	Portuguese, creole	Roman Catholic, Protestant	Cape Verde escudo
CENTRAL AFRICAN REPUBLIC		622 436	240 324	3 844 000	Bangui	French, Sango, Banda, Baya, local languages	Protestant, Roman Catholic, traditional beliefs, Sunni Muslim	CFA franc*
CHAD		1 284 000	495 755	8 390 000	Ndjamena	Arabic, French, Sara, local languages	Sunni Muslim, Roman Catholic, Protestant, traditional beliefs	CFA franc*
COMOROS		1 862	719	749 000	Moroni	Comorian, French, Arabic	Sunni Muslim, Roman Catholic	Comoros franc
CONGO		342 000	132 047	3 206 000	Brazzaville	French, Kongo, Monokutuba, local languages	Roman Catholic, Protestant, traditional beliefs, Sunni Muslim	CFA franc*
CONGO, DEMOCRATIC REP. OF		2 345 410	905 568	54 275 000	Kinshasa	French, Lingala, Swahili, Kongo, local languages	Christian, Sunni Muslim	Congolese franc
CÔTE D'IVOIRE		322 463	124 504	16 691 000	Yamoussoukro	French, creole, Akan, local languages	Sunni Muslim, Roman Catholic, traditional beliefs, Protestant	CFA franc*
DJIBOUTI		23 200	8 958	652 000	Djibouti	Somali, Afar, French, Arabic	Sunni Muslim, Christian	Djibouti franc
EGYPT		1 000 250	386 199	70 278 000	Cairo	Arabic	Sunni Muslim, Coptic Christian	Egyptian pound
EQUATORIAL GUINEA		28 051	10 831	483 000	Malabo	Spanish, French, Fang	Roman Catholic, traditional beliefs	CFA franc*
ERITREA		117 400	45 328	3 993 000	Asmara	Tigrinya, Tigre	Sunni Muslim, Coptic Christian	Nakfa
ETHIOPIA		1 133 880	437 794	66 040 000	Addis Ababa	Oromo, Amharic, Tigrinya, local languages	Ethiopian Orthodox, Sunni Muslim, traditional beliefs	Birr
GABON		267 667	103 347	1 293 000	Libreville	French, Fang, local languages	Roman Catholic, Protestant, traditional beliefs	CFA franc*
THE GAMBIA		11 295	4 361	1 371 000	Banjul	English, Malinke, Fulani, Wolof	Sunni Muslim, Protestant	Dalasi
GHANA		238 537	92 100	20 176 000	Accra	English, Hausa, Akan, local languages	Christian, Sunni Muslim, traditional beliefs	Cedi
GUINEA		245 857	94 926	8 381 000	Conakry	French, Fulani, Malinke, local languages	Sunni Muslim, traditional beliefs, Christian	Guinea franc
GUINEA-BISSAU		36 125	13 948	1 257 000	Bissau	Portuguese, crioulo, local languages	Traditional beliefs, Sunni Muslim, Christian	CFA franc*
KENYA		582 646	224 961	31 904 000	Nairobi	Swahili, English, local languages	Christian, traditional beliefs	Kenyan shilling
LESOTHO		30 355	11 720	2 076 000	Maseru	Sesotho, English, Zulu	Christian, traditional beliefs	Loti, S. African rand
LIBERIA		111 369	43 000	3 298 000	Monrovia	English, creole, local languages	Traditional beliefs, Christian, Sunni Muslim	Liberian dollar
LIBYA		1 759 540	679 362	5 529 000	Tripoli	Arabic, Berber	Sunni Muslim	Libyan dinar
MADAGASCAR		587 041	226 658	16 913 000	Antananarivo	Malagasy, French	Traditional beliefs, Christian, Sunni Muslim	Malagasy franc
MALAWI		118 484	45 747	11 828 000	Lilongwe	Chichewa, English, local languages	Christian, traditional beliefs, Sunni Muslim	Malawian kwacha
MALI		1 240 140	478 821	12 019 000	Bamako	French, Bambara, local languages	Sunni Muslim, traditional beliefs, Christian	CFA franc*
MAURITANIA		1 030 700	397 955	2 830 000	Nouakchott	Arabic, French, local languages	Sunni Muslim	Ouguiya
MAURITIUS		2 040	788	1 180 000	Port Louis	English, creole, Hindi, Bhojpuri, French	Hindu, Roman Catholic, Sunni Muslim	Mauritius rupee
MOROCCO		446 550	172 414	30 988 000	Rabat	Arabic, Berber, French	Sunni Muslim	Moroccan dirham
MOZAMBIQUE		799 380	308 642	18 986 000	Maputo	Portuguese, Makua, Tsonga, local languages	Traditional beliefs, Roman Catholic, Sunni Muslim	Metical
NAMIBIA		824 292	318 261	1 819 000	Windhoek	English, Afrikaans, German, Ovambo, local languages	Protestant, Roman Catholic	Namibian dollar
NIGER		1 267 000	489 191	11 641 000	Niamey	French, Hausa, Fulani, local languages	Sunni Muslim, traditional beliefs	CFA franc*
NIGERIA		923 768	356 669	120 047 000	Abuja	English, Hausa, Yoruba, Ibo, Fulani, local languages	Sunni Muslim, Christian, traditional beliefs	Naira
RWANDA		26 338	10 169	8 148 000	Kigali	Kinyarwanda, French, English	Roman Catholic, traditional beliefs, Protestant	Rwandan franc
SÃO TOMÉ AND PRÍNCIPE		964	372	143 000	São Tomé	Portuguese, creole	Roman Catholic, Protestant	Dobra
SENEGAL		196 720	75 954	9 908 000	Dakar	French, Wolof, Fulani, local languages	Sunni Muslim, Roman Catholic, traditional beliefs	CFA franc*
SEYCHELLES		455	176	83 000	Victoria	English, French, creole	Roman Catholic, Protestant	Seychelles rupee

*Communauté Financière Africaine

AFRICA continued

		area sq km	area sq miles	population	capital	languages	religions	currency
SIERRA LEONE		71 740	27 699	4 814 000	Freetown	English, creole, Mende, Temne, local languages	Sunni Muslim, traditional beliefs	Leone
SOMALIA		637 657	246 201	9 557 000	Mogadishu	Somali, Arabic	Sunni Muslim	Somali shilling
SOUTH AFRICA, REPUBLIC OF		1 219 090	470 693	44 203 000	Pretoria/Cape Town	Afrikaans, English, nine official local languages	Protestant, Roman Catholic, Sunni Muslim, Hindu	Rand
SUDAN		2 505 813	967 500	32 559 000	Khartoum	Arabic, Dinka, Nubian, Beja, Nuer, local languages	Sunni Muslim, traditional beliefs, Christian	Sudanese dinar
SWAZILAND		17 364	6 704	948 000	Mbabane	Swazi, English	Christian, traditional beliefs	Emalangeni, S. African rand
TANZANIA		945 087	364 900	36 820 000	Dodoma	Swahili, English, Nyamwezi, local languages	Shi'a Muslim, Sunni Muslim, traditional beliefs, Christian	Tanzanian shilling
TOGO		56 785	21 925	4 779 000	Lomé	French, Ewe, Kabre, local languages	Traditional beliefs, Christian, Sunni Muslim	CFA franc*
TUNISIA		164 150	63 379	9 670 000	Tunis	Arabic, French	Sunni Muslim	Tunisian dinar
UGANDA		241 038	93 065	24 780 000	Kampala	English, Swahili, Luganda, local languages	Roman Catholic, Protestant, Sunni Muslim, traditional beliefs	Ugandan shilling
ZAMBIA		752 614	290 586	10 872 000	Lusaka	English, Bemba, Nyanja, Tonga, local languages	Christian, traditional beliefs	Zambian kwacha
ZIMBABWE		390 759	150 873	13 076 000	Harare	English, Shona, Ndebele	Christian, traditional beliefs	Zimbabwean dollar

*Communauté Financière Africaine

OCEANIA

		area sq km	area sq miles	population	capital	languages	religions	currency
AUSTRALIA		7 682 395	2 966 189	19 536 000	Canberra	English, Italian, Greek	Protestant, Roman Catholic, Orthodox	Australian dollar
FIJI		18 330	7 077	832 000	Suva	English, Fijian, Hindi	Christian, Hindu, Sunni Muslim	Fiji dollar
KIRIBATI		717	277	85 000	Bairiki	Gilbertese, English	Roman Catholic, Protestant	Australian dollar
MARSHALL ISLANDS		181	70	53 000	Delap-Uliga-Djarrit	English, Marshallese	Protestant, Roman Catholic	United States dollar
MICRONESIA, FEDERATED STATES OF		701	271	129 000	Palikir	English, Chuukese, Pohnpeian, local languages	Roman Catholic, Protestant	United States dollar
NAURU		21	8	13 000	Yaren	Nauruan, English	Protestant, Roman Catholic	Australian dollar
NEW ZEALAND		270 534	104 454	3 837 000	Wellington	English, Maori	Protestant, Roman Catholic	New Zealand dollar
PAPUA NEW GUINEA		462 840	178 704	5 032 000	Port Moresby	English, Tok Pisin (creole), local languages	Protestant, Roman Catholic, traditional beliefs	Kina
SAMOA		2 831	1 093	159 000	Apia	Samoan, English	Protestant, Roman Catholic	Tala
SOLOMON ISLANDS		28 370	10 954	479 000	Honiara	English, creole, local languages	Protestant, Roman Catholic	Solomon Islands dollar
TONGA		748	289	100 000	Nuku'alofa	Tongan, English	Protestant, Roman Catholic	Pa'anga
TUVALU		25	10	10 000	Vaiaku	Tuvaluan, English	Protestant	Australian dollar
VANUATU		12 190	4 707	207 000	Port Vila	English, Bislama (creole), French	Protestant, Roman Catholic, traditional beliefs	Vatu

NORTH AMERICA

		area sq km	area sq miles	population	capital	languages	religions	currency
ANTIGUA AND BARBUDA		442	171	65 000	St John's	English, creole	Protestant, Roman Catholic	East Caribbean dollar
THE BAHAMAS		13 939	5 382	312 000	Nassau	English, creole	Protestant, Roman Catholic	Bahamian dollar
BARBADOS		430	166	269 000	Bridgetown	English, creole	Protestant, Roman Catholic	Barbados dollar
BELIZE		22 965	8 867	236 000	Belmopan	English, Spanish, Mayan, creole	Roman Catholic, Protestant	Belize dollar
CANADA		9 970 610	3 849 674	31 268 000	Ottawa	English, French	Roman Catholic, Protestant, Eastern Orthodox, Jewish	Canadian dollar
COSTA RICA		51 100	19 730	4 200 000	San José	Spanish	Roman Catholic, Protestant	Costa Rican colón
CUBA		110 860	42 803	11 273 000	Havana	Spanish	Roman Catholic, Protestant	Cuban peso
DOMINICA		750	290	70 000	Roseau	English, creole	Roman Catholic, Protestant	East Caribbean dollar
DOMINICAN REPUBLIC		48 442	18 704	8 639 000	Santo Domingo	Spanish, creole	Roman Catholic, Protestant	Dominican peso
EL SALVADOR		21 041	8 124	6 520 000	San Salvador	Spanish	Roman Catholic, Protestant	El Salvador colón, United States dollar
GRENADA		378	146	94 000	St George's	English, creole	Roman Catholic, Protestant	East Caribbean dollar
GUATEMALA		108 890	42 043	11 995 000	Guatemala City	Spanish, Mayan languages	Roman Catholic, Protestant	Quetzal, United States dollar
HAITI		27 750	10 714	8 400 000	Port-au-Prince	French, creole	Roman Catholic, Protestant, Voodoo	Gourde
HONDURAS		112 088	43 277	6 732 000	Tegucigalpa	Spanish, Amerindian languages	Roman Catholic, Protestant	Lempira
JAMAICA		10 991	4 244	2 621 000	Kingston	English, creole	Protestant, Roman Catholic	Jamaican dollar
MEXICO		1 972 545	761 604	101 842 000	Mexico City	Spanish, Amerindian languages	Roman Catholic, Protestant	Mexican peso
NICARAGUA		130 000	50 193	5 347 000	Managua	Spanish, Amerindian languages	Roman Catholic, Protestant	Córdoba
PANAMA		77 082	29 762	2 942 000	Panama City	Spanish, English, Amerindian languages	Roman Catholic, Protestant, Sunni Muslim	Balboa
ST KITTS AND NEVIS		261	101	38 000	Basseterre	English, creole	Protestant, Roman Catholic	East Caribbean dollar
ST LUCIA		616	238	151 000	Castries	English, creole	Roman Catholic, Protestant	East Caribbean dollar
ST VINCENT AND THE GRENADINES		389	150	115 000	Kingstown	English, creole	Protestant, Roman Catholic	East Caribbean dollar
TRINIDAD AND TOBAGO		5 130	1 981	1 306 000	Port of Spain	English, creole, Hindi	Roman Catholic, Hindu, Protestant, Sunni Muslim	Trinidad and Tobago dollar
UNITED STATES OF AMERICA		9 809 378	3 787 422	288 530 000	Washington DC	English, Spanish	Protestant, Roman Catholic, Sunni Muslim, Jewish	United States dollar

SOUTH AMERICA

		area sq km	area sq miles	population	capital	languages	religions	currency
ARGENTINA		2 766 889	1 068 302	37 944 000	Buenos Aires	Spanish, Italian, Amerindian languages	Roman Catholic, Protestant	Argentinian peso
BOLIVIA		1 098 581	424 164	8 705 000	La Paz/Sucre	Spanish, Quechua, Aymara	Roman Catholic, Protestant, Baha'i	Boliviano
BRAZIL		8 547 379	3 300 161	174 706 000	Brasília	Portuguese	Roman Catholic, Protestant	Real
CHILE		756 945	292 258	15 589 000	Santiago	Spanish, Amerindian languages	Roman Catholic, Protestant	Chilean peso
COLOMBIA		1 141 748	440 831	43 495 000	Bogotá	Spanish, Amerindian languages	Roman Catholic, Protestant	Colombian peso
ECUADOR		272 045	105 037	13 112 000	Quito	Spanish, Quechua, other Amerindian languages	Roman Catholic	US dollar
GUYANA		214 969	83 000	765 000	Georgetown	English, creole, Amerindian languages	Protestant, Hindu, Roman Catholic, Sunni Muslim	Guyana dollar
PARAGUAY		406 752	157 048	5 778 000	Asunción	Spanish, Guarani	Roman Catholic, Protestant	Guarani
PERU		1 285 216	496 225	26 523 000	Lima	Spanish, Quechua, Aymara	Roman Catholic, Protestant	Sol
SURINAME		163 820	63 251	421 000	Paramaribo	Dutch, Surinamese, English, Hindi	Hindu, Roman Catholic, Protestant, Sunni Muslim	Suriname guilder
URUGUAY		176 215	68 037	3 385 000	Montevideo	Spanish	Roman Catholic, Protestant, Jewish	Uruguayan peso
VENEZUELA		912 050	352 144	25 093 000	Caracas	Spanish, Amerindian languages	Roman Catholic, Protestant	Bolívar

ABBREVIATION KEY

A.	ANDORRA	**HUN.**	HUNGARY	**S.**	SERBIA AND MONTENEGRO
AL.	ALBANIA	**ISR.**	ISRAEL	**ROM.**	ROMANIA
ARM.	ARMENIA	**JOR.**	JORDAN	**SL.**	SLOVENIA
AUST.	AUSTRIA	**L.**	LUXEMBOURG	**SLA.**	SLOVAKIA
AZER.	AZERBAIJAN	**LAT.**	LATVIA	**SUR.**	SURINAME
B.	BURUNDI	**LEB.**	LEBANON	**SW.**	SWITZERLAND
BEL.	BELGIUM	**LITH.**	LITHUANIA	**TAJIK.**	TAJIKISTAN
B.H.	BOSNIA-HERZEGOVINA	**M.**	MACEDONIA	**TURKM.**	TURKMENISTAN
BULG.	BULGARIA	**MOL.**	MOLDOVA	**U.A.E.**	UNITED ARAB EMIRATES
CR.	CROATIA	**NETH.**	NETHERLANDS	**U.K.**	UNITED KINGDOM
CZ.R.	CZECH REPUBLIC	**N.Z.**	NEW ZEALAND	**U.S.A.**	UNITED STATES OF AMERICA
EST.	ESTONIA	**R.**	RWANDA	**UZBEK.**	UZBEKISTAN
GEOR.	GEORGIA	**R.F.**	RUSSIAN FEDERATION		

World's largest countries (area)

COUNTRY	AREA	
Russian Federation, Europe/Asia	17 075 400 sq km	6 592 849 sc miles
Canada, North America	9 970 610 sq km	3 849 674 sc miles
United States of America, North America	9 809 378 sq km	3 787 422 sc miles
China, Asia	9 584 492 sq km	3 700 593 sc miles
Brazil, South America	8 547 379 sq km	3 300 161 sc miles
Australia, Oceania	7 682 395 sq km	2 966 189 sc miles
India, Asia	3 065 027 sq km	1 183 414 sc miles
Argentina, South America	2 766 889 sq km	1 068 302 sc miles
Kazakhstan, Asia	2 717 300 sq km	1 049 155 sc miles
Sudan, Africa	2 505 813 sq km	967 500 sc miles

World's largest countries (population)

COUNTRY	POPULATION
China, Asia	1 279 557 000
India, Asia	1 041 144 000
United States of America, North America	288 530 000
Indonesia, Asia	217 534 000
Brazil, South America	174 706 000
Pakistan, Asia	148 721 000
Russian Federation, Europe/Asia	143 752 000
Bangladesh, Asia	143 364 000
Japan, Asia	127 538 000
Nigeria, Africa	120 047 000

World's largest cities

CITY	POPULATION
Tōkyō, Japan	26 444 000
Mexico City, Mexico	18 066 000
São Paulo, Brazil	17 962 000
New York, United States of America	16 732 000
Mumbai, India	16 086 000
Los Angeles, United States of America	13 213 000
Kolkata, India	13 058 000
Shanghai, China	12 887 000
Dhaka, Bangladesh	12 519 000
Delhi, India	12 441 000

World capitals

Largest national capital (population)	Tōkyō, Japan	26 444 000
Smallest national capital (population)	Vatican City	524
Most northerly national capital	Reykjavík, Iceland	64° 08'N
Most southerly national capital	Wellington, New Zealand	41° 18'S
Highest capital	La Paz, Bolivia	3 630 m 11 909 ft
Joint capital (Netherlands)	Amsterdam/The Hague	
Joint capital (Malaysia)	Kuala Lumpur/Putrajaya	
Joint capital (Bolivia)	La Paz/Sucre	
Joint capital (South Africa)	Pretoria/Cape Town	

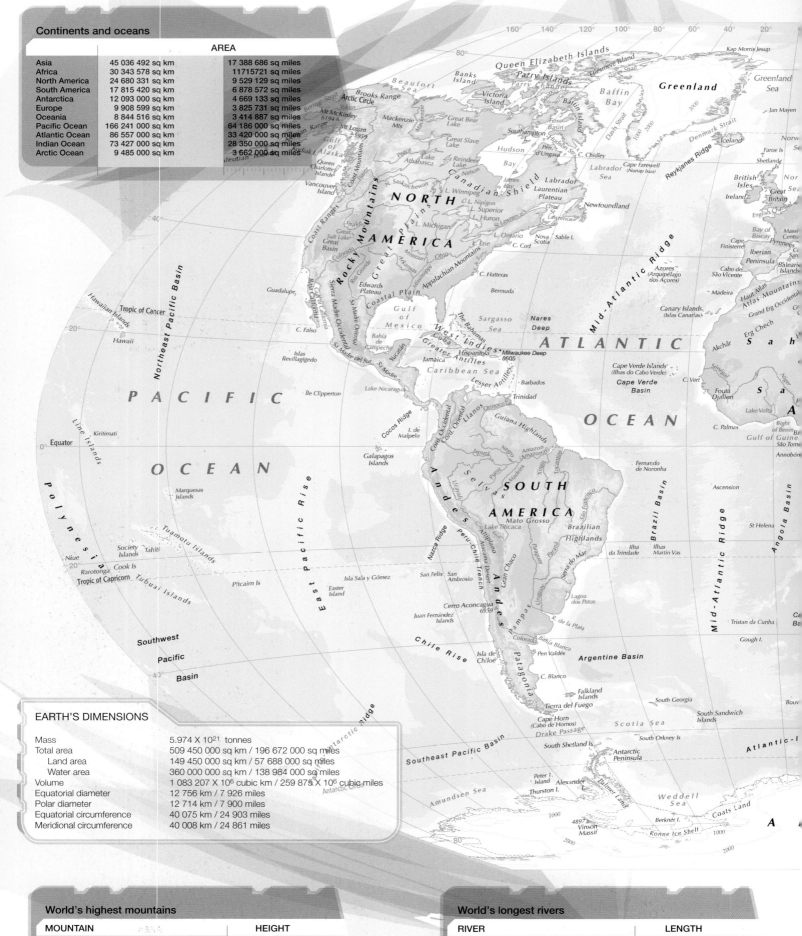

Continents and oceans

	AREA	
Asia	45 036 492 sq km	17 388 686 sq miles
Africa	30 343 578 sq km	11 715 721 sq miles
North America	24 680 331 sq km	9 529 129 sq miles
South America	17 815 420 sq km	6 878 572 sq miles
Antarctica	12 093 000 sq km	4 669 133 sq miles
Europe	9 908 599 sq km	3 825 731 sq miles
Oceania	8 844 516 sq km	3 414 887 sq miles
Pacific Ocean	166 241 000 sq km	64 186 000 sq miles
Atlantic Ocean	86 557 000 sq km	33 420 000 sq miles
Indian Ocean	73 427 000 sq km	28 350 000 sq miles
Arctic Ocean	9 485 000 sq km	3 662 000 sq miles

EARTH'S DIMENSIONS

Mass	5.974 X 10^{21} tonnes
Total area	509 450 000 sq km / 196 672 000 sq miles
Land area	149 450 000 sq km / 57 688 000 sq miles
Water area	360 000 000 sq km / 138 984 000 sq miles
Volume	1 083 207 X 10^6 cubic km / 259 875 X 10^6 cubic miles
Equatorial diameter	12 756 km / 7 926 miles
Polar diameter	12 714 km / 7 900 miles
Equatorial circumference	40 075 km / 24 903 miles
Meridional circumference	40 008 km / 24 861 miles

World's highest mountains

MOUNTAIN	HEIGHT	
Mt Everest, China/Nepal	8 848 m	29 028 ft
K2, China/Jammu and Kashmir	8 611 m	28 251 ft
Kangchenjunga, India/Nepal	8 586 m	28 169 ft
Lhotse, China/Nepal	8 516 m	27 939 ft
Makalu, China/Nepal	8 463 m	27 765 ft
Cho Oyu, China/Nepal	8 201 m	26 906 ft
Dhaulagiri, Nepal	8 167 m	26 794 ft
Manaslu, Nepal	8 163 m	26 781 ft
Nanga Parbat, Jammu and Kashmir	8 126 m	26 660 ft
Annapurna I, Nepal	8 091 m	26 545 ft

World's longest rivers

RIVER	LENGTH	
Nile, Africa	6 695 km	4 160 miles
Amazon, South America	6 516 km	4 049 miles
Yangtze, Asia	6 380 km	3 964 miles
Mississipi-Missouri, North America	5 969 km	3 709 miles
Ob'-Irtysh, Asia	5 568 km	3 459 miles
Yenisey-Angara-Selenga, Asia	5 550 km	3 448 miles
Yellow, Asia	5 464 km	3 395 miles
Congo, Africa	4 667 km	2 900 miles
Rio de la Plata - Paraná, South America	4 500 km	2 796 miles
Irtysh, Asia	4 440 km	2 759 miles

World's largest lakes

LAKE	AREA	
Caspian Sea, Asia/Europe	371 000 sq km	143 243 sq miles
Lake Superior, North America	82 100 sq km	31 698 sq miles
Lake Victoria, Africa	68 800 sq km	26 563 sq miles
Lake Huron, North America	59 600 sq km	23 011 sq miles
Lake Michigan, North America	57 800 sq km	22 316 sq miles
Aral Sea, Asia	33 640 sq km	12 988 sq miles
Lake Tanganyika, Africa	32 900 sq km	12 702 sq miles
Great Bear Lake, North America	31 328 sq km	12 095 sq miles
Lake Baikal, Asia	30 500 sq km	11 776 sq miles
Lake Nyasa, Africa	30 044 sq km	11 600 sq miles

World's largest islands

ISLAND	AREA	
Greenland, North America	2 175 600 sq km	840 004 sq miles
New Guinea, Oceania	808 510 sq km	312 167 sq miles
Borneo, Asia	745 561 sq km	287 863 sq miles
Madagascar, Africa	587 040 sq km	266 657 sq miles
Baffin Island, North America	507 451 sq km	195 927 sq miles
Sumatra, Asia	473 606 sq km	182 860 sq miles
Honshū, Asia	227 414 sq km	87 805 sq miles
Great Britain, Europe	218 476 sq km	84 354 sq miles
Victoria Island, North America	217 291 sq km	83 897 sq miles
Ellesmere Island, North America	196 236 sq km	75 767 sq miles

europe
scandinavia and the baltic states

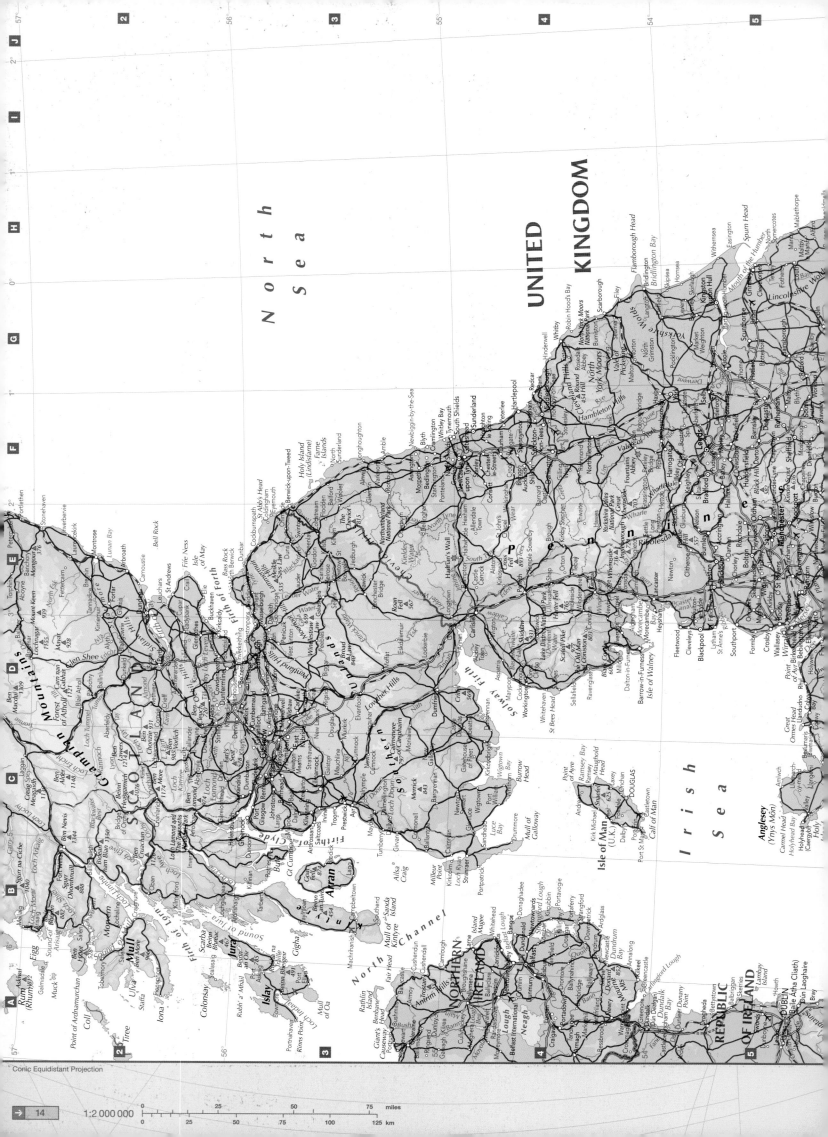

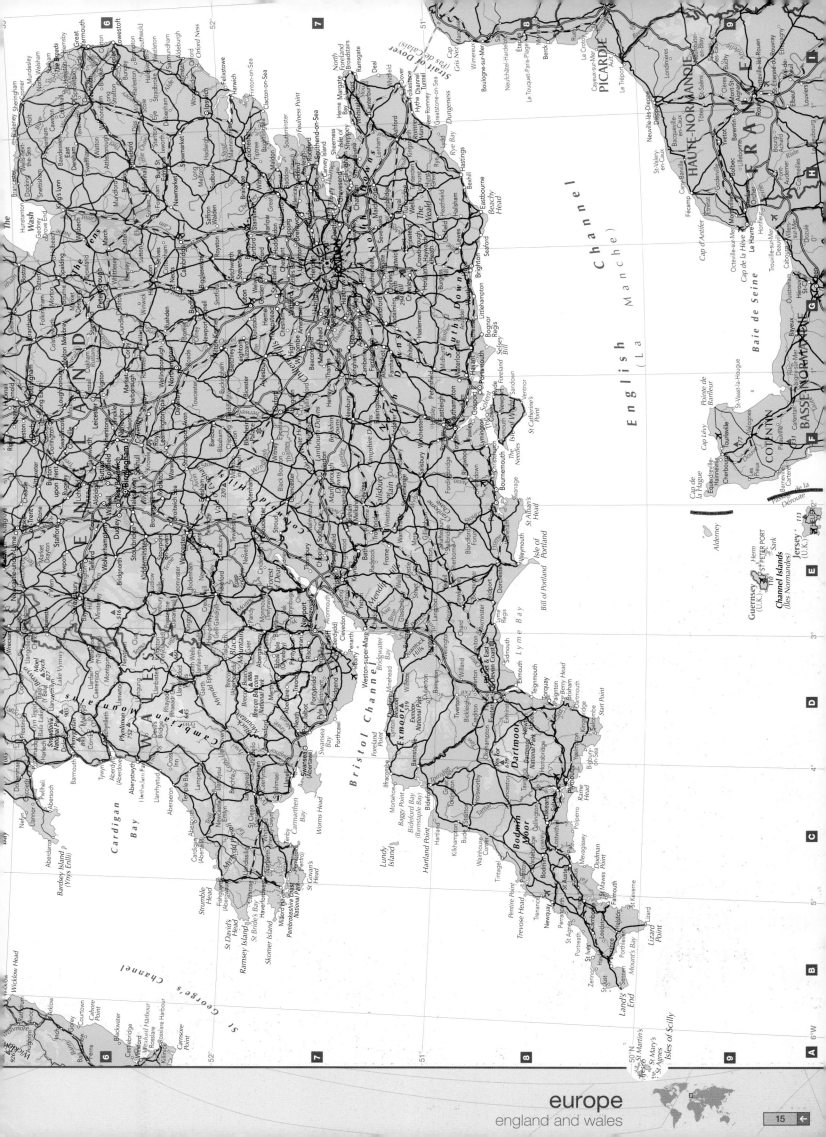

europe

england and wales

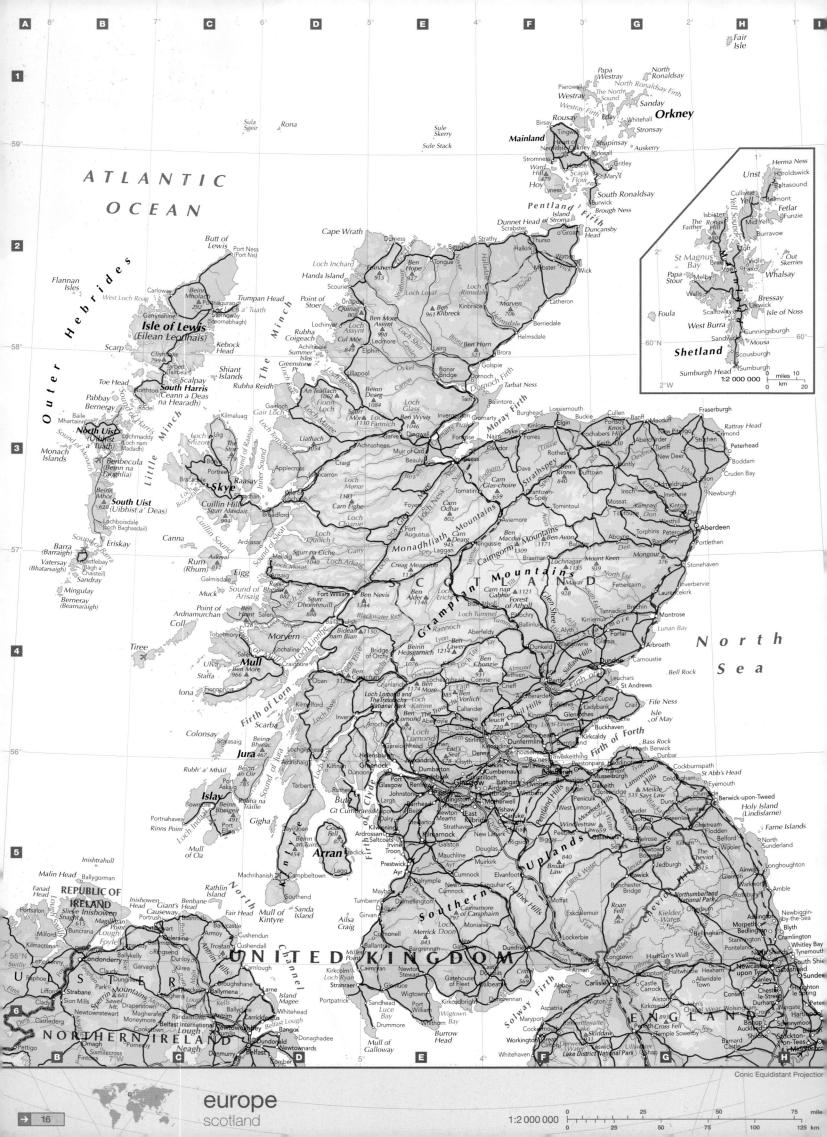

europe
france

Conic Equidistant Projection

1:5 000 000

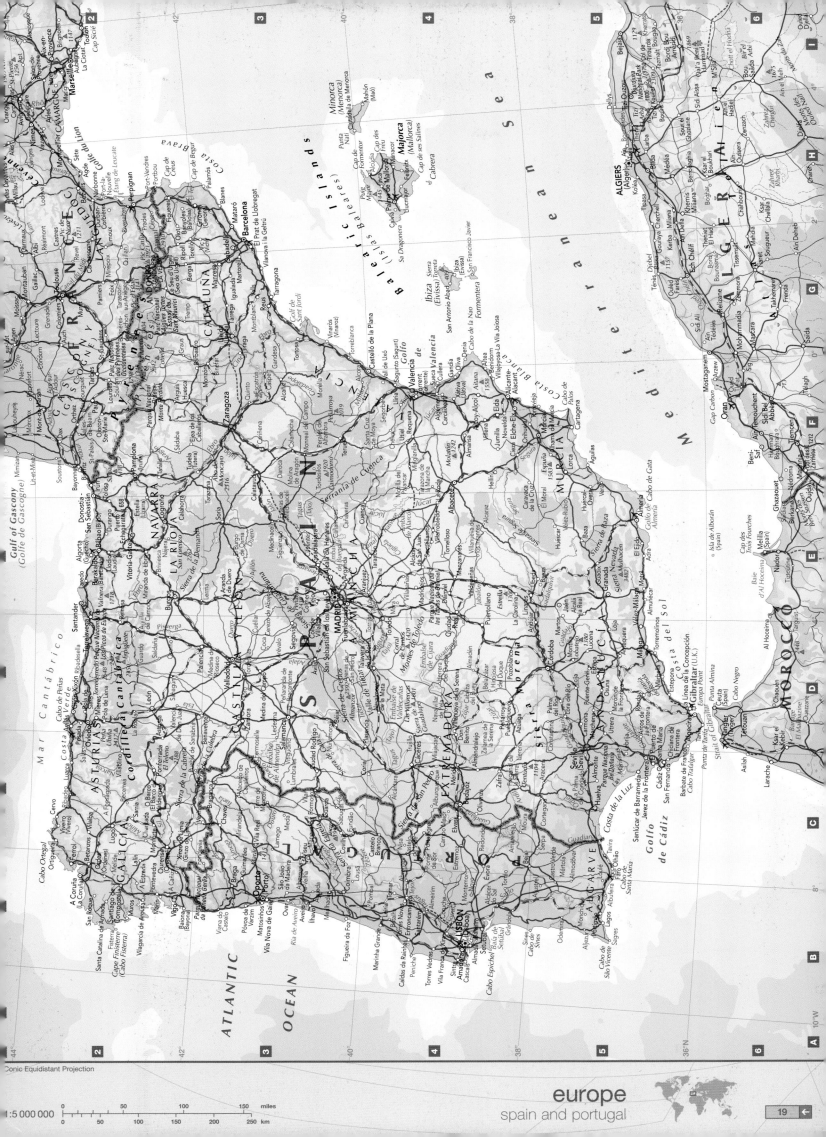

Conic Equidistant Projection

Conic Equidistant Projection

1:5 000 000

europe
italy and the balkans

Conic Equidistant Projection

1:7 500 000

asia
northern asia

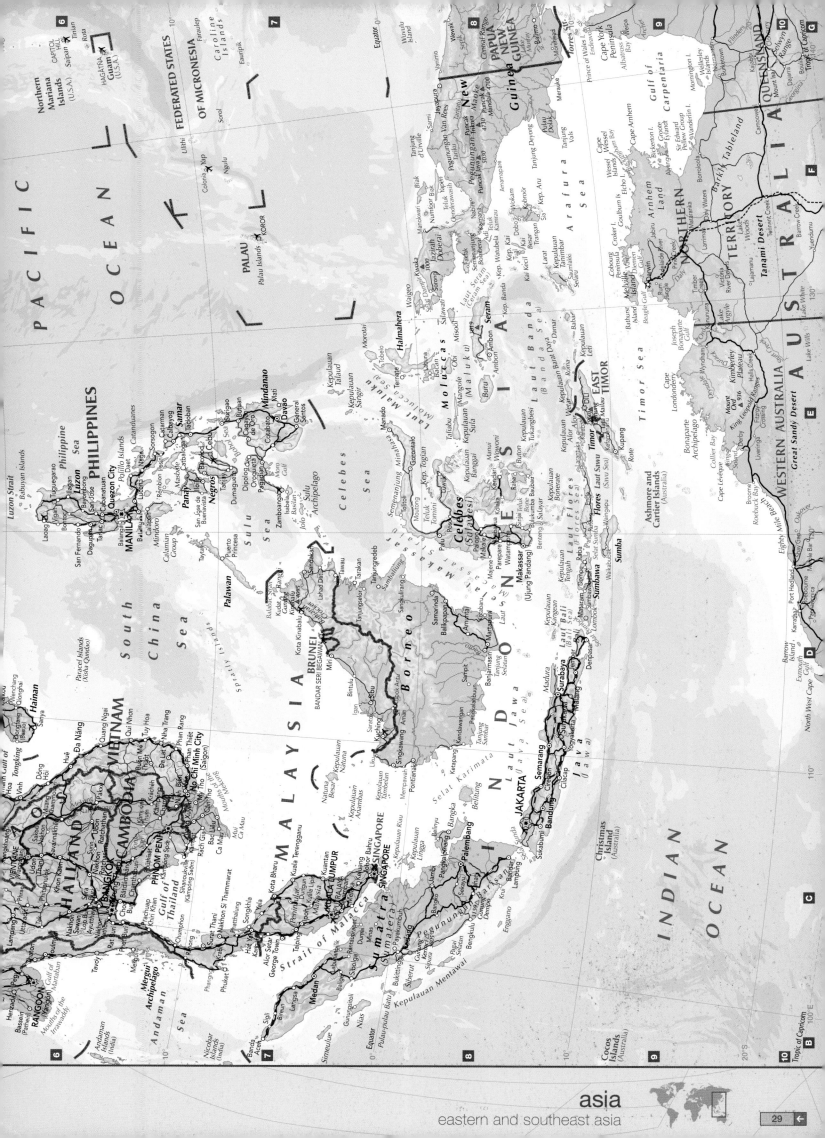

asia
eastern and southeast asia

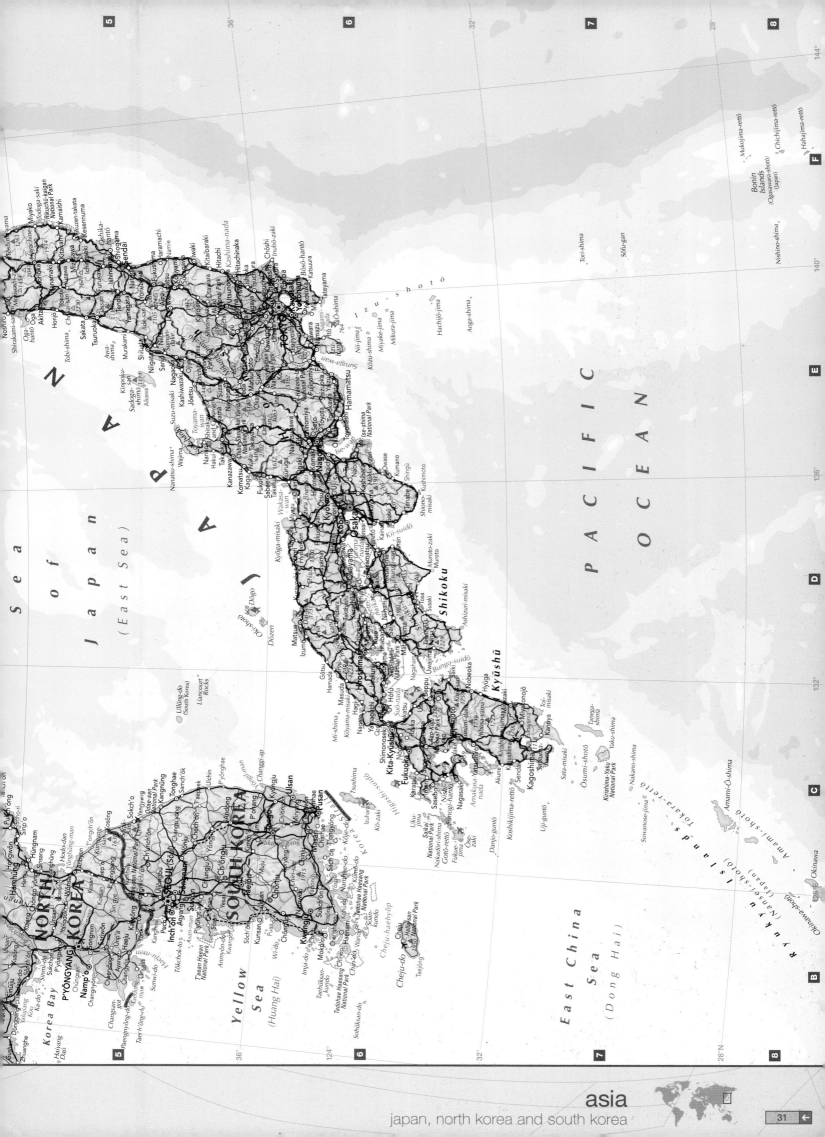

asia

japan, north korea and south korea

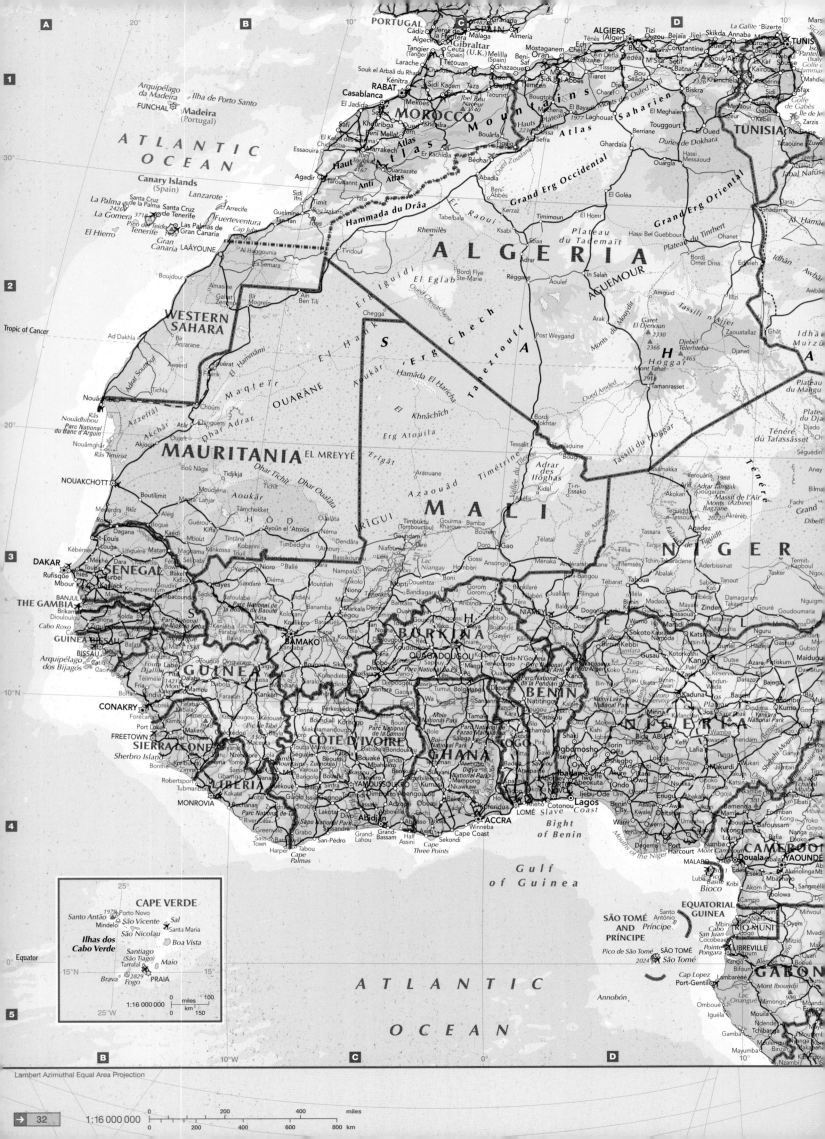

G   160°   170°   H   180°   I   170°   J

1

0°

2

10°

3

20°

Tropic of Capricorn

4

30°

5

40°

G   160°   170°   H   180°   I   170°   J   160°   K   150°W   L

6

Howland Island (U.S.A.)
Baker Island (U.S.A.)

NAURU
Nauru YAREN
Aranuka
Banaba (Ocean Island)
Nonouti
Beru
Nikunau
Tabiteuea
Onotoa
Tamana
Arorae
Kingsmill Group

K I R I B A T I

Phoenix Islands
Kanton
McKean
Rawaki
Nikumaroro
Orona
Manra

Tauu Islands
Nukumanu Islands

SOLOMON ISLANDS
Ontong Java Atoll
Roncador Reef
Choiseul
Georgia Sound
Santa Isabel
Buala
Malu'u
New Georgia
Rangata
Florida Islands
Malaita
Georgia Islands
Avuavu
Maramasike
Ulawa Island
Guadalcanal
Kirakira
Santa Ana
San Cristobal (Makira)
Rennell
Indispensable Reefs

Nanumea
Nanumanga
Niutao
Nui
Vaitupu
Nukufetau

TUVALU
Funafuti VAIAKU
Nukulaelae
Niulakita

Tokelau (New Zealand)
Atafu
Nukunono
Fakaofo
Swains Island

SAMOA
Wallis and Futuna Islands (France)
Îles Wallis
MATA'UTU
Savai'i
Upolu
APIA
Manua Islands
American Samoa (U.S.A.)
Tutuila
FAGATOGO
Rose Island

Pukapuka (Danger Islands)
Nassau
Suwarrow

al Sea

Nupani
Swallow Island
Duff Islands
Santa Cruz Islands (Solomon Islands)
Ndeni
Utupua
Vanikoro Islands
Mitre Island
Torres Islands
Tikopia
Cherry Island
Uréparapara
Banks Islands
Vanua Lava
Santa María Island

VANUATU
Espíritu Santo
Mount Tabwémasana 1879
Aoba
Maéwo
Norsup
Pentecost Island
Malakula
Ambrym
Émaé 1270 Epi
Shepherd Islands
PORT VILA
Éfaté
Erromango

Récifs d'Entrecasteaux
Grand Passage
Îles Belep
Grand Récif de Cook
Récif des Français
Koumac
Nouvelle Calédonie
Ouvéa
Îles Loyauté (France)
Lifou
New Caledonia (France)
Bourail
Tadin
Maré
Yaté
NOUMÉA
Île des Pins
Grand Récif du Sud

Rotuma (Fiji)

Îles de Hoorn
Niuafo'ou 210
Tafahi
Niuatoputapu

Yasawa Group
Great Sea Reef
Vanua Levu
Labasa (Lambasa)
Bligh Water
Tomanivi
Mt Victoria
Taveuni
Lautoka
Koro
Northern Lau Group
Viti Levu
Koro Sea
SUVA
Gau
Vava'u Group
Kadavu Passage
FIJI
Moala
Lakeba
Kadavu
Matuku
Southern Lau Group
Kabara
Vatoa

Vava'u Group
ALOFI
Niue (New Zealand)

Cook Islands (New Zealand)

Tanna 361
Futuna
Anatom (Aneityum)
Ceva-i-Ra (Conway Reef)
Doi
Ono-i-Lau
TONGA
NUKU'ALOFA
Tongatapu Group
Tofua 500
Ha'apai Group
Ata

Palmerston

Hunter Island 100

Minerva Reefs

P A C I F I C   O C E A N

Norfolk Island (Australia)
KINGSTON

Lord Howe Island (Australia)

Raoul Island
Kermadec Islands (New Zealand)
Macauley Island
Curtis Island
Havre Rock
L'Espérance Rock

Three Kings Islands
North Cape
Maria van Diemen
Cape Maria van Diemen
Awanui
Whangarei
Great Barrier Island
North Island
Takapuna
Auckland
Manukau
Hamilton
Tauranga
East Cape
Te Kuiti
Tokoroa
Taupo
Whakatane
NEW ZEALAND
New Plymouth
Mount Taranaki (Mount Egmont)
Mount Ruapehu
Wairoa
Gisborne
Mahia Peninsula
Hawera
Wanganui
Napier
Hastings
Palmerston North
Cape Farewell
Tasman Bay
Nelson
Masterton
Picton
Blenheim
Upper Hutt
Lower Hutt
WELLINGTON
Westport
South Island
Hokitika
Greymouth
Southern Alps
Aoraki (Mount Cook) 3754
Christchurch
Banks Peninsula
Mount Aspiring 3030
Ashburton
Mount Christina 2502
Timaru
Queenstown
Oamaru
Cape Providence
Gore
Dunedin
Stewart Island
Invercargill
South West Cape
Foveaux Strait
Snares Islands

Cook Strait

Chatham Islands (New Zealand)
Chatham Island
Waitangi
Pitt Island

Bounty Islands (New Zealand)

an Sea

Tasman Sea

Auckland Islands (New Zealand)
Antipodes Islands (New Zealand)

oceania
southeast australia

1:5 000 000

Lambert Azimuthal Equal Area Projection

NEW ZEALAND

Tasman Sea

PACIFIC OCEAN

North Island

South Island

Three Kings Islands
Cape Maria van Diemen
North Cape
Te Paki
Ninety Mile Beach
Cape Karikari
Doubtless Bay
Ahipara Bay
Tauroa Point
Bay of Islands
Cape Brett
Kaitaia
Kerikeri
Broadwood
Russell
Kawakawa
Poor Knights Islands
Donnellys Crossing
Dargaville
Whangarei
Maungaturoto
Bream Bay
Mokohinau Islands
Welsford
Leigh
Port Fitzroy
Great Barrier Island
North Head
Kaipara Harbour
Kawau Island
Colville Channel
Helensville
Orewa
Hauraki Gulf
Waiheke Island
Colville
Mercury Islands
East Coast Bays
Takapuna
Whitianga
Coromandel Peninsula
Auckland
Manukau
The Aldermen Islands
Manukau Harbour
Papakura
Thames
Whangamata
Pukekohe
Waiuku
Mayor Island
Port Waikato
Waihi
Matakana Island
Whakaari
1075
Cape Runaway
Huntly
Tauranga
Hicks Bay
Te Araroa
Hamilton
Cambridge
Lake Rotorua
East Cape
Ruatoria
Kawhia Harbour
Te Awamutu
Rotorua
Raukumara Range
1754
Hikurangi
Otorohanga
Te Kuiti
Mount Tarawera (Tarawera)
Opotiki
Tokomaru Bay
Piopio
Mangakino
Whakatane
Urewera National Park
Tolaga Bay
Awakino
Mokau
Okahukura
Ohura
Taupo
Matawai
Gisborne
North Taranaki Bight
Whanganui National Park
Lake Taupo
Poverty Bay
New Plymouth
Mount Taranaki (Mount Egmont)
Kaimanawa Mountains
Wairoa
Table Cape
Cape Egmont
Egmont National Park
Tongariro National Park
Mahia Peninsula
Opunake
Taihape
Hawke Bay
Hawera
Ruahine Range
Hastings
Napier
South Taranaki Bight
Waiouru
Cape Kidnappers
Wanganui
Havelock North
Turakina
Tikokino
Waimarama
Marton
Feilding
Dannevirke
Palmerston North
Waipukurau
Porangahau
Cape Farewell
Farewell Spit
Cape Stephens
Cook Strait
Levin
Cape Turnagain
Kahurangi Point
Collingwood
Golden Bay
D'Urville Island
Otaki
Kapiti Island
Abel Tasman National Park
Tasman Bay
Paraparaumu
Masterton
Castlepoint
Tasman Mountains
Kahurangi National Park
Riwaka
Porirua
Upper Hutt
Karamea
Richmond
Nelson
Takaka
Lower Hutt
WELLINGTON
Karamea Bight
Seddonville
Hope Saddle
Motueka
Wakefield
Havelock
Blenheim
Mount Ross
Palliser Bay
Waimangaroa
Owen River
Buller
Wairau
983
Cape Palliser
Charleston
Westport
Seddon
Mount Travers
2131
Awatere
Inland Kaikoura Range
Cape Campbell
Paparoa National Park
Reefton
2338
Tapuaenuku
Manakau
Greymouth
Victoria Range
Nelson Lakes Nat. Park
2885
Clarence
2610
Springs Junction
Lewis Pass
Hanmer Springs
Kaikoura
Hokitika
Lake Brunner
Rotomanu
Hope
Ross
Arthur's Pass National Park
Lake Sumner
Culverden
Parnassus
Cheviot
Abut Head
Harihari
Puketeraki Range
Waitari
Waipara
Pegasus Bay
Westland National Park
Franz Josef Glacier
Oxford
Rangiora
Fox Glacier
3117
Mount Arrowsmith
2795
Kaiapoi
Sheffield
Southern Alps
Christchurch
Aoraki (Mount Cook)
3754
Mount Cook National Park
Canterbury Plains
Aylesbury
Sumner
Cascade Point
L. Tekapo
Rakaia
Banks Peninsula
Jackson Head
Lake Paringa
Mount Ward
2614
Lake Tekapo
Pleasant Point
Akaroa
Lake Pukaki
Mayfield
Taitapu
Lake Ellesmere
Mount Aspiring National Park
Mount Aspiring
3030
Ashburton
Longbeach
Canterbury Bight
South Island
Milford Sound
Mount Aspiring
2347
The Hunters Hills
Temuka
Milford Sound
Mount Earnslaw
2819
Timaru
Mount Christina
Kinloch
Lake Hawea
Otematata
Pareora
George Sound
1969
Lake Wanaka
Kurow
Waimate
Secretary Island
Fiordland
Lake Te Anau
Richardson Mts
Wanaka
Studholme Junction
Doubtful Sound
Mount Alta
2350
Dunstan Mts
Cascade
Waimate
Breaksea Sound
Fiordland National Park
Te Anau
Eyre Mountains
James Peak
1969
Hawkdun Range
Duntroon
Oamaru
Lake Manapouri
2171
Alexandra
Lammerlaw Range
Cape Wanbrow
Resolution Island
Lake Manapouri
Mossburn
Ranfurly
Moeraki Point
Caroline Peak
1722
Hyde
Shag Point
Cape Providence
Lumsden
Roxburgh
Middlemarch
Palmerston
Puysegur Point
Ohai
Mandeville
Beaumont
Warrington
Waikouaiti
Gore
Waitahuna
Mosgiel
Port Chalmers
Te Waewae Bay
Orepuki
Waipahi
Dunedin
Otago Peninsula
Solander Island
Riverton
Edendale
Mount Pye
720
Balclutha
Henley
Milton
Invercargill
Wyndham
Mataura
Nugget Point
Bluff
Fortrose
Kaitangata
Long Point
Foveaux Strait
Ruapuke Island
Chaslands Mistake
Codfish Island
Mason Bay
Halfmoon Bay
Muttonbird Islands
Stewart Island
Shelter Point
South West Cape
North Trap

Conic Equidistant Projection

1:5 250 000

0   50   100   150   miles
0   50   100   150   200   250   km

north america
canada

north america
northeast united states

1 : 3 500 000

Lambert Conformal Conic Projection

north america

central america and the caribbean

south america
northern south america

53

south america
southern south america

1:14 000 000

Lambert Azimuthal Equal Area Projection

Lambert Azimuthal Equal Area Projection

1 : 7 000 000

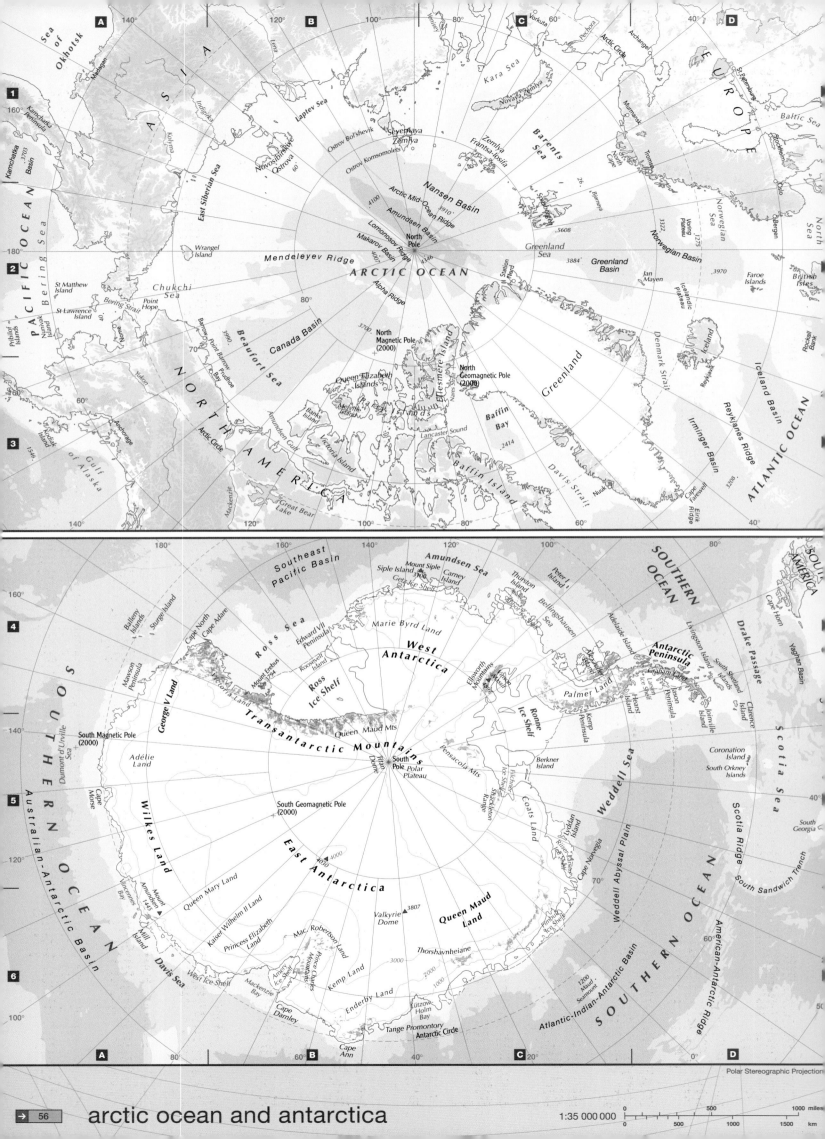

arctic ocean and antarctica

1:35 000 000

Polar Stereographic Projection

INDEX

The index includes the most significant names on the maps in the atlas. The names are generally indexed to the largest scale map on which they appear. For large physical features this will be the largest scale map on which they appear in their entirety or in the majority. Names can be located using the grid reference letters and numbers around the edges of the map. Names located on insets have a symbol □.

Abbreviations used to describe features in the index:

admin. dist.	administrative district	g.	gulf	prov.	province
admin. div.	administrative division	hd.	headland	pt	point
admin. reg.	administrative region	i.	island	r.	river
aut. reg.	autonomous region	imp. lake	impermanent lake	r. mouth	river mouth
aut. rep.	autonomous republic	is.	islands	reg.	region
b.	bay	l.	lake	resr.	reservoir
c.	cape	lag.	lagoon	salt l.	salt lake
depr.	depression	mt.	mountain	sea chan.	sea channel
des.	desert	mts	mountains	terr.	territory
esc.	escarpment	pen.	peninsula	vol.	volcano
est.	estuary	plat.	plateau		
for.	forest	pref.	prefecture		

1

54D5 9 de Julio
54D5 25 de Mayo

A

13K5 Aachen
13M6 Aalen
12J5 Aalst
45M3 Aasiaat
32D4 Aba
33H1 Ābādān
26E3 Abādeh
26E3 Abādeh
32C1 Abadla
55B2 Abaeté
53I4 Abaetetuba
32D4 Abakaliki
24K4 Abakan
24J4 Abakanskiy Khrebet mts
52D6 Abancay
26E3 Abarqū
30G3 Abashiri
11H8 Abay
47I6 Abbeville
33F3 Abéché
32C4 Abengourou
11F9 Abenrá
32D4 Abeokuta
15D7 Aberdare
16G3 Aberdeen
42E4 Aberdeen
46H2 Aberdeen
15D7 Aberdovey
15C6 Aberystwyth
33H1 Abhā
33H1 Abhar
32C4 Abidjan
46H5 Abilene
15F7 Abingdon
23H7 Abinsk
45J5 Abitibi, Lake
32C4 Aboisso
32D4 Abomey
32E4 Abong Mbang
16G3 Aboyne
34E1 Abqaiq
19B4 Abrantes
46E3 Absaroka Range mts
34E2 Abū 'Arīsh
26E4 Abu Dhabi
33G3 Abu Hamed
32D4 Abuja
33H1 Abū Kamāl
27G4 Abu Road
53I5 Açailândia
50C4 Acaponeta
50C4 Acapulco
53I4 Acaraú
53I4 Acaraú
52E2 Acarigua
50E5 Acatlán
32C4 Accra
14E5 Accrington
52E2 Achaguas
30B3 Acheng
24K4 Achinsk
21M6 Açıpayam
20I6 Acireale
47M7 Acklins Island
15B4 Acle
53K5 Aconcagua, Cerro mt.
19B2 A Coruña
20C2 Acqui Terme
20G5 Acri
47H5 Ada
33G2 Adamantina
48E1 Adams
33G1 Adana
34E1 Ad Dafinah
34E1 Ad Dahnā' des.
32B2 Ad Dakhla
34D1 Ad Dār al Hamrā'
34E2 Ad Darb
34E1 Ad Dawādimī
34D3 Addis Ababa
33H1 Ad Dīwānīyah
15G7 Addlestone
41H6 Adelaide
34E2 Aden
34E2 Aden, Gulf of
34D2 Adigrat
33E2 Adirī
48D1 Adirondack Mountains
21L1 Adjud
40F2 Admiralty Gulf
38E2 Admiralty Islands
32D4 Ado-Ekiti
20F6 Adrano
32C2 Adrar
20E2 Adriatic Sea
32C4 Adzopé
21K5 Aegean Sea
19B2 A Estrada
19B2 Afanas'yevo
22I4 Afghanistan
34E3 Afgooye
53K5 Afogados da Ingazeira
55C3 Afonso Cláudio
53H4 Afuá
32C1 Agadir
27G2 Agadyr'
23I8 Agara
27I4 Agartala
32C4 Agboville
23I8 Ağcabādi
18F5 Agde
18E4 Agen
21J6 Agios Dimitrios
21H7 Agios Nikolaos
21K2 Agirtós (?)
27G4 Agra
23I8 Ağri
20E6 Agrigento
21I5 Agrinio
51K5 Aguadilla
46F5 Agua Prieta
50D4 Aguascalientes
55A3 Agudos

19F5 Águilas
36E8 Agulhas, Cape
26D3 Ahar
27G4 Ahmadabad
34E3 Ahmar mts
23I7 Aleksandrovskoye
11O7 Ahtme
21J5 Aigio
47K5 Aiken
20B7 Aïn Beïda
19H5 Aïn Defla
19G6 Aïn Deheb
22K5 Alekseyevskoye
19H6 Aïn el Hadjel
19H6 Aïn Oussera
32C1 Aïn Sefra
18E2 Aïn Taya
19G6 Aïn Témouchent
19F6 Aïn Temouchent
16F5 Airdrie
33G1 Aleppo
21J1 Aiud
18G4 Alès
21J1 Aiud
20C2 Alessandria
18G5 Aix-en-Provence
18G4 Aix-les-Bains
10E5 Alesund
11N8 Aizkraukle
31E5 Aizu-wakamatsu
36C5 Alexander Bay
18I6 Ajaccio
42B6 Alexandra
33F1 Ajdābiyā
16E5 Ajka
21K3 Alexandria
27G4 Ajmer
33F1 Alexandria
21N4 Akçakoca
47I5 Alexandria
23H6 Akçakale
48C3 Alexandria
23H6 Akhisar
21K4 Alexandroupoli
23I6 Akhtubinsk
24J4 Aleysk
23I8 Akhty
33G2 Al Fayyūm
11K7 Akita
55B3 Alfenas
11K7 Akita
23H6 Al Fujayrah
27G1 Akkol'
34J2 Al Ghaydah
20C4 Alghero
20C4 Alghero
33G2 Al Ghurdaqah
23H8 Akkus
33G2 Al Ghurdaqah
32E4 Akom II
19H5 Algiers
19H5 Algiers
37G7 Algoa Bay
55B3 Americana
46E3 American Fork
39J3 American Samoa terr.
33H1 Al Hadīthah
23H7 Aksay
47K5 Americus
21N5 Akşehir
12J4 Amersfoort
27H2 Aksu
15G7 Amersham
23K5 Aksubayevo
47J1 Ames
26E2 Aktau
33H1 Al Hayy
27I4 Aktobe
33H1 Al Hayy
23F5 Aktsyabrski
21J5 Amfissa
19E6 Akune
25O3 Amga
34E1 Al Hoceima
17F3 Antrim
34E1 Al Hufūf
21J5 Amiens
27H4 Akwanga
21I5 Alicante-Alacant
46G6 Amistad Reservoir
53K4 Akyazı
14C5 Amlwch
40G4 Alice Springs
12J5 Amman
31E1 Al Hufūf
21I5 Amlwch

27J4 Bhutan
23D5 Biała Podlaska
13D4 Białogard
11M10 Białystok
18D5 Biarritz
30F4 Bibai
13L6 Biberach an der Riß
55C3 Bicas
15F7 Bicester
32D4 Bida
48F1 Biddeford
15C7 Bideford
15C7 Bideford Bay
18H3 Biel
13N6 Böhmer Wald mts
13L4 Bielefeld
20C2 Biella
13O6 Bielsko-Biała
29C6 Biên Hoa
35B5 Bié Plateau
21L4 Biga
21M5 Bigadiç
21L5 Biga Yarımadası pen.
46F1 Biggar
15G6 Biggleswade
46F3 Bighorn Mountains
32B3 Bioko
47J3 Big Rapids
46G5 Big Spring
45I4 Big Trout Lake
20F2 Bihać
33H1 Bijār
21H2 Bijeljina
21H3 Bijelo Polje
27G4 Bikaner
30D3 Bikin
23F6 Bila Tserkva
19E2 Bilbao
21M4 Bilecik
23D6 Bilhoraj
21N1 Bilhorod-Dnistrovs'kyy
25R3 Bilibino
15H7 Billericay
14F4 Billingham
46F2 Billings
15E8 Bill of Portland hd
23G7 Bilohirs'k
23E6 Bilohir''ya
23H6 Bilovods'k
47J5 Biloxi
33F3 Biltine
21N1 Bilyayivka
47L6 Bimini Islands
35D5 Bindura
48D1 Binghamton
29D7 Bintulu
30B3 Binxian
32D4 Bioco i.
34C2 Birao
27I6 Bireun
55A3 Birigüi
26E3 Bīrjand
14D5 Birkenhead
20F7 Birkirkara
15F6 Birmingham
47J5 Birmingham
32D3 Birnin-Gwari
32D3 Birnin-Kebbi
32D3 Birnin Konni
30D2 Birobidzhan
11N8 Biržai
46F5 Bisbee
18B4 Biscay, Bay of sea
27G2 Bishkek
37H7 Bisho
14F4 Bishop Auckland
15H7 Bishop's Stortford
32D1 Biskra
46G2 Bismarck
38E2 Bismarck Archipelago is
38E2 Bismarck Sea
32B3 Bissau
21K1 Bistrița
21I4 Bitola
20G4 Bitonto
46D2 Bitterroot Range mts
32E3 Biu
31D6 Biwa-ko l.
24J4 Biysk
20C6 Bizerte
10K5 Bjästa
20G2 Bjelovar
11F8 Bjerringbro
11J6 Björklinge
24C2 Bjørnøya i.
32C3 Bla
38E4 Blackall
14E5 Blackburn
13I7 Black Forest mts
14D5 Blackpool
48A4 Blacksburg
23H8 Black Sea
17F3 Blackwater r.
23I7 Blagodarnyy
21J3 Blagoevgrad
30B2 Blagoveshchensk
18H4 Blanc, Mont mt.
54D5 Blanca, Bahía b.
41H5 Blanche, Lake salt flat
19J3 Blanes
13P6 Blansko
35D5 Blantyre
42D4 Blayney
43D5 Blenheim
17F4 Blessington Lakes
15G6 Bletchley
19H5 Blida
37H5 Bloemfontein
37H4 Bloemhof
47J3 Bloomington
48C2 Bloomsburg
15F6 Bloxham
48A4 Bluefield
51H6 Bluefields
42D4 Blue Mountains
33G3 Blue Nile r.
48B4 Blue Ridge
48A4 Blue Ridge mts
55A4 Blumenau
32B4 Bo
52F3 Boa Esperança
32C5 Bobo-Dioulasso
23I6 Bobrov
23G6 Bobrovytsya
52E5 Boca do Acre
55C2 Bocaiúva
51I7 Bocas del Toro
13R6 Bochnia
13L5 Bochum
37I2 Bochum
15C8 Bodmin
15C8 Bodmin Moor
10I3 Bodø
33F5 Boende
32C3 Bogandé

17C5 Boggeragh Mts hills
15G8 Bognor Regis
23H5 Bogoroditsk
52D3 Bogotá
24J4 Bogotol
25K4 Boguchany
23I6 Boguchar
32B3 Bogué
27K3 Bo Hai g.
27K3 Bohai Wan b.
37H6 Bohlokong
13N6 Böhmer Wald mts
23I6 Bohodukhiv
29E7 Bohol Sea
27H2 Bohu
46D3 Boise
26E3 Bojnūrd
17D4 Boyle
21L5 Bozcaada i.
32B3 Bozdoğan
21M6 Bozdoğan
46E2 Bozeman
34B3 Bozoum
21L5 Bozüyük
24J4 Boguchany
19G7 Brač i.
27K3 Bohu
52C3 Buga
30A2 Bugt
21L1 Buhuşi
15D6 Builth Wells
23K5 Buinsk
21I3 Bujanovac
34C4 Bujumbura
34C4 Bukavu
26F3 Bukhara
29C8 Bukittinggi
46E5 California, Gulf of
48C2 Carlisle
14F5 Carlisle
46G5 Carlsbad
16F5 Carluke
44H5 Carlyle
3584 Calulo
35B5 Caluquembe
15D7 Camaçari
35B5 Camacupa
51I4 Camagüey
53H7 Camaná
35C5 Camanongue
53H7 Camapuã
35C5 Camaquã
55B2 Camaquã
29C6 Buôn Mê Thuột
34E3 Burao
34E1 Buraydah
49C3 Burbank
21N6 Burdur
34D2 Burē
10L4 Burea
11O9 Braslaw
21K2 Braşov
10L4 Brea
21N1 Bratislava
25L4 Bratsk
13N6 Braunau am Inn
13M4 Braunschweig
46H6 Bravo del Norte, Río r.
49E4 Brawley
17F4 Bray
55A3 Brazil
53G5 Brazil r.
47H6 Brazos r.
34C4 Brazzaville
13P6 Brčko
35B4 Brazzaville

42B3 Bourke
15F8 Bournemouth
16F4 Buckhaven
41H2 Buckingham Bay
23F5 Buda-Kashalyova
21H1 Budapest
15C8 Bude
23J7 Budennovsk
42F1 Buderim
52C3 Buenaventura
54E4 Buenos Aires
55D1 Buerarema
48B1 Buffalo
23L2 Bug r.
13S5 Bug r.
52C3 Buga
30A2 Bugt
21L1 Buhuşi
15D6 Builth Wells
23K5 Buinsk
21I3 Bujanovac
34C4 Bujumbura
34C4 Bukavu
26F3 Bukhara
29C8 Bukittinggi
46E5 Bukoba
18I3 Bülach
52C6 Callao
15C8 Callington
20F6 Caltagirone
20F6 Caltanissetta
35B4 Calulo
35B5 Caluquembe
18I5 Calvi
55D1 Camaçari
35B5 Camacupa
51I4 Camagüey
53H7 Camaná
35C5 Camanongue
53H7 Camapuã
35C5 Camaquã
55B2 Camaquã
34D3 Camarón
48D3 Camarillo
34E3 Ca Mau
15G7 Camberley
29C6 Camboriú
15B8 Camborne
18F1 Cambrai
15D6 Cambrian Mountains hills
34B3 Cambridge
47I2 Cambridge
15G8 Cambridge
48A1 Cambridge
48C3 Cambridge
45H3 Cambridge Bay
35C4 Cambulo
55A2 Cambuquira
53J5 Buriti Bravo
55B3 Cambuquira
47I5 Camden
48F1 Camden
49B1 Cameroon
55B3 Cameroun, Mont vol.
47I5 Camden

48A3 Buckhannon
52C5 Cajamarca
16F4 Buckhaven
16G6 Buckhaven
41H2 Buckingham Bay
20C1 Čakovec
32D4 Calabar
20C5 Carbondale
21I3 Calafat
18E1 Calais
54C2 Calama
19F3 Calamocha
21I3 Calaf
18E1 Calais
54C2 Calama
19F3 Calamocha
21K3 Calafat
33B5 Calaguembe
29E6 Calapan
21L2 Călăraşi
52C3 Calbayog
53H3 Calçoene
19B4 Caldas da Rainha
53I7 Caldas Novas
46D3 Caldwell
49E4 Calexico
44G4 Calgary
52I3 Cali
27G5 Calicut
37H4 Carletonville
46E5 California state
48C2 California, Gulf of
48B2 Carlisle
21I3 Calafat
18E1 Calais
54C2 Calama
19F3 Calamocha
21K3 Calama
33B5 Calulo
29E6 Calapan
21L2 Calbayog

33G1 Cairo
52C5 Cajamarca
52C5 Cajuru
20C1 Cakovec
32D4 Calabar
20C5 Carbondale
20C5 Carbonia
55C2 Carbonita
19E4 Carcaixent
18F5 Carcassonne
47K7 Cárdenas
50E4 Cárdenas
15D7 Cardiff
15C6 Cardigan
15C6 Cardigan Bay
55A3 Cardoso
51I3 Calçoene
21I1 Carei
23G8 Çerkeş
53H3 Cariacica
52C4 Carauari
52C6 Cariaco
44G4 Caribou
51H5 Caribbean Sea
46E5 California state
46E5 California, Gulf of
48B2 Carlisle
14F5 Carlisle
46G5 Carlsbad
16F5 Carluke
44H5 Carlyle
20B2 Carmagnola
15C7 Carmarthen
15C7 Carmarthen Bay
18F4 Carmaux
54C5 Carmen de Patagones
46G3 Carmo r.
26F3 Carmo da Cachoeira
55B2 Carmo do Paranaíba
54E4 Carnarvon
40E5 Carnarvon Range hills
40E5 Carnegie, Lake salt flat
18G3 Carnot
16G4 Carnoustie
35D5 Carolina
29G7 Caroline Islands
52F2 Caroni r.
23C6 Carpathian Mountains
41H2 Carpentaria, Gulf of
18G4 Carpentras
20D2 Carpi
50F5 Carrantuohill mt.
17C6 Carrara
27G3 Carrickfergus
17D4 Carrick-on-Shannon
17E5 Carrick-on-Suir
46H6 Carrizo Springs
47J3 Carroll
47J5 Carrollton
32A3 Carson City
19F5 Cartagena
51I7 Cartagena
47I7 Carthage
53I6 Caruaru

34B3 Central African Republic
46H3 Central City
38E2 Central Range mts
20C5 Carbondale
23H5 Central Russian Upland hills
25M3 Central Siberian Plateau
21I5 Cephalonia i.
36D7 Ceres
49B2 Ceres
54D3 Ceres
55A1 Ceres
23G8 Cerkeş
21M2 Cernavodă
50D4 Cerritos
51H4 Cerro Azul
45I3 Cerro de Pasco
20E2 Cesena
11N8 Cēsis
13O6 České Budějovice
13O6 Českomoravská Vysočina hills
13O6 Český Krumlov
46G3 Cheyenne
21L5 Cessnock
20H3 Cetinje
19D6 Ceuta
26F4 Chābahār
55C2 Chachapoyas
33E3 Chad
33E3 Chad, Lake
24K4 Chadan
46G3 Chadron
35B5 Chad7leev r.
26F3 Chaghcharān
22G4 Chagoda
19H6 Chahbounia
54E4 Chajari
52D7 Chala
50G6 Chalatenango
21J5 Chalkida
34D2 Chalatenango
40E5 Châlons-en-Champagne
18G3 Chalon-sur-Saône
35C5 Chibia
18G3 Chillán

25M3 Chernyshevskiy
23I6 Chernyshkovskiy
23J7 Chernye Zemli reg.
23I6 Chernyy Yar
48D3 Chervel r.
23I6 Cherven Bryag
23I6 Chervonohrad
21I5 Chervyen'
15F7 Cherwell r.
47L4 Chesapeake
48C3 Chesapeake Bay
15G7 Chesham
14F5 Chester
15G7 Cheshunt
55A1 Chester
14E5 Chesterfield
45I3 Chesterfield Inlet
14F5 Chester-le-Street
46H3 Chetumal
44F4 Chetwynd
14E4 Cheviot Hills
46G3 Cheyenne
26F3 Chhapra
28B6 Chiang Mai
28B6 Chiang Rai
31F6 Chiba
31E6 Chichibu
46H4 Chickasha
19C5 Chiclana de la Frontera
52C5 Chiclayo
48E1 Chico r.
48E1 Chicopee
45K5 Chicoutimi
18F4 Chieti
27K2 Chifeng
46F6 Chihuahua
21J5 Childers
41K5 Childress
54B4 Chile
35C5 Chile Chico
35C5 Chililabombwe
14F4 Cleveland Hills

20E3 Città di Castello
23I6 Chernyshkovskiy
23J7 Chernye Zemli reg.
52F2 Ciudad
18B2 Compiègne
21M1 Comrat
52F2 Ciudad Altamirano
52F2 Ciudad Bolívar
46F6 Ciudad Camargo
46F6 Ciudad Constitución
55C2 Ciudad del Carmen
52F2 Ciudad Delicias
50E4 Ciudad de Valles
51H5 Ciudad Guayana
46F6 Ciudad Guzmán
46F5 Ciudad Juárez
50E4 Ciudad Mante
46H4 Ciudad Obregón
50E4 Ciudad Real
19E4 Ciudad Real
19D3 Ciudad Rodrigo
14E5 Ciudad Victoria
19C3 Civa
20D3 Civitanova Marche
20D3 Civitavecchia
34C4 Congo
21I5 Congleton
15I7 Clacton-on-Sea
17E4 Clara
41H6 Clare
48E1 Claremont
46E1 Claresholm
48A3 Clarksburg
47I5 Clarksdale
47I5 Clarksville
50C6 Clervaux
48E1 Clevedon
40G5 Cleveland
47K4 Cleveland
48A2 Cleveland
14F4 Cleveland Hills
14C5 Cleveleys
47I3 Clinton
42C5 Clonakilty
47J3 Cloncurry
41H5 Clones
16C5 Clovelly
46G4 Clovis
21I4 Cluj-Napoca
18H3 Clwydian Range hills
21K3 Coari
15I6 Clyde r.
16E5 Clyde, Firth of est.
16E5 Clydebank
42F2 Coraki
24J5 Coari

15F6 Coventry
19C3 Covilhã
48A4 Covington
40E6 Cowan, Lake
19C3 Covilhã
16F4 Cowdenbeath
15F8 Cowes
42D4 Cowra
53H7 Coxim
51G4 Cozumel
46E3 Craig
17F3 Craigavon
42B6 Craigieburn
13M6 Crailsheim
21I2 Craiova
21I2 Cramlington
44G5 Cranbrook
15E6 Credenhill
20C2 Crema
15E6 Cremona
20C2 Crewe
15E5 Criciúma
15E5 Crieff
21I2 Crimea pen.
53I6 Cristalândia
55A2 Cristalina
20I3 Crna Gora aut. rep.
20F2 Croatia
15G7 Crawley
15E6 Crediton
20C2 Crema
20C2 Cremona
20C2 Crewe
47J5 Crestview
47I5 Creswick
21K7 Crete i.
15E5 Crewe
53I6 Criciúma
20C2 Crestview
39J3 Cook Islands terr.
42D5 Crookwell
14D5 Crosby
20G5 Crotone
48A3 Crowborough
42F1 Crows Nest
40E6 Coolgardie
48B3 Coonabarabran
42D3 Coonamble
46F1 Crossett
47I3 Coos Bay
41H6 Crystal Brook
46H6 Crystal City
21I1 Csongrád
46F6 Cuauhtémoc
51H4 Cuba
35C5 Cubango r.
55B3 Cubatão
52C2 Cúcuta
27G5 Cuddalore
27G5 Cuddapah
19E3 Cuenca
52C4 Cuenca
52C4 Cuernavaca
21J2 Cugir
53G7 Cuiabá
16C3 Cuillin Hills
16C3 Cuillin Sound sea chan.
30C3 Cuiluan
42C5 Culcairn
46F7 Culiacán
46H5 Cullera
17I5 Cullybackey
17G2 Culpeper
52C1 Cumaná
48B3 Cumberland
47J4 Cumberland Plateau
45I3 Cumberland Sound sea chan.
42C5 Cumnock
35C5 Cunnamulla
51G4 Curaçao i.
51K6 Curaçao i.
55A4 Curitiba
55A4 Curitibanos
53K5 Currais Novos
55B2 Curvelo
52C6 Cusco
27H4 Cuttack
51J4 Cuxhaven
47H5 Cuyahoga Falls
34C4 Cyangugu
21K6 Cyclades is
33G1 Cyprus
15D7 Cwmbran
13O5 Częstochowa

D
30B3 Da'an
33A4 Dabakala
32B3 Dabola
13M6 Dachau
29E6 Daet
32B3 Dagana
30A2 Da Hinggan Ling mts
32B3 Dakar
33F2 Dākhilah, Wāhāt ad oasis
21I3 Đakovica
32B3 Dalaba
30B3 Dalain Hob
11J6 Dälälven r.
32D2 Dalandzadgad
29C6 Đa Lat
54D3 Dale City
52D7 Dali
47H5 Dallas
47H5 Dallas
30C3 Dal'negorsk
30D3 Dal'nerechensk
30D4 Daloa
49B2 Daly City
32E3 Damanhūr
16D3 Damascus
32E3 Damaturu
40D4 Dampier
40D4 Dampier Archipelago is

58

29F8 Dampir, Selat *sea chan.*
32C4 Danané
29C6 Đa Năng
48E2 Danbury
31B4 Dandong
50G5 Dangriga
22I4 Danilov
23J6 Danilovka
23H5 Dankov
51G6 Danlí
32C3 Dano
23F7 Danube *r.*
47J3 Danville
47L4 Danville
48C2 Danville
32C4 Daoukro
32D3 Dapaong
27I3 Da Qaidam Zhen
30B3 Daqing
32B3 Dara
33G1 Dar'ā
26E4 Dārāb
32E3 Darazo
21L4 Dardanelles *strait*
35D4 Dar es Salaam
43D2 Dargaville
27J2 Darhan
52C2 Darién, Golfo del *g.*
27H4 Darjiling
42B3 Darling *r.*
42D1 Darling Downs *hills*
40D6 Darling Range *hills*
14F4 Darlington
13L6 Darmstadt
33F1 Darnah
19F3 Daroca
22J4 Darovskoy
15H7 Dartford
15C8 Dartmoor *hills*
15D8 Dartmouth
45L5 Dartmouth
38E2 Daru
14E5 Darwen
40G2 Darwin
26E2 Dashoguz
23J8 Daşkäsän
21L6 Datça
30F4 Date
27K2 Datong
11N8 Daugava *r.*
11O9 Daugavpils
29E7 Davao
47I3 Davenport
15F6 Daventry
37I4 Daveyton
51H7 David
49B1 Davis
45M3 Davis Strait
26E5 Dawqah
44F4 Dawson Creek
18D5 Dax
42B6 Daylesford
33H1 Dayr az Zawr
47K4 Dayton
47K6 Daytona Beach
27J3 Dazhou
33G1 Dead Sea *salt l.*
15I7 Deal
15E7 Dean, Forest of
54D4 Deán Funes
14F5 Dearne *r.*
49D2 Death Valley *depr.*
15H9 Deauville
21I4 Debar
21I1 Debrecen
34D3 Debre Zeyit
47J4 Decatur
47J5 Decatur
27G5 Deccan *plat.*
42F1 Deception Bay
13O5 Děčín
47I3 Decorah
32C3 Dédougou
22F4 Dedovichi
14D5 Dee *est.*
15D5 Dee *r.*
16G3 Dee *r.*
32D4 Degema
13N6 Deggendorf
33H1 Dehlorān
21J1 Dej
47J3 De Kalb
34B3 Dékoa
7 Delap-Uliga-Djarrit
37G4 Delareyville
48D3 Delaware *r.*
48D3 Delaware *state*
48D3 Delaware Bay
18H3 Delémont
12J4 Delft
13K4 Delfzijl
27G4 Delhi
19H5 Dellys
49D4 Del Mar
13L4 Delmenhorst
20F2 Delnice
25Q2 De-Longa, Ostrova *is*
46G6 Del Rio
11J6 Delsbo
46F4 Delta
35C4 Demba
23F5 Demidov
46F5 Deming
21M5 Demirci
21L4 Demirköy
33H3 Denakil *reg.*
14D5 Denbigh
27J2 Dengkou
12J4 Den Helder
19G4 Denia
47H3 Denison
21M6 Denizli
42E4 Denman
11F8 Denmark
45P3 Denmark Strait
16F4 Denny
29D8 Denpasar
47H5 Denton
40D6 D'Entrecasteaux, Point
41K1 D'Entrecasteaux Islands
46F4 Denver
48C2 Denver
25O3 Deputatskiy
27G3 Dera Ghazi Khan
15F6 Derby
48E2 Derby
17D5 Derg, Lough *l.*
23K6 Dergachi
23H6 Derhachi
47I5 De Ridder
48E1 Derry
36F7 De Rust
14F6 Derwent *r.*
14G5 Derwent *r.*
26F1 Derzhavinsk
34D2 Desē
47I3 Des Moines
23F6 Desna *r.*
23G5 Desnogorsk
13N5 Dessau
35C5 Dete
13L5 Detmold
47K3 Detroit
47H2 Detroit Lakes
13O7 Deutschlandsberg
21J2 Deva
13K4 Deventer
46H2 Devil's Lake
15F7 Devizes
21L3 Devnya
45I2 Devon Island
41J8 Devonport
21N4 Devrek
27G4 Dewas
14F5 Dewsbury
27J3 Deyang
33H1 Dezfūl
25T3 Dezhneva, Mys *c.*
27K3 Dezhou
34F1 Dhahran
27I4 Dhaka
34E2 Dhamār
27H4 Dhanbad
32B3 Dhar Adrar *hills*
32C3 Dhar Oualâta *hills*
32C3 Dhar Tîchît *hills*
27G5 Dharwad
27G4 Dhule
34E3 Dhuusa Marreeb
49B2 Diablo, Mount
49B2 Diablo Range *mts*
54D4 Diamante
55C2 Diamantina
55C1 Diamantina, Chapada *plat.*
53G6 Diamantino
53I6 Dianópolis
32D3 Diapaga
35C4 Dibaya
27I4 Dibrugarh
46G2 Dickinson
32C3 Didiéni
32C3 Diébougou
32C3 Diéma
15I9 Dieppe
18I3 Dietikon
32E3 Diffa
18H4 Digne-les-Bains
18G3 Dijon
34E2 Dikhil
21L5 Dikili
24J2 Dikson
34D3 Dīla
29E8 Dili
44C4 Dillingham
46E2 Dillon
35C5 Dilolo
27I4 Dimapur
32C4 Dimbokro
21K3 Dimitrovgrad
23K5 Dimitrovgrad
18C2 Dinan
12J5 Dinant
21N5 Dinar
20G2 Dinaric Alps *mts*
27G5 Dindigul
17B5 Dingle Bay
32B3 Dinguiraye
16E3 Dingwall
32C3 Dioïla
54F3 Dionísio Cerqueira
32B3 Diourbel
29E7 Dipolog
32C3 Diré
34E3 Dirē Dawa
40C5 Dirk Hartog Island
34E2 Dirs
41I7 Discovery Bay
55B1 Distrito Federal *admin. dist.*
36F5 Ditloung
55B3 Divinópolis
23I7 Divnoye
32C4 Divo
49B1 Dixon
44E4 Dixon Entrance *sea chan.*
26D3 Diyarbakır
32E2 Djado, Plateau du
34B4 Djambala
19H6 Djelfa
32C3 Djenné
32C3 Djibo
34E2 Djibouti
34E2 Djibouti *country*
32D4 Djougou
32E4 Djoum
23G5 Dmitriyev-L'govskiy
22H4 Dmitrov
26C2 Dnieper *r.*
23F7 Dniester *r.*
23G6 Dniprodzerzhyns'k
23G6 Dnipropetrovs'k
22F4 Dno
33E4 Doba
11M8 Dobele
29F8 Doberai, Jazirah *pen.*
20H2 Doboj
21L3 Dobrich
23I5 Dobrinka
23H5 Dobroye
23F5 Dobrush
21L7 Dodecanese *is*
46G4 Dodge City
35D4 Dodoma
32D3 Dogondoutchi
21M6 Doğu Menteşe Dağları *mts*
34F1 Doha
13J4 Dokkum
11O9 Dokshytsy
23H7 Dokuchayevs'k
18G3 Dole
15D6 Dolgellau
23H5 Dolgorukovo
30F3 Dolinsk
20D2 Dolomites *mts*
54E4 Dolores
54E5 Dolores
23D6 Dolyna
13N6 Domažlice
20H1 Dombóvár
54B3 Domeyko
51L5 Dominica
51J5 Dominican Republic
21J5 Domokos
29D8 Dompu
16G3 Don *r.*
23H7 Don *r.*
17G3 Donaghadee
42A6 Donald
19D4 Don Benito
14F5 Doncaster
35B4 Dondo
17D3 Donegal
17D3 Donegal Bay
23H7 Donets'k
23H6 Donets'kyy Kryazh *hills*
27J4 Dongchuan
27J5 Dongfang
31B5 Donggang
29C6 Đông Hôi
30C3 Dongning
33G3 Dongola
27K4 Dongting Hu *l.*
27K3 Dongying
19F2 Donostia - San Sebastián
23I7 Donskoye
41H3 Doomadgee
15E8 Dorchester
18D4 Dordogne *r.*
12J5 Dordrecht
55B2 Dores do Indaiá
32C3 Dori
15G7 Dorking
16E3 Dornoch Firth *est.*
32C3 Doro
23G5 Dorogobuzh
23E7 Dorohoi
42F3 Dorrigo
13K5 Dortmund
32D3 Dosso
47J5 Dothan
18F1 Douai
32D4 Douala
43A7 Doubtful Sound *inlet*
32C3 Douentza
14C4 Douglas
46F3 Douglas
46F5 Douglas
47K5 Douglas
54F2 Dourados
19B3 Douro *r.*
15I7 Dover
48A2 Dover
48D2 Dover
48D3 Dover
48F1 Dover
15I8 Dover, Strait of
17G3 Downpatrick
48D2 Doylestown
55A3 Dracena
13K4 Drachten
21K2 Drăgănești-Olt
21K2 Drăgășani
18H5 Draguignan
11N10 Drahichyn
37I3 Drakensberg *mts*
21K4 Drama
11G7 Drammen
20H2 Drava *r.*
20B6 Dréan
13N5 Dresden
18E2 Dreux
21J2 Drobeta - Turnu Severin
17F4 Drogheda
23D6 Drohobych
15E6 Droitwich Spa
17F3 Dromore
14F5 Dronfield
45K5 Drummondville
11N10 Druskininkai
11O7 Druzhnaya Gorka
21K3 Dryanovo
55A3 Duartina
26E4 Dubai
45H3 Dubawnt Lake
42D4 Dubbo
17F4 Dublin
47K5 Dublin
22H4 Dubna
23E6 Dubno
23J6 Dubovka
23I7 Dubovskoye
20H3 Dubrovnik
23E6 Dubrovytsya
47I3 Dubuque
24J3 Dudinka
15E6 Dudley
32C4 Duékoué
19C3 Duero *r.*
18H4 Dufourspitze *mt.*
20G3 Dugi Rat
13K5 Duisburg
37H6 Dukathole
23K5 Dukhovnitskoye
21L3 Dulovo
47I2 Duluth
29E7 Dumaguete
27J6 Dumai
46G4 Dumas
16E5 Dumbarton
16F5 Dumfries
33G1 Dumyāṭ
13P7 Dunajská Streda
21H1 Dunakeszi
20H1 Dunaújváros
23E6 Dunayivtsi
46H5 Duncan
16F2 Duncansby Head
11M8 Dundaga
17F3 Dundalk
48C3 Dundalk
17F4 Dundalk Bay
48B1 Dundas
16G4 Dundee
37J5 Dundee
17G3 Dundonald
43C7 Dunedin
16F4 Dunfermline
17F3 Dungannon
17E5 Dungarvan
15H8 Dungeness *hd*
17F3 Dungiven
42E4 Dungog
34C3 Dungu
29C7 Dungun
30C4 Dunhua
18F1 Dunkirk
48B1 Dunkirk
17F4 Dún Laoghaire
48D2 Dunmore
17G3 Dunmurry
16F2 Dunnet Head
48B1 Dunnville
16G5 Duns
15G7 Dunstable
21J3 Dupnitsa
23G8 Durağan
19E2 Durango
46F4 Durango
46G7 Durango
47H5 Durant
54E4 Durazno
37J5 Durban
18F5 Durban-Corbières
36D7 Durbanville
14F4 Durham
47L4 Durham
21M1 Durlești
21H4 Durrës
15F7 Durrington
21M5 Dursunbey
27F3 Dushanbe
13K5 Düsseldorf
32D3 Dutse
32D3 Dutsin-Ma
27J4 Duyun
21N4 Düzce
27F4 Dwarka
23G5 Dyat'kovo
47J4 Dyersburg
15D6 Dyfi *r.*
23H6 Dymytrov
35E5 Dzaoudzi
22I4 Dzerzhinsk
23G7 Dzhankoy
26F2 Dzhizak
26F2 Dzhusaly
13R4 Działdowo
27J2 Dzuunmod
11O10 Dzyarzhynsk

E

46G6 Eagle Pass
16E4 Earn, Loch *l.*
15H8 Eastbourne
28E4 East China Sea
15H6 East Dereham
6 Easter Island
37H6 Eastern Cape *prov.*
33G2 Eastern Desert
27G5 Eastern Ghats *mts*
54E8 East Falkland *i.*
13K4 East Frisian Islands
15G7 East Grinstead
48E1 Easthampton
48E2 East Hartford
16E5 East Kilbride
48A2 Eastlake
15F8 Eastleigh
48A2 East Liverpool
37H7 East London
45K4 Eastmain *r.*
48C3 Easton
48D2 Easton
48D2 East Orange
48F2 East Providence
25P2 East Siberian Sea
29E8 East Timor
48B1 East York
47I3 Eau Claire
15D7 Ebbw Vale
32E4 Ebebiyin
13N4 Eberswalde-Finow
30F4 Ebetsu
20F4 Eboli
32E4 Ebolowa
19G3 Ebro *r.*
19G5 Ech Chélif
19D5 Écija
13L3 Eckernförde
52C4 Ecuador
33H3 Ed
16G1 Eday *i.*
33G3 Ed Damazin
33G3 Ed Damer
33G3 Ed Dueim
32E4 Edéa
55A2 Edéia
42D6 Eden
17E4 Edenderry
21J4 Edessa
46H6 Edinburg
16F5 Edinburgh
21L4 Edirne
44G4 Edmonton
45L5 Edmundston
21L5 Edremit
34C4 Edward, Lake
46G5 Edwards Plateau
47J4 Effingham
13R7 Eger
11E7 Egersund
10□1 Egilsstaðir
21N6 Eğirdir
43D4 Egmont, Cape
25T3 Egvekinot
33G2 Egypt
27J3 Ehen Hudag
13L6 Ehingen (Donau)
13K5 Eifel *hills*
16C4 Eigg *i.*
40E3 Eighty Mile Beach
33G2 Eilat
12J5 Eindhoven
18I3 Einsiedeln
52E5 Eirunepé
13M5 Eisenach
13O4 Eisenhüttenstadt
13P7 Eisenstadt
11M7 Ekenäs
27G1 Ekibastuz
11I8 Eksjö
20B7 El Aouinet
20B6 El Arrouch
26C3 Elazığ
20D3 Elba, Isola d' *i.*
30E2 El'ban
21I4 Elbasan
32D1 El Bayadh
13L4 Elbe *r.*
46F4 Elbert, Mount
15I9 Elbeuf
13Q3 Elbląg
23I8 El'brus *mt.*
26D3 Elburz Mountains
49D4 El Cajon
52F2 El Callao
47H6 El Campo
49E4 El Centro
52F7 El Cerro
19F4 Elche-Elx
19F4 Elda
25O3 El'dikan
47H4 El Dorado
47I5 El Dorado
54F3 Eldorado
55A4 Eldorado
34D3 Eldoret
19E5 El Ejido
34D3 Elemi Triangle *terr.*
47L6 Eleuthera *i.*
33F3 El Fasher
46F6 El Fuerte
33F3 El Geneina
16F3 Elgin
47J3 Elgin
32D1 El Goléa
26C6 Elgon, Mount
20B6 El Hadjar
32C2 El Ḥank *esc.*
51J5 Elías Piña
23J7 Elista
48D2 Elizabeth
47L4 Elizabeth City
47J4 Elizabethtown
32C1 El Jadida
20D7 El Jem
13S4 Ełk
20C6 El Kala
46H4 Elk City
32C1 El Kelaâ des Srarhna
46E1 Elkford
49B1 Elk Grove
47J3 Elkhart
21L3 Elkhovo
48B3 Elkins
46D3 Elko
48D3 Elkton
46C2 Ellensburg
45J2 Ellesmere Island
14E5 Ellesmere Port
48C3 Ellicott City
37H6 Elliot
47N3 Ellsworth
21M6 Elmalı
32D1 El Meghaïer
48C1 Elmira
13L4 Elmshorn
33F3 El Muglad
33G3 El Obeid
32D1 El Oued
46F5 El Paso
46F5 El Porvenir
51I7 El Porvenir
19H3 El Prat de Llobregat
50G5 El Progreso
19C5 El Puerto de Santa María
46H4 El Reno
46F7 El Salto
54C3 El Salvador
50G6 El Salvador *country*
49D4 Elsinore
20C6 El Tarf
52F2 El Tigre
23J6 El'ton
19C4 Elvas
11G6 Elverum
15H6 Ely
47K3 Elyria
26E2 Emba
37I4 Embalenhle
54D2 Embarcación
34D4 Embu
13K4 Emden
21M5 Emet
37J3 eMijindini
33E3 Emi Koussi *mt.*
50F5 Emiliano Zapata
21N5 Emirdağ
11I8 Emmaboda
48D2 Emmaus
13K4 Emmen
18I3 Emmen
37J5 Empangeni
20D3 Empoli
47H4 Emporia
47L4 Emporia
37I4 Emzinoni
54E3 Encarnación
49D4 Encinitas
55C1 Encruzilhada
41I2 Endeavour Strait
48C1 Endicott
23G7 Enerhodar
23J6 Engel's
15E6 England *admin. div.*
15F9 English Channel
46H4 Enid
30F4 Eniwa
11J7 Enköping
20F6 Enna
17D5 Ennis
47H5 Ennis
17F5 Enniscorthy
17E3 Enniskillen
13K4 Enschede
46D5 Ensenada
27J3 Enshi
34D3 Entebbe
55B3 Entre Rios de Minas
19B4 Entroncamento
32D4 Enugu
52D5 Envira
48C2 Ephrata
18H2 Épinal
15G7 Epsom
32D4 Equatorial Guinea
20H1 Érd
21L4 Erdek
54F3 Erechim
21N4 Ereğli
33G1 Ereğli
27K2 Erenhot
13M5 Erfurt
32C2 'Erg Chech *des.*
11N8 Ērgļi
48A1 Erie
48A1 Erie, Lake
34D2 Eritrea
13M6 Erlangen
37I4 Ermelo
33G1 Ermenek
21K6 Ermoupoli
27G5 Erode
36B1 Erongo *admin. reg.*
32C1 Er Rachidia
23I6 Ertil'
13N5 Erzgebirge *mts*
26C3 Erzincan
26D3 Erzurum
11F9 Esbjerg
47J2 Escanaba
50F5 Escárcega
13M5 Eschwege
49D4 Escondido
50C4 Escuinapa
50F6 Escuintla
32E4 Eséka
26E3 Eşfahān
37K5 Esikhawini
11J7 Eskilstuna
23G8 Eskipazar
21N5 Eskişehir
33H1 Eslāmābād-e Gharb
11H9 Eslöv
21M5 Eşme
52C3 Esmeraldas
40E6 Esperance
46F6 Esperanza
55C2 Espinhaço, Serra do *mts*
55C1 Espinosa
55C2 Espírito Santo *state*
39G3 Espíritu Santo *i.*
11N6 Espoo
54B6 Esquel
32C1 Essaouira
32B2 Es Semara
13K5 Essen
53G2 Essequibo *r.*
48C3 Essex
53K6 Estância
37I5 Estcourt
51G6 Estelí
19D5 Estepona
46G2 Estevan
47I3 Estherville
11N7 Estonia
55A5 Estrela
19C3 Estrela, Serra da *mts*
55B2 Estrela do Sul
19C4 Estremoz
18F2 Étampes
37J4 eThandakukhanya
34D3 Ethiopia
20F6 Etna, Mount *vol.*
48B1 Etobicoke
35B5 Etosha Pan *salt pan*
48A2 Euclid
53K6 Euclides da Cunha
46C3 Eugene
26D3 Euphrates *r.*
11M6 Eura
46C3 Eureka
46D2 Eureka
42B6 Euroa
35E6 Europa, Île *i.*
19D5 Europa Point
48A2 Evans City
46E3 Evanston
47J4 Evansville
37H4 Evaton
40G5 Everard Range *hills*
27H4 Everest, Mount
46C2 Everett
47K6 Everglades *swamp*
15F6 Evesham
19C4 Évora
18E2 Évreux
21K5 Evvoia *i.*
16D3 Ewe, Loch *b.*
34B4 Ewo
15D8 Exe *r.*
15D8 Exeter
48F1 Exeter
15D7 Exmoor *hills*
15D8 Exmouth
40C4 Exmouth
40C4 Exmouth Gulf
48D2 Exton
19D4 Extremadura *reg.*
34D4 Eyasi, Lake *salt l.*
16G5 Eyemouth
10□1 Eyjafjörður *inlet*
15F7 Eynsham
41H5 Eyre (North), Lake *salt flat*
41H6 Eyre Peninsula
41H5 Eyre (South), Lake *salt flat*
37J5 Ezakheni
22K3 Ezhva
21L5 Ezine

F

11G9 Fåborg
20E3 Fabriano
32D3 Fada-N'Gourma
20D2 Faenza
21K2 Făgăraș
39I3 Fagatogo
11I7 Fagersta
44D3 Fairbanks
48C3 Fairfax
49A1 Fairfield
17F2 Fair Head
16H1 Fair Isle *i.*
47I3 Fairmont
48A3 Fairmont
27G3 Faisalabad
22K4 Falenki
11H8 Falkenberg
16F5 Falkirk
54E8 Falkland Islands *terr.*
54D8 Falkland Sound *sea chan.*
11H7 Falköping
49D4 Fallbrook
46D4 Fallon
48F2 Fall River
15B8 Falmouth
48C3 Falmouth
36D8 False Bay
11G9 Falster *i.*
23E7 Fălticeni
11I6 Falun
33G1 Famagusta
35E6 Fandriana
30C3 Fangzheng
20E3 Fano
32B3 Faraba
35E6 Farafangana
33F2 Farāfirah, Wāḥāt al *oasis*
26F3 Farāh
32B3 Faranah
15F8 Fareham
43D5 Farewell, Cape
45N3 Farewell, Cape
47H2 Fargo
47I3 Faribault
46F4 Farmington
48B4 Farmville
15G7 Farnborough
15G7 Farnham
19C5 Faro
53G4 Faro
10□2 Faroe Islands *terr.*
35F5 Farquhar Group *is*
11E7 Farsund
20G4 Fasano
23F6 Fastiv
27H4 Fatehpur
32B3 Fatick
10I3 Fauske
15F8 Fawley
10□1 Faxaflói *b.*
33E3 Faya
47I4 Fayetteville
47L4 Fayetteville
32B2 Fdérik
47L5 Fear, Cape
15H9 Fécamp
48D3 Federalsburg
52D5 Feijó
55D1 Feira de Santana
13L7 Feldkirch
13O7 Feldkirchen in Kärnten
50G5 Felipe C. Puerto
55B2 Felixlândia
15I7 Felixstowe
35E5 Fenoarivo Atsinanana
23G7 Feodosiya
21L4 Feres
47H2 Fergus Falls
20C7 Fériana
32C4 Ferkessédougou
20E3 Fermo
19C3 Fermoselle
47K5 Fernandina Beach
55A3 Fernandópolis
20D2 Ferrara
19B2 Ferrol
55C2 Ferros
32C1 Fès
21M6 Fethiye
16□ Fetlar *i.*
27G3 Feyzābād
15D6 Ffestiniog
35E6 Fianarantsoa
21H4 Fier
16G4 Fife Ness *pt*
18F4 Figeac
19B3 Figueira da Foz
19H2 Figueres
32C1 Figuig
33E4 Figuil
39H3 Fiji
54D2 Filadelfia
14G4 Filey
32D3 Filingué
21I5 Filippiada
11I7 Filipstad
49C3 Fillmore
47K3 Findlay
48C1 Finger Lakes
21N6 Finike
19B2 Finisterre, Cape
10O5 Finland
11M7 Finland, Gulf of
10H2 Finnmarksvidda *reg.*
11I7 Finspång
54D4 Firmat
18G4 Firminy
36C5 Fish *watercourse*
45J3 Fisher Strait
15C7 Fishguard
37I6 Flagstaff
46E4 Flagstaff
14G4 Flamborough Head
46C2 Flattery, Cape
14D5 Fleetwood
11E7 Flekkefjord
11J7 Flen
13L3 Flensburg
41J7 Flinders Island
41H6 Flinders Ranges *mts*
44H4 Flin Flon
14D5 Flint
47K3 Flint
20D3 Florence
46E5 Florence
47J5 Florence
47L5 Florence
52C3 Florencia
50G5 Flores
29E8 Flores *i.*
29D8 Flores, Laut *sea*
53K5 Floresta
53J5 Floriano
55A4 Florianópolis
54E4 Florida
47K5 Florida *state*
47K7 Florida, Straits of
49B1 Florin
21I4 Florina
11D6 Florø
21L5 Foça
21L2 Focșani
20F4 Foggia
18E5 Foix
10I3 Folda *sea chan.*
20E3 Foligno
15I7 Folkestone
20D3 Follonica
35E5 Fomboni
47J3 Fond du Lac
20E4 Fondi
52E4 Fonte Boa
10□1 Fontur *pt*
44C3 Foraker, Mount
13M6 Forchheim
15H6 Fordham
15F8 Fordingbridge
32B4 Forécariah
47J5 Forest
42C5 Forest Hill
49A1 Forestville
16G4 Forfar
48D3 Forked River
20E2 Forlì
14D5 Formby
55B3 Formiga
54E3 Formosa
55B1 Formosa
55A1 Formoso *r.*
47I4 Forrest City
11M6 Forssa
42F4 Forster
53K4 Fortaleza
51L6 Fort-de-France
47I3 Fort Dodge
48E1 Fort Edward
16F4 Forth *r.*
16F4 Forth, Firth of *est.*
47K6 Fort Lauderdale
46E2 Fort Macleod
44G4 Fort McMurray
47K6 Fort Myers
47J5 Fort Payne
47K6 Fort Pierce
34D3 Fort Portal
47I4 Fort Scott
44G3 Fort Smith
47I4 Fort Smith
46G5 Fort Stockton
47J3 Fort Wayne
16D4 Fort William
47H5 Fort Worth
20B2 Fossano
42C7 Foster
18D2 Fougères
16□ Foula *i.*
32E4 Foumban
32B3 Fouta Djallon *reg.*
43A8 Foveaux Strait
46G4 Fowler
44G4 Fox Creek
45K3 Foxe Basin *g.*
17E3 Foyle *r.*
17E2 Foyle, Lough *b.*
54F3 Foz do Iguaçu
48F1 Framingham
55B3 Franca
20G4 Francavilla Fontana
18F3 France
34B4 Franceville
35C6 Francistown
47K4 Frankfort
13L5 Frankfurt am Main
13O4 Frankfurt an der Oder
13M6 Fränkische Alb *hills*
48B2 Franklin
48F1 Franklin
46D2 Franklin D. Roosevelt Lake *resr*
42B7 Frankston
24G2 Frantsa-Iosifa, Zemlya *is*
20E4 Frascati
44F5 Fraser *r.*
45L4 Fraser *r.*
16G3 Fraserburgh
18I3 Frauenfeld
54E4 Fray Bentos
14E5 Freckleton
11F9 Fredericia
48C3 Frederick
46H5 Fredericksburg
48C3 Fredericksburg
45L5 Fredericton
11G8 Frederikshavn
11H9 Frederiksværk
48B1 Fredonia
11G7 Fredrikstad
48D2 Freehold
47H6 Freeport
47L6 Freeport City
37H5 Free State *prov.*
32B4 Freetown
13K6 Freiburg im Breisgau
13M6 Freising
13O6 Freistadt
18H5 Fréjus
40D6 Fremantle
47H3 Fremont
49B2 Fremont
53H3 French Guiana *terr.*
6 French Polynesia *terr.*
7 French Southern and Antarctic Lands
19G6 Frenda
50D4 Fresnillo
49C2 Fresno
13L6 Freudenstadt
32B3 Fria
54C3 Frias
18H3 Fribourg
13L7 Friedrichshafen
45L3 Frobisher Bay
10F5 Frohavet *b.*
23I6 Frolovo
15E7 Frome
41H6 Frome, Lake *salt flat*
50F5 Frontera
46F5 Fronteras
48B3 Front Royal
20E4 Frosinone
13Q6 Frýdek-Místek
19E3 Fuenlabrada
54E2 Fuerte Olimpo
32B2 Fuerteventura *i.*
26E4 Fujairah
31E6 Fuji
30C3 Fujin
31E6 Fujinomiya
31E6 Fuji-san *vol.*
31E6 Fujiyoshida
31D6 Fukuchiyama
31E5 Fukui
31C6 Fukuoka
31F5 Fukushima
13L5 Fulda
49D4 Fullerton
47I4 Fulton
48C1 Fulton
31E6 Funabashi
39H2 Funafuti *atoll*
32B1 Funchal
19C3 Fundão
55C2 Fundão
45L5 Fundy, Bay of *g.*
32D3 Funtua
22I4 Furmanov
55B3 Furnas, Represa *resr*
41J8 Furneaux Group *is*
13O4 Fürstenwalde
13M6 Fürth
31F5 Furukawa
30A4 Fushun
30B4 Fusong
27K3 Fuyang
30B3 Fuyu
30B3 Fuyu
27H2 Fuyun
27K4 Fuzhou
28D5 Fuzhou
11G9 Fyn *i.*
16D5 Fyne, Loch *inlet*

G

34E3 Gaalkacyo
35B5 Gabela
32E1 Gabès
32E1 Gabès, Golfe de *g.*
34B4 Gabon
37G3 Gaborone
21K3 Gabrovo
32B3 Gabú
47J5 Gadsden
21K2 Găești
20E4 Gaeta
20C7 Gafsa
23G5 Gagarin
32C4 Gagnoa
23I8 Gagra
47H5 Gainesville
47K5 Gainesville
47K6 Gainesville
14G5 Gainsborough
41H6 Gairdner, Lake *salt flat*
13P6 Galanta
16G5 Galashiels
21M2 Galați
20H4 Galatina
47I3 Galesburg
36G5 Galeshewe
22I4 Galich
19C2 Galicia *reg.*
47J4 Gallatin
27H6 Galle
52D1 Gallinas, Punta *pt*
20H4 Gallipoli
21L4 Gallipoli
10L3 Gällivare
46F4 Gallup
17D5 Galtee Mountains *hills*
47I6 Galveston
47I6 Galveston Bay
17C4 Galway
17C4 Galway Bay
37J6 Gamalakhe
32B3 Gambia, The
34D3 Gambēla
34B4 Gamboma
11J8 Gamleby
23J8 Gäncä
35B5 Ganda
35C4 Gandajika
45M5 Gander
19G3 Gandesa
27G4 Gandhinagar
19F4 Gandía
27G4 Ganganagar
27H3 Gangdisê Shan *mts*
27I4 Ganges *r.*
27H4 Ganges, Mouths of the
30A3 Gannan
44H5 Gannett Peak
32E4 Ganye
32C3 Gao
32C3 Gaoua
32B3 Gaoual
18H4 Gap
32C3 Garalo
53K5 Garanhuns
37H3 Ga-Rankuwa
34E3 Garbahaarey
13L4 Garbsen
55A3 Garça
20D2 Garda, Lake
46G4 Garden City
27F3 Gardēz
48F1 Gardner
11L9 Gargždai
37G6 Gariep Dam *resr*
36C6 Garies
34D4 Garissa
18D4 Garonne *r.*
34E3 Garoowe
55A5 Garopaba
32E4 Garoua
47J3 Gary
46G6 Garza García
18D5 Gascony *reg.*
18C5 Gascony, Gulf of
40C5 Gascoyne *r.*
32E3 Gashua
47N2 Gaspé, Péninsule de *pen.*
47K4 Gastonia
11Q7 Gatchina
14F4 Gateshead
46H5 Gatesville
37I4 Gauteng *prov.*
21K7 Gavdos *i.*
11J6 Gävle
22H4 Gavrilov-Yam
41H6 Gawler
41H6 Gawler Ranges *hills*
32D3 Gaya
32D3 Gayéri
41K5 Gayndah
22L3 Gayny
26C3 Gaza
37K2 Gaza *prov.*
33G1 Gaziantep
32C4 Gbarnga
13Q3 Gdańsk
13Q3 Gdańsk, Gulf of
11O7 Gdov
13Q3 Gdynia
33G3 Gedaref
42B7 Geelong
11F6 Geilo
27J4 Gejiu
20F6 Gela
23H7 Gelendzhik
34B3 Gemena
21M4 Gemlik
54D5 General Acha
54C5 General Alvear
54E5 General Juan Madariaga
54D5 General Pico
54C5 General Roca
55A3 General Salgado
29E7 General Santos
54D5 General Villegas
48C1 Geneseo
18H3 Geneva
48C1 Geneva
18H3 Geneva, Lake
30A2 Genhe
13J5 Genk
20C2 Genoa
20C2 Genoa, Gulf of
40D6 Geographe Bay
40C4 Geographe Channel
36F7 George
29C7 George Town
32B3 Georgetown
46H5 Georgetown
47L5 Georgetown
51H5 George Town
53G2 Georgetown
23I8 Georgia
47K5 Georgia *state*
45J5 Georgian Bay
27H2 Georgiyevka
23I7 Georgiyevsk
13N5 Gera
55B1 Geral de Goiás, Serra *hills*
55B1 Geral do Paraná, Serra *hills*
40C5 Geraldton
23G8 Gerede
13L5 Germany
23G8 Gerze
48C3 Gettysburg
21J4 Gevgelija
21N4 Geyve
32D1 Ghadāmis
32C4 Ghana
35C6 Ghanzi
36F2 Ghanzi *admin. dist.*
32D1 Ghardaïa
33E1 Gharyān
33E3 Ghazal, Bahr el *watercourse*
19F6 Ghazaouet
27G4 Ghaziabad
26F3 Ghaznī
12I5 Ghent
21K1 Gheorgheni
21J1 Gherla
18I5 Ghisonaccia
23I7 Giaginskaya
21J4 Giannitsa
17F2 Giant's Causeway *lava field*
20F6 Giarre
19D5 Gibraltar *terr.*
19C6 Gibraltar, Strait of
40E4 Gibson Desert
13L5 Gießen
31E6 Gifu
19D2 Gijón-Xixón
49E4 Gila *r.*
53I5 Gilbués
42D3 Gilgandra
27G3 Gilgit
46F3 Gillette
15H7 Gillingham
49B2 Gilroy
20G4 Ginosa
20G4 Gioia del Colle
42B7 Gippsland *reg.*
23H8 Giresun
19H3 Girona
18D4 Gironde *est.*
16E5 Girvan
43G4 Gisborne
11H8 Gislaved
34C4 Gitarama
34C4 Gitega
20E3 Giulianova
21K3 Giurgiu
37J2 Giyani
33G2 Giza
21I4 Gjirokastër
11G6 Gjøvik
45M5 Glace Bay
41K4 Gladstone
20G2 Glamoč
16E5 Glasgow
47J4 Glasgow
15E7 Glastonbury
22L4 Glazov
46E5 Glendale
49C3 Glendale
42E2 Glen Innes
16E3 Glen More *valley*
16F4 Glenrothes
48E1 Glens Falls
13Q5 Gliwice
46E5 Globe
13P5 Głogów
10H3 Glomfjord
15E7 Gloucester
42E3 Gloucester
48F1 Gloucester
48D1 Gloversville
23I6 Glubokiy
27H1 Glubokoye
13O6 Gmünd
13N7 Gmunden
13P4 Gniezno
21I3 Gnjilane
34E3 Goba
36D2 Gobabis
27J2 Gobi *des.*
31D6 Gobō
36D3 Gochas
15G7 Godalming
27H5 Godavari *r.*
53L5 Goiana
55A1 Goianésia
55A2 Goiânia
55A1 Goiás
55A2 Goiás *state*
54F2 Goio-Erê
21K4 Gökçeada *i.*
21M4 Gölcük
42F2 Gold Coast
43D5 Golden Bay
47L4 Goldsboro
23I8 Göle
49C3 Goleta
23H8 Gölköy
27I3 Golmud
21N4 Gölpazarı
34C4 Goma
32E3 Gombe
46G6 Gómez Palacio
51J5 Gonaïves
26E3 Gonbad-e Kavus
34D2 Gonder
21L4 Gönen
47H6 Gonzales
36D8 Good Hope, Cape of
14G5 Goole
42E2 Goondiwindi
13L6 Göppingen
27H4 Gorakhpur
21M5 Gördes
34D3 Gorē
17F5 Gorey
26E3 Gorgān
20E2 Gorizia
23D6 Gorlice
13O5 Görlitz
21K3 Gorna Oryakhovitsa
21I2 Gornji Milanovac
20G3 Gornji Vakuf
24J4 Gorno-Altaysk
30F3 Gornozavodsk
24J4 Gornyak
23K6 Gornyy
22I4 Gorodets
23J5 Gorodishche
23J6 Gorodishche
23I7 Gorodovikovsk
38E2 Goroka
22I4 Gorokhovets
32C3 Gorom Gorom
29E7 Gorontalo
23H6 Gorshechnoye
23H7 Goryachiy Klyuch
13O4 Gorzów Wielkopolski
14F3 Gosforth
48D2 Goshen
20F2 Gospić
15F8 Gosport
32C3 Gossi
21I4 Gostivar
11H7 Götene
13M5 Gotha
11G8 Gothenburg
11K8 Gotland *i.*
21J4 Gotse Delchev
31D6 Gōtsu
13L5 Göttingen
12J4 Gouda
45K5 Gouin, Réservoir
42D5 Goulburn
32C3 Goundam
19G5 Gouraya
32C3 Gourcy
32E3 Gouré
55C2 Governador Valadares
27I2 Govĭ Altayn Nuruu *mts*
54E3 Goya
23J8 Göyçay
20F6 Gozo *i.*
36G7 Graaf-Reinet
36D8 Grabouw
20F2 Gračac
42F2 Grafton
48A3 Grafton
46H5 Graham
37H7 Grahamstown
53I5 Grajaú
16E4 Grampian Mountains
19E5 Granada
51G6 Granada
45K5 Granby
32B2 Gran Canaria *i.*
54D3 Gran Chaco *reg.*
47L6 Grand Bahama *i.*
45M5 Grand Bank
45M5 Grand Banks of Newfoundland *sea feature*
32C4 Grand-Bassam
49F2 Grand Canyon *gorge*
51H5 Grand Cayman *i.*
54C8 Grande, Bahía *b.*
44G4 Grande Prairie
32E3 Grand Erg de Bilma *des.*
32C1 Grand Erg Occidental *des.*
32D2 Grand Erg Oriental *des.*
54C4 Grandes, Salinas *salt marsh*
45M5 Grand Falls
47H2 Grand Forks
46H3 Grand Island
46F4 Grand Junction
32C4 Grand-Lahou
19B4 Grândola
47I2 Grand Rapids
47J3 Grand Rapids
51J4 Grand Turk
11I6 Grängesberg
53J4 Granja
11I7 Gränna
15G6 Grantham
16F3 Grantown-on-Spey
46F4 Grants
46C3 Grants Pass
48C2 Grantville
55C2 Grão Mogol
37J3 Graskop
18H5 Grasse
19G2 Graus
55A5 Gravataí
15H7 Gravesend
20G4 Gravina in Puglia
15H7 Grays
13O7 Graz
47L6 Great Abaco *i.*
40F6 Great Australian Bight *g.*
47L6 Great Bahama Bank *sea feature*
43E3 Great Barrier Island
41I2 Great Barrier Reef
46D4 Great Basin
44G3 Great Bear Lake
11G9 Great Belt *sea chan.*
46H4 Great Bend
12G4 Great Britain *i.*
42B6 Great Dividing Range *mts*
51H4 Greater Antilles *is*
47L7 Great Exuma *i.*
46E2 Great Falls
47M7 Great Inagua *i.*
36F7 Great Karoo *plat.*
15E6 Great Malvern
27I6 Great Nicobar *i.*
15H6 Great Ouse *r.*
34D4 Great Rift Valley
46E3 Great Salt Lake
46E3 Great Salt Lake Desert
33F2 Great Sand Sea *des.*
40E4 Great Sandy Desert
44G3 Great Slave Lake
15I7 Great Stour *r.*
15C8 Great Torrington
40F5 Great Victoria Desert
15H7 Great Waltham
15I6 Great Yarmouth
48C1 Greece
21I5 Greece *country*
46G3 Greeley
47J3 Green Bay
47J2 Green Bay *b.*
47K4 Greeneville
48E1 Greenfield
45N2 Greenland *terr.*
24A2 Greenland Sea
16E5 Greenock
46F3 Green River
48B2 Greensburg
32C4 Greenville
47H5 Greenville
47I5 Greenville
47J5 Greenville
47K5 Greenville
48E2 Greenwich
47K5 Greenwood
40F4 Gregory, Lake *salt flat*
40E4 Gregory Range *hills*
41I3 Gregory Range *hills*
13N3 Greifswald
11G8 Grenå
47J5 Grenada
51L6 Grenada *country*
42D4 Grenfell
18G4 Grenoble
16F6 Gretna
21I4 Grevena
46F3 Greybull
43C6 Greymouth
42A2 Grey Range *hills*
23I6 Gribanovskiy
47K5 Griffin
42C5 Griffith
34C3 Grimari
14G5 Grimsby
44G4 Grimshaw
11F7 Grimstad
10□1 Grindavík
11F9 Grindsted
20G2 Grmeč *mts*
37I3 Groblersdal
30C3 Grodekovo
13K4 Groningen
41H2 Groote Eylandt *i.*
35B5 Grootfontein
36E7 Groot Swartberge *mts*
36E5 Grootvloer *salt pan*
20D3 Grosseto
13L6 Groß-Gerau
13N7 Großglockner *mt.*
49B3 Grover Beach
23J8 Groznyy
20G2 Grubišno Polje
13Q4 Grudziądz
23H5 Gryazi
22I4 Gryazovets
13O4 Gryfice
13O4 Gryfino
19E3 Guadalajara
50D4 Guadalajara
41M1 Guadalcanal *i.*
19C5 Guadalquivir *r.*
46G7 Guadalupe Victoria
19D3 Guadarrama, Sierra de *mts*
51L5 Guadeloupe *terr.*
19E5 Guadix
55A5 Guaíba
54F2 Guaíra
54E4 Gualeguay
54E4 Gualeguaychu
29G6 Guam *terr.*
46F6 Guamúchil
50D4 Guanajuato
55C1 Guanambi
52E2 Guanare
51H4 Guane
27J3 Guangyuan
27K4 Guangzhou
55C2 Guanhães
51I4 Guantánamo
55B3 Guapé
55A5 Guaporé
52E6 Guaporé *r.*
53K5 Guarabira
52C4 Guaranda
55C3 Guarapari
55A4 Guarapuava
55A3 Guararapes
55B3 Guaratinguetá
55A4 Guaratuba
19C3 Guarda
55B3 Guarujá
46F6 Guasave
50F5 Guatemala
50F6 Guatemala City
55B3 Guaxupé
52C4 Guayaquil
52B4 Guayaquil, Golfo de *g.*
46E6 Guaymas
23H6 Gubkin
23J8 Gudermes
32B4 Guéckédou
20B6 Guelma
32B2 Guelmine
48A1 Guelph
18E3 Guéret
15E9 Guernsey *terr.*
32B3 Guérou
52E2 Guiana Highlands *mts*
33E4 Guider
20E4 Guidonia-Montecelio
32C4 Guiglo
15G7 Guildford
27K4 Guilin
19B3 Guimarães
53J4 Guimarães
32B3 Guinea
32D4 Guinea, Gulf of
32B3 Guinea-Bissau
51H4 Güines
53H7 Guiratinga
27J4 Guiyang
27G3 Gujranwala
23H6 Gukovo
27G5 Gulbarga
11O8 Gulbene
47J5 Gulfport
27F2 Gulistan
23I7 Gul'kevichi
34D3 Gulu
35C5 Gumare
32D3 Gumel
27G4 Guna
42D5 Gundagai
21M5 Güney
46F4 Gunnison
27G5 Guntakal
29B7 Gunungsitoli
55A2 Gurinhatã
53H4 Gurupá
53I6 Gurupi
11L9 Gur'yevsk
32D3 Gusau
11M9 Gusev
31A5 Gushan
25L4 Gusinoozersk
22I5 Gus'-Khrustal'nyy
13N4 Güstrow
13L5 Gütersloh
27I4 Guwahati
53G2 Guyana
46G4 Guymon
42E3 Guyra
26F3 Guzar
11L9 Gvardeysk
27G4 Gwalior
35C6 Gwanda
34F2 Gwardafuy, Gees *c.*
35C5 Gweru
35C6 Gweta
32E3 Gwoza
24I2 Gydan Peninsula
41K5 Gympie
13Q7 Gyöngyös
20G1 Győr
21J6 Gytheio
21I1 Gyula
23I8 Gyumri
26E3 Gyzylarbat

H

11M7 Haapsalu
12J4 Haarlem
34E2 Habban
30F4 Hachinohe
48D2 Hackensack
16G5 Haddington
32E3 Hadejia
11F3 Haderslev
23G6 Hadyach
31B5 Haeju
31B6 Haenam
29G6 Hagátña
13K5 Hagen
48C3 Hagerstown
11H6 Hagfors
31C6 Hagi
18H2 Haguenau
33G1 Haifa
27K4 Haikou
26D4 Ha'il
27K2 Hailar
30C3 Hailin
15H8 Hailsham
30B3 Hailun
27K5 Hainan i.
28C5 Hai Phong
51J5 Haiti
21I1 Hajdúböszörmény
34E2 Hajjah
30F4 Hakodate
31E5 Hakui
33G2 Halaib Triangle terr.
13M5 Halberstadt
11G7 Halden
13M4 Haldensleben
15E6 Halesowen
15I6 Halesworth
14F5 Halifax
45L5 Halifax
11I7 Hällefors
13N7 Hallein
13M5 Halle (Saale)
11I7 Hallsberg
40F3 Halls Creek
29E7 Halmahera i.
11H8 Halmstad
11G8 Hals
14E4 Haltwhistle
31D6 Hamada
33H1 Hamadān
33G1 Hamah
31E6 Hamamatsu
11G6 Hamar
27H6 Hambantota
13L4 Hamburg
48B1 Hamburg
11N6 Hämeenlinna
13L4 Hameln
40D4 Hamersley Range mts
31B5 Hamhŭng
27I2 Hami
16E5 Hamilton
43E3 Hamilton
47K4 Hamilton
48B1 Hamilton
51L2 Hamilton
11O6 Hamina
31B5 Hamju
13K5 Hamm
32C2 Hammada du Drâa plat.
20D6 Hammamet
20D6 Hammamet, Golfe de g.
10M1 Hammerfest
48D3 Hammonton
15F7 Hampshire Downs hills
48C4 Hampton
34D1 Hanak
31F5 Hanamaki
27K3 Handan
35D4 Handeni
49C2 Hanford
27I2 Hangayn Nuruu mts
28E4 Hangzhou
28E4 Hangzhou Wan b.
11M7 Hanko
44G4 Hanna
47I4 Hannibal
13L4 Hannover
11I9 Hanöbukten b.
28C5 Ha Nôi
48C3 Hanover
11O10 Hantsavichy
27J3 Hanzhong
10N4 Haparanda
45L4 Happy Valley – Goose Bay
34E1 Haradh
23F5 Haradok
31F5 Haramachi
35D5 Harare
30B3 Harbin
11D7 Hardangerfjorden sea chan.
36C3 Hardap admin. reg.
34E3 Harer
34E3 Hargeysa
31D6 Harima-nada b.
11M6 Harjavalta
15I6 Harleston
15H7 Harlow
46C3 Harney Basin
10J5 Härnösand
32C4 Harper
16F3 Harris, Sound of sea chan.
48D2 Harrisburg
47I4 Harrison
48B3 Harrisonville
14F5 Harrogate
21L2 Hârșova
10J2 Hartau
13O7 Hartberg
48E2 Hartford
14F4 Hartlepool
46G2 Harvey
15G7 Harwich
27G5 Hassan
12J5 Hasselt
11H8 Hässleholm
15H8 Hastings
43F4 Hastings
46H3 Hastings
47I3 Hastings
14G5 Hatfield
47L4 Hatteras, Cape
47L5 Hattiesburg
29C7 Hat Yai
34E3 Haud reg.
11D7 Haugesund
10P5 Haukivesi i.
40F3 Hauraki Gulf
15I9 Haute-Normandie admin. reg.
32C1 Hauts Plateaux
15H8 Havana
15G8 Havant
15W5 Haverfordwest
48F1 Haverhill
21L5 Havlíčkův Brod
21L5 Havre
39I5 Havre Rock i.

23G8 Havza
46◻ Hawaii i.
16G5 Hawick
43F4 Hawke Bay
14F4 Haxby
42B5 Hay
41H4 Hay watercourse
26E5 Haymâ'
21L4 Hayrabolu
44G3 Hay River
46H4 Hays
23F6 Haysyn
49A2 Hayward
15G8 Haywards Heath
48D2 Hazleton
15F5 Heanor
7 Heard and McDonald Islands terr.
41J6 Hearst
42B6 Heathcote
12J4 Hechi
11I6 Hedemora
30C3 Hegang
13L3 Heide
47J4 Heidelberg
13L6 Heidelberg
37I4 Heidelberg
23H6 Heihe
13M4 Heilbronn
13L6 Heilbronn
30C3 Heilong Jiang prov.
11N6 Heinola
10◻1 Hekla vol.
48E2 Helena
16E4 Helena
13L3 Helgoländer Bucht g.
19F4 Hellín
12J5 Helmond
13M4 Helmstedt
30C4 Helong
11H8 Helsingborg
11N6 Helsinki
15G7 Hemel Hempstead
49D4 Hemet
21N4 Hendek
47L5 Henderson
49E2 Henderson
12J4 Hengelo
27J1 Hengshan
14G5 Hengyang
42D6 Henley-on-Thames
37J5 Henzada
39I1 Herât
42C5 Herford
13L5 Herisau
16F2 Herkimer
13O5 Herma Ness (?)
13O5 Hermes, Cape
23J8 Hermosillo
23G6 Hernandarias
11M10 Herne Bay
28E5 Hérouville-St-Clair
52C5 Herrera del Duque
30B4 Hershey
27K3 Hertford
27J4 Hesperia
46◻ Hettstedt
19B3 Hexham
55D1 Heysham
15F6 Heywood
33G1 Heze
32C4 Hibbing
14F5 Hidalgo del Parral
54B4 Hidrolândia
33O2 Highlands
22F4 Highland Springs
47I4 High Level
47J4 High Point
47K3 High Prairie
19J1 High Wycombe
18G5 Higüey
14E4 Hiiumaa i.
18E4 Hikone
14E5 Hildesheim
27K3 Hillah
47I2 Hillston
54B3 Hilo
46F6 Hilton Head Island
31F5 Hilversum
27G5 Himalaya mts
55A4 Himarë
48E2 Himeji
48C4 Hinckley
14F5 Hindley
14E5 Hindu Kush mts
51I5 Hinesville
15F5 Hirosaki
15D7 Hiroshima
46C3 Hirson
10J5 Hirtshals
32C4 Hisar
11G8 Hispaniola i.
11G8 Hitachi
10H1 Hitachinaka
21I2 Hjälmaren l.
25P2 Hjørring
32D5 Hlotse
48B2 Hluhluwe
17F4 Hlybokaye
47H5 Hobart
13M6 Hobbs
37J2 Hobro
19H4 Ho Chi Minh City
31B5 Hoddesdon
12J4 Hodeidah
46B3 Hódmezővásárhely
32D4 Hoek van Holland
31E5 Hof
34E3 Hofsjökull ice cap
34E3 Hōfu
31D6 Hoggar plat.
11M6 Hoh Xil Shan mts
15I6 Hokkaidō i.
15H7 Holbox
46C3 Holbrook
10J5 Holguín
32C4 Holíč (?)
16F3 Hollister
48D2 Holly Springs
47I4 Hollywood
48B3 Hollywood
14F5 Holmestrand
21L2 Holmsund
10J2 Holt
13O7 Holyhead
48E2 Holyhead Bay
14F4 Holy Island
46G2 Holy Island

32C3 Hombori
45L3 Home Bay
48C1 Homer
33G1 Homs
23F5 Homyel'
21M6 Honaz
46H6 Hondo
51G6 Honduras
11G6 Hønefoss
27J4 Hongjiang
27K4 Hong Kong
31B4 Hongwŏn
28D4 Hongze Hu l.
15D8 Honiton
46◻ Honolulu
31D6 Honshū i.
13K4 Hoogeveen
37G4 Hoopstad
11H9 Höör
12J4 Hoorn
49E2 Hoover Dam
23I8 Hope
48C4 Hopewell
47J4 Hopkinsville
11H9 Hörby
23F5 Horki
23H6 Horlivka
26E4 Hormuz, Strait of
13O6 Horn
54C9 Horn, Cape
14G5 Horncastle
10K5 Hörnefors
42I4 Horodenka (?)
23E6 Horodenka
23D6 Horodnya
23E6 Horodok
11F9 Horsens
15G7 Horsham
41I7 Horsham
11G7 Horten
27G3 Hoshiarpur
27H3 Hotan
11H8 Hot Springs
19G3 Houghton
14F4 Houghton le Spring
53K5 Houma
47H6 Houston
27I2 Hov
15G8 Hove
11I8 Hovmantorp
32D4 Hövsgöl Nuur l.
27J1 Howe, Cape
13J4 Howick
42D6 Howland Island terr.
37J5 Howlong
39I1 Höxter
13L5 Hoy i.
16F2 Hoyerswerda
13O5 Hradec Králové
23J8 Hrazdan
23G6 Hrebinka
11M10 Hrodna
13Q4 Hsinchu
35C4 Huacho
22I3 Huadian
34C3 Huaide
31B6 Huainan
32D4 Huajuápan de León
32D4 Hualien
31B6 Huallaga r.
15I7 Huambo
11F8 Huanan
19D4 Huancavelica
50E5 Huancayo
19C5 Huánuco
47I3 Huaráz
52C4 Huarmey
47J3 Huasco
47K3 Huatabampo
47L5 Hubli
47L5 Hucknall
49G3 Huddersfield
11I8 Hudson
46D3 Hudson
46E2 Hudson r.
11M8 Hudson Bay sea
46C3 Hudson Falls
20F4 Hudson Strait
31B6 Huê
32D4 Huehuetenango
31F5 Huelva
33H1 Huesca
13Q4 Hughenden
35C4 Hughson
22I3 Hugo
35C4 Huhudi
34C3 Huib-Hoch Plateau
27G3 Huila Plateau
27H3 Huimanguillo
11H8 Huittinen
19G3 Hulan
14F4 Hulan Ergi
53K5 Hulayfah
47H6 Hulin
27I2 Hull
15G8 Hultsfred
11I8 Hulun Nur l.
32D4 Humaitá
27J1 Humber, Mouth of the
13J4 Hume Reservoir
42D6 Húnaflói b.
37J5 Hunedoara
39I1 Hungary
13L5 Húngnam
13O5 Hunstanton
13O5 Huntingdon
23J8 Huntington
23G6 Huntington
11M10 Huntington Beach
52C5 Huntsville
30B4 Huntsville
27K3 Hurghada
31B6 Huron
52C5 Huron, Lake
19D4 Húsavík
52C4 Husn
52C5 Husum
47K3 Husum
46F6 Hutchinson
27G5 Huzhou
11I9 Hvar i.
18G5 Hwange
14E4 Hyargas Nuur l. (?)
18E4 Hyderabad
14E5 Hyderabad
27K3 Hyesan
47I2 Hythe
54B3 Hyūga
46F6 Hyvinkää

I

34E2 Ibb
19 Iberian Peninsula
55B2 Ibiá
53J4 Ibiapaba, Serra da hills
55C1 Ibiassucê
55D1 Ibicaraí
55A4 Ibirama
55A3 Ibitinga
19G4 Ibiza
19G4 Ibiza i.
53J6 Ibotirama
26E4 Ibrâ'
26E4 Ibri
52C6 Ica
53J4 Icatu
33G1 İçel
10◻1 Iceland
31E6 Ichinomiya
31F5 Ichinoseki
23G6 Ichnya
53K5 Icó
55C3 Iconha
32D4 Idah
46E3 Idaho state
46E3 Idaho Falls
13K6 Idar-Oberstein
33G2 Idfū
35B4 Idiofa
33G1 Idlib
55A3 Iepê
35D4 Ifakara
35E6 Ifanadiana
32D4 Ife
33E3 Ifenat
32D3 Iférouâne
32D3 Ifôghas, Adrar des hills
33G4 Iganga
55B3 Igarapava
24J3 Igarka
11J6 Iggesund
20C5 Iglesias
11O9 Ignalina
21I5 Igoumenitsa
55C1 Iguaí
48C1 Iguala
19G3 Igualada
55B4 Iguape
54F2 Iguatemi
53K5 Iguatu
35E6 Ihosy
27G1 Iisalmi
19F2 Iizuka
16E5 Ijebu-Ode
49D4 Ijevan (?)
23J8 IJssel r.
13J4 Ikare
29E7 Ikageng
37H4 Ikare
24J4 Ikhtiman (?)
21I6 Ikaria i.
11B8 Ikast
21J3 Ikhtiman
32D4 Ikom
20F4 Iksan
31B6 Iseyin
31E6 Ishinomaki
33H1 Īlām
13Q4 Iława
35C4 Ilebo
22I3 Ileza
34C3 Ileza
22I3 Ilfracombe
23G8 Ilgaz
54F2 Ilha Grande, Represa resr
19B3 Ilhavo
55D1 Ilhéus
15F6 Ilkeston
14F5 Ilkley
54B4 Illapel
30B4 Illinois state
52C5 Illizi
32D2 Ilmen', Ozero l.
22F4 Il'men', Ozero l.
12G5 Ilminster
15E8 Ilo
29E6 Iloilo
32D4 Ilorin
49B2 Ilovlya
49H3 Iltur...
23H7 Imabari
14E5 Imaichi
31C6 Imari
55A5 Imatra
20D2 Imbituba
53I5 Imperatriz
20C3 Imperia
49B2 Imperial
47J5 Imperial Beach
31C6 Impfondo
21K4 Imphal
31E6 İmroz
31E6 Ina
19H4 Inarijärvi l.
31B5 Inch'ŏn
16C5 Indaal, Loch b.
34D2 Indalsälven r.
47I4 Inda Silasé
47I4 Independence
55A3 Inder
26E2 Inderborskiy
27G4 Indiana state
47J3 Indianapolis
55B3 Indianola
47I3 Indigirka r.
25P2 Indigirka r.
19H4 Indonesia
19H4 Indore
55A2 Indus r.
26F4 Indus, Mouths of the
23G8 Inebolu
21M4 Inegöl
14H5 Ingleborough h.
48B2 Inglewood
47H5 Inglewood
14H5 Ingoldmells
13M6 Ingolstadt
43F4 Inhambane prov.
37I2 Inhambane
55A2 Inhumas
16D3 Inner Sound sea chan.
21J3 Innisfail
34B4 Innsbruck
13Q4 Inongo
23I5 Inowrocław
23I5 In Salah
13Q4 Inscription, Cape
24H3 Inta
31E5 International Falls
12G5 Inukjuak
47H4 Inuvik
47I4 Invercargill
43B8 Invergordon
16E3 Inverkeithing
16E4 Inverness
40G6 Investigator Group is
14G5 Inyonga
23I5 Iņça
41H7 Inverell
13M7 Inyonga
35D4 Iona
23I5 Iona i.

16C4 Iona i.
21H5 Ionian Islands
20H5 Ionian Sea
21K6 Ios i.
47I3 Iowa state
47I3 Iowa City
55A2 Ipameri
55C2 Ipanema
55C2 Ipatinga
23I7 Ipatovo
37G4 Ipelegeng
52C3 Ipiales
55A4 Ipiaú
55D1 Ipirá
55A4 Ipiranga
29C7 Ipoh
55A2 Iporá
34C3 Ippy
21L4 Ipsala
15I6 Ipswich
42F1 Ipswich
53J4 Ipu
45L3 Iqaluit
52B4 Iquique
52C4 Iquitos
21K7 Iraklion
55C1 Iramaia
26E3 Iran
26F4 Īrānshahr
50D4 Irapuato
33H1 Iraq
55A4 Irará
55A4 Irati
33G1 Irbid
24I4 Irbit
17E4 Ireland i.
17E4 Ireland, Republic of
26F2 Irgiz
35D4 Iringa
53H4 Iriri r.
17G4 Irish Sea
53I4 Irituia
25L4 Irkutsk
48C1 Irondequoit
24J4 Iron Mountain
47J2 Irosin
29E6 Irpin'
23F6 Irrawaddy r.
27I5 Irtysh r.
27G1 Irún
19F2 Irvine
16E5 Irvine
49D4 Isa
32D3 Isabela
29E7 Isafjörður est.
10◻1 Isafjörður
31E6 Ise
18G4 Isère r.
20F4 Isernia
31E6 Ise-wan b.
32D4 Iseyin
31F5 Ishinomaki
31F5 Ishinomaki
13Q4 Ishikari
35C4 Isil'kul'
34C3 Isipingo
22I3 Isiro
29F7 Islamabad
43E2 Islands, Bay of
16C5 Islay i.
23D6 Isoka
21N6 Isparta
21J3 Isperikh
33G1 Israel
32C4 Issia
18F4 Issoire
32D3 Istanbul
13J6 İller r.
21N1 Illichivs'k
47I4 Illinois r.
47J4 Illinois state
32D2 İlizi
55A3 Itaberaba
55A2 Itaberaí
55C2 Itabira
55C3 Itabirito
55D1 Itabuna
55B3 Itacajá
55B1 Itacarambi
55C1 Itambé
55C1 Itaobím
55A3 Itaí
55A4 Itaiópolis
53G4 Itaituba
55B4 Itajaí
55B3 Itajubá
20E3 Italy
55C2 Itamarandiba
55C1 Itambé
55C2 Itambé
54D1 Itaobím
21I4 Itaobím
31E6 Itaberá
53B3 Itabira
55A4 Itabira
55B3 Itaituba
55A4 Itajaí
55B3 Itajubá
14H5 Itaperuna
42C2 Itapetinga
33E2 Itapetininga
55B2 Itapeva
53J6 Itapicuru Mirim
53J4 Itapipoca
55B3 Itapira
55A5 Itaporanga
54E3 Itararé
55B3 Itatiba
55A4 Itaúna
55B3 Itaúna
26E2 Itinga
27G4 Ithaca
55C2 Itinga
55B3 Itiruçu
31E6 Itō
55B3 Itu
34E3 Ituaçu
34E3 Ituberá
30B4 Ituiutaba
23I6 Itumbiara
23H7 Ituporanga
52F2 Iturama
19H4 Iturbide
11N10 Itzehoe
23I5 Ivanava
40G6 Ivangorod (?)
41H7 Ivano-Frankivs'k
11N10 Ivanovo
50E4 Ivatsevichy
48D4 Ivrea
53J5 Ivujivik
34E2 Ivyanets
47H4 Iwaki
35C4 Iwamizawa
31E6 Iwo
33G1 Ixmiquilpan
32D2 Ixtlán
50C4 Izberbash
35D4 Izhevsk

24G4 Izhevsk
21M2 Izmayil
21L5 İzmir
21L5 İzmir Körfezi g.
21K4 İztochni Rodopi mts
31D6 Izumo
23E6 Izyaslav
22M2 Iz''yayu
23H6 Izyum

J

27G4 Jabalpur
20G3 Jablanica
53L5 Jaboatão
55A3 Jabotical
55C1 Jacaraci
55B3 Jacareí
55A3 Jacarézinho
55C2 Jacinto
47I5 Jackson
47J4 Jackson
47K3 Jackson
47K5 Jacksonville
47K5 Jacksonville
47L5 Jacksonville
51J5 Jacmel
26F4 Jacobabad
53J6 Jacobina
53I4 Jacunda
19E5 Jaén
41H7 Jaffa, Cape
27G6 Jaffna
27H5 Jagdalpur
55A4 Jaguaraíva
32D4 Jaguaripe
26E4 Jahrom
27G4 Jaipur
27G4 Jaisalmer
29C8 Jakarta
10M5 Jakobstad
33G4 Jalālābād
27G3 Jalandhar
50E5 Jalapa
55A3 Jalapa (?)
50E5 Juchitán
32E4 Jalingo
51G6 Jalingo
50D4 Jalpa
27H4 Jalpaiguri
51I5 Jamaica
51I5 Jamaica Channel
29C8 Jambi
47H4 James r.
41H6 Jamestown
46H2 Jamestown
42C5 Junee
18H3 Jungfrau mt.
31C6 Jungfrau
11N8 Juodupė
16D4 Jura r.
21J3 Jura, Sound of sea chan.
55C1 Janaúba
47I3 Janesville
55B1 Januária
31D5 Japan
31D5 Japan, Sea of
52F4 Japurá r.
55A1 Jaraguá
55A4 Jaraguá do Sul
55B3 Jardinópolis
13P5 Jarocin
23D6 Jarosław
48C3 Jarrettsville
52F6 Jarú
11N6 Järvenpää
26E4 Jäsk
23D6 Jasło
35C4 Jasper
21M4 Jasper
13J6 Jastrzębie-Zdrój
21H1 Jászberény
55A2 Jataí
55A3 Jaú
52C6 Jauja
29C8 Java i.
29D8 Jawa, Laut sea
34E3 Jawhar
13P5 Jawor
29E8 Jaya, Puncak mt.
29G8 Jayapura
34D1 Jeddah
47I4 Jefferson City
36B8 Jeffrey's Bay
11N8 Jēkabpils
13P5 Jelenia Góra
11M8 Jelgava
13M5 Jena
34B3 Jendouba
47I5 Jennings
31C7 Jequié
51J5 Jérémie
50D4 Jerez
26C3 Jerez de la Frontera
46E3 Jerome
15E9 Jersey terr.
48D2 Jersey City
53J5 Jerumenha
33G1 Jervis Bay
42E5 Jervis Bay Territory admin. div.
20F1 Jesenice
20E3 Jesi
11G6 Jessheim
47K5 Jesup
27G4 Jhansi
35C6 Jiamusi
10M4 Ji'an
27K4 Jianyang
47J3 Jiaxing
27H3 Jiayuguan
13Q6 Jieznas (?)
13O6 Jihlava
32D1 Jijel
34C4 Jijiga
11L9 Jilib
23I6 Jilin
30B4 Jilin prov.
11I8 Jīma
37J2 Jiménez
23I6 Jinan
29D8 Jiexi (?)
27G4 Jingdezhen
42C5 Jingle
22H4 Jinhua
47J3 Jining
34B4 Jining
36B8 Jinja
20O7 Jinotepe
22J4 Jinzhou
19G2 Jixi
21L5 Jixi
27J2 Jixian
11H8 Jīzān
21K4 Jiujiang

55A4 Joaçaba
29C6 João Pessoa
53L5 João Pinheiro
55B2 Jodhpur
34D3 Joensuu
31E5 Jõetsu
23E6 Jõgeva
37H4 Johannesburg
46D3 John Day
16F2 John o'Groats
48B2 Johnstone
16H5 Johnstown
48D1 Johnstown
29C7 Johor Bahru
31E6 Jõhvi
18G2 Joinville
10R3 Joinville
55A4 Joliet
11N9 Jonava
47I4 Jonesboro
45J2 Jones Sound sea chan.
55A2 Jönköping
45K5 Jonquière
47I4 Joplin
33G1 Jordan
27I4 Jorhat
29C7 Jorpeland
54B6 José de San Martín
19E5 Joseph Bonaparte Gulf
32D4 Jos Plateau
37H4 Jouberton
11M6 Joutseno
46G7 Juan Aldama
44F5 Juan de Fuca Strait
53J5 Juàzeiro
53K5 Juàzeiro do Norte
33G4 Juba
34E4 Jubba r.
19F4 Júcar r.
55A1 Juçara
50E5 Juchitán
31C7 Judenburg
51I6 Juigalpa
23F6 Juina
55C3 Juiz de Fora
52D7 Juliaca
19F4 Jumilla
55A1 Junagadh
47H4 Junction City
55B3 Jundiaí
44E4 Juneau
42C5 Junee
18H3 Jungfrau mt.
11N8 Juodupė
16D4 Jura r.
21J3 Jura, Sound of sea chan.
55C1 Jurbarkas
55B1 Jürmala
53G4 Juruti
55A3 Juruá r.
51I6 Juticalpa
11F8 Jutland pen.
10N5 Jyväskylä

K

27G3 K2 mt.
11M6 Kaarina
34C4 Kabale
35C4 Kabalo
21M4 Kabardino
13Q6 Kabinda
35C5 Kabompo
27F3 Kābul
35C5 Kabwe
27G4 Kachchh, Rann of marsh
32D4 Kachia
31C6 Kachret'i
29C8 Kachug
34E3 Kadıköy
27H5 Kadoma
29G8 Kadugli
32D3 Kaduna
34D1 Kadzherom
36B8 Kaédi
11N8 Kaélé
13P5 Kaesŏng
11M8 Kafanchan
13M5 Kafue
34B3 Kafue r.
47I5 Kaga
31C7 Kaga Bandoro
51J5 Kagoshima
26C3 Kagoshima pref.
15E9 Kaharlyk
48D2 Kahramanmaraş
53J5 Kaifeng
46E3 Kainan
15E9 Kaiyuan
48D2 Kaiyuan
53J5 Kajaani
33G1 Kakata
42E5 Kakhovka
20F1 Kakinada
20E3 Kakogawa
11G6 Kala
47K5 Kalaç Kebira
27G4 Kalach
35C6 Kalach-na-Donu
10M4 Kalahari Desert
27K4 Kalajoki
47J3 Kalamata
47J3 Kalamazoo
34B4 Kalanchak
11L9 Kale
23I6 Kalecik
30B4 Kalemie
29D8 Kalgoorlie
27G4 Kali
42C5 Kaliakra, Nos pt (?)
22H4 Kalinin
47J3 Kaliningrad
47J3 Kalininskaya
34B4 Kalinkavichy
36B8 Kalispell
33G1 Kalisz
27G4 Kaliua
31E5 Kalix
35C6 Kalixälven r.
10M4 Kalkan
27K4 Kallavesi l.
47J3 Kallsjön l.
11H8 Kalmar
21K4 Kaluga
23I6 Kalundborg
35C5 Kalush
24J4 Kalyazin
23I8 Kama r.
44F4 Kamaishi
23I8 Kamakura
15H6 Kambos
16D3 Kamchatka pen.
34D2 Kamchia r.
37J2 Kamen'-na-Obi
11L9 Kamenka
16D3 Kamen'-na-Obi
25T3 Kamenka
43I3 Kamensk-Shakhtinskiy
34B4 Kamensk-Ural'skiy
31E5 Kamina
23I5 Kamloops
50D4 Kamo
16H3 Kampala
47H4 Kampene

29C6 Kâmpóng Cham
29C6 Kâmpóng Spœ
29C6 Kâmpóng Thum
42E4 Katoomba
13Q5 Katowice
33G2 Katrînah, Jabal mt.
16E4 Katrine, Loch l.
11J7 Katrineholm
34D1 Katsina
32D4 Katsina-Ala
31F6 Katsuura
11G8 Kattegat strait
46◻ Kauai Channel
10M5 Kauhajoki
10M5 Kauhava
23K5 Khvalynsk
11M9 Kaunas
22G4 Kaura-Namoda
27G3 Khyber Pass
21K4 Kavadarci
42E5 Kiama
21I4 Kavala
30D3 Kaavalerovo
21M3 Kavarna
26E3 Kavīr, Dasht-e des.
27H6 Kandy
31E6 Kandygash
31E6 Kawaguchi
31E6 Kawasaki
54C3 Kaya
32B3 Kayes
26C3 Kayseri
27G1 Kazakhskiy Melkosopochnik plain
26F2 Kazakhstan
22K5 Kazan'
21K3 Kazanlŭk
21I3 Kazincbarcika
17F3 Kazbek
22H4 Kcad
46H3 Kearney
32D1 Kebili
21N6 Keçiborlu
21I3 Kecskemét
33G1 Kediri (?)
30B3 Kedong
10R2 Kędzierzyn-Koźle
48E1 Keene
11N7 Keetmanshoop
32D4 Kefti
17E5 Keflavik
27G2 Kegen
11N7 Kehra
46H5 Keighley
16E5 Keith
22K4 Kel'mez'
42B6 Kelmë
35D4 Kelo
44G5 Kelowna
29C7 Kelso
22G2 Kem'
23G8 Kemalpaşa
21N6 Kemer
24J4 Kemerovo
21L5 Kemi
10O3 Kemijärvi
35B4 Kemijoki r.
10N4 Kempele
13M7 Kempten (Allgäu)
31E6 Kempton Park
16F4 Kendal
48B1 Kendari
32B3 Kendawangan
34C4 Kenema
26E3 Kenge
26F3 Kenhardt
32C3 Kenitra
42E4 Kennewick
46D2 Kenora
47J3 Kenosha
49E4 Kent admin. reg.
35C5 Kentucky state
24J2 Kentucky r.
43C5 Kenya
27F4 Kenya, Mount
24I4 Keokuk
47I3 Keppel Bay
27G2 Kepsut
35C4 Kerala admin. reg.
27G2 Kerang
15H6 Kerava (?)
26E4 Kerch
46D3 Kerema
23H6 Kerguelen Islands
11N7 Kerkerabé (?)
21H5 Kerkrade
34C4 Kerman
27G3 Kermānshāh
27G2 Kerme Körfezi g.
13P5 Kerpen
23D6 Kerry admin. dist.
31B5 Keşan
32E4 Kesennuma
11N7 Kesh
16H5 Kestenga
22J4 Keszthely
13M5 Ketapang
15G6 Kettering
32D4 Keweenaw Peninsula
31B5 Key Largo
11I8 Key West
16D3 Kgalagadi admin. dist.
35C4 Kgatleng admin. dist.
37J2 Khabarovsk
35C6 Khabarovsk Kray admin. div.
24J3 Khairpur
10R2 Khamar-Daban, Khrebet mts
21J4 Khamgaon
21J3 Khamis Mushayt
35D5 Khandwa
21L4 Khanewal
11M6 Khanh Hoa
35D5 Khanka, Lake
11M6 Khanty-Mansiysk
34D3 Kharagpur
23G8 Khārān
31E5 Khārijah, Wāḥāt al oasis
23E6 Kharkiv
21M4 Kharmanli
17F3 Kharovsk
22H4 Khartoum
25M4 Khashuri
11G9 Khāsh
23I6 Khaskovo
23I6 Khatanga
21K4 Khaybar
37J2 Khaydarken (?)
35C6 Khāsh
23G7 Khelvnoye
23I6 Khmel'nyts'kyy
23I6 Khmil'nyk
23I6 Khodzheyli
31D6 Kholm
23G6 Kholm
23G6 Khomas admin. reg.
46D3 Khon Kaen
27H4 Khong
23J6 Khorol

30D3 Khorol
32C4 Khorramābād
21I5 Khorramshahr
27G3 Khorugh
13Q5 Khouribga
33G2 Khromtau
16E4 Khrystynivka
11J7 Khulays
34D1 Khulna
27H4 Khuma
37H4 Khŭrays
34E1 Khŭraysh
23G5 Khust
23I6 Khvalynsk
23K5 Khvoynaya
27G3 Khyber Pass
42E5 Kiama
30D3 Kiboga
34D3 Kibungo
34D4 Kichmengskiy Gorodok
32D3 Kidal
15E6 Kidderminster
15E6 Kidsgrove
31E5 Kiel
13R5 Kielce
27G1 Kielder Water resr
13M3 Kieler Bucht b.
23F6 Kiev
11N10 Kiffa
23J8 Kigali
21M4 Kigoma
22I4 Kiira
31D6 Kikinda
31C6 Kikwit
22I4 Kilbrannan Sound sea chan.
47I3 Kildare admin. reg.
10R2 Kilimanjaro vol.
34D4 Kilingi-Nõmme
11N7 Kilis
11N7 Kilkee
17F3 Kilkeel
17F5 Kilkenny
10M5 Kilkís
27G2 Killarney
17C5 Killeen (?)
22K4 Killarney
17F3 Killiney
22K4 Kil'mez'
27I1 Kilrush
31I6 Kilwinning
11M9 Kolari (?)
16E5 Kimberley
27H2 Kimberley Plateau
23E6 Kimch'aek
23J4 Kimch'ŏn
23L5 Kemalpaşa (dup)
23J4 Kinabalu, Gunung mt.
13M7 Kincardine
37I4 Kindersley
16F4 Kindia
46I1 Kindu
48B2 Kineshma
32B3 King Island
23K5 King Leopold Ranges hills
13Q7 Kingman
26E1 King's Lynn
11J7 King Sound b.
32D4 Kingston
24J4 Kingston
10O3 Kingston
35B4 Kingston upon Hull
29D7 Kingussie
32C3 Kingwilliamstown
16F4 King William's Town
48B2 Kinloss
35C4 Kinna
22I5 Kinross
23I6 Kinshasa
24J4 Kintore
21M5 Kinyeti mt.
14G5 Kippax
19G5 Kirby in Ashfield
15F7 Kirkby
10O2 Kirkcaldy
16E5 Kirkcudbright
10O2 Kirkintilloch
45J5 Kirkland Lake
16G5 Kirkstall
41J6 Kirksville
20G1 Kirkuk
22K4 Kirkwall
32D2 Kirov
23K5 Kirov
22I4 Kirovo-Chepetsk
10N5 Kirovohrad
21L5 Kirov's'ke
15H7 Kirovsk
16F4 Kirriemuir
22J4 Kirs
23I5 Kiruna
23I8 Kiryū
21J7 Kisangani
31C6 Kiselëvsk
29D7 Kishi
34D4 Kiskőrös
23K5 Kiskunfélegyháza
23I6 Kiskunhalas
23I8 Kislovodsk
31F5 Kismaayo
33G5 Kiso r.
33G4 Kisoro
35C5 Kissidougou
27G4 Kissimmee
23I5 Kisumu
14F3 Kita
37H7 Kitakami
29C6 Kitakyūshū
21J4 Kital (?)
34C4 Kitchener
24H4 Kitee
21M4 Kithira
27H4 Kitimat
32C3 Kittanning
11P7 Kittery
40E3 Kitunda (?)
41I7 Kitwe
49E3 Kivu, Lake
21J8 Kizel

23J8 Kizil''yurt
23J8 Kizlyar
22K4 Kizner
11I9 Kladno
32C1 Khourïbga (dup)
26E1 Khromtau (dup)
23F6 Khrystynivka
11J7 Klagenfurt
13O7 Klaipėda
10◻2 Klaksvík
44F5 Klamath r.
46C3 Klamath Falls
13N6 Klazienaveen (?)
37H4 Klerksdorp
23G5 Kletnya
23I6 Kletskaya
23G5 Klimavichy
22I4 Klimovo
32H4 Klin
23G5 Klintsy
20G2 Ključ
13P5 Kłodzko
13P6 Klosterneuburg
20F4 Kluczbork
11O10 Klyetsk
25R4 Klyuchevskaya, Sopka vol.
14F4 Knaresborough
15D6 Knighton
17D5 Knittelfeld
17D5 Knockmealdown Mts hills
37H4 Knoxville
36F8 Knysna
31D6 Kōbe
13K5 Koblenz
11N10 Kobryn
21J6 Kočani
21I4 Kočevje
21I4 Kodaikanal
31D6 Kochi
23I7 Kochubeyevskoye
14F4 Kodiak
44C4 Kodiak Island
22H3 Kodino
32C4 Kōforidua
31E6 Kōfu
10R2 Kohima
11H9 Kohtla-Järve
11N7 Kokand
27C2 Kōkkola
10M5 Kokkola
47J3 Kokomo
23I6 Kokosi
37H4 Kokosi
27H1 Kökshetau
23I6 Kokstad
10R2 Kola
22H2 Kola Peninsula
22H4 Kol'chugino
32B3 Kolda
11F9 Kolding
29E8 Koléa
13M7 Kolhapur
27G5 Kolhapur
27H4 Kolkata
13Q3 Kolkata
22C3 Kolokani
23I6 Kolomna
23E6 Kolomyya
26E3 Kolondiéba
32C3 Kolonedale
38C2 Kolpashevo
46I1 Kolpino
32B3 Kolpny
33H3 Kolwezi
35C5 Kolyma r.
25R3 Kolymskiy, Khrebet mts
23J5 Kolyshley
31E6 Komárno
31I6 Komaki
31N1 Kominternivs'ke
11N1 Komatsu
20I1 Komló
21K4 Komotini
35O2 Komsomol'sk
30E2 Komsomol'sk-na-Amure
22G3 Kondoa
22G3 Kondopoga
23G5 Kondrovo
45P2 Kong Christian X Land reg.
45M3 Kong Frederik IX Land reg.
45O3 King William Town
11F7 Kongsberg
11G6 Kongsvinger
11H6 Konin
22I3 Konotop
30B2 Konstantinovka
13I7 Konstanz
33G1 Konya
22G3 Kondopoga
23G5 Konz
33J4 Konya
33J4 Köping
11I7 Köping
20G1 Koprivnica
23I5 Korablino
21I4 Korçë
21I4 Korčula i.
31B5 Korea, North
31B5 Korea, South
23I6 Korea Bay g.
23I6 Korea Strait
14F5 Korenovsk
15F7 Korets'
16E4 Korhogo
31F5 Koryazhma
31F6 Korosten'
10O3 Koror
13Q7 Korsakov
11G9 Korsør
35D5 Korsun'-Shevchenkivs'kyy
12J5 Kortrijk
23G7 Koryŏng
30F3 Kosan
31B5 Kosan
31B5 Kościan
42D6 Kościuszko, Mount
23K5 Košice
23K5 Kosovo prov.
21I3 Kosovska Mitrovica
26F1 Kostanay
32H4 Kostenets
10O4 Kostomuksha
10O4 Kostopil'
23H6 Kostyantynivka
22H4 Kostroma
30F4 Kosŭng
29D8 Kota
23I6 Kota Baharu
29C7 Kota Kinabalu
29D7 Kota

60

25O2 Kotel'nyy, Ostrov i.
33G4 Kotido
11O6 Kotka
22J3 Kotlas
32D3 Kotorkoshi
23J6 Kotovo
23I5 Kotovsk
32C3 Koudougou
32C3 Koulikoro
39G4 Koumac
32B3 Koundâra
32C3 Koupéla
53H2 Kourou
32C3 Kouroussa
33E3 Kousséri
32C3 Koutiala
11O6 Kouvola
10Q3 Kovdor
23E6 Kovel'
22I4 Kovernino
22I4 Kovrov
23I5 Kovylkino
41I3 Kowanyama
21M6 Köyceğiz
21I4 Kozani
20G2 Kozara mts
23F6 Kozelets'
23G5 Kozel'sk
21N4 Kozlu
22J4 Koz'modem'yansk
21J4 Kožuf mts
23F6 Kozyatyn
32D4 Kpalimé
29B7 Krabi
29C6 Krâchéh
11F7 Kragerø
21I2 Kragujevac
13Q5 Kraków
23H6 Kramators'k
10J5 Kramfors
21J6 Kranidi
20F1 Kranj
11O9 Krāslava
22I5 Krasnaya Gorbatka
23J6 Krasnoarmeysk
23H6 Krasnoarmiys'k
22J3 Krasnoborsk
23H7 Krasnodar
23H6 Krasnodon
11P8 Krasnogorodskoye
23I7 Krasnogvardeyskoye
23G6 Krasnohrad
23G7 Krasnohvardiys'ke
23G7 Krasnoperekops'k
23I5 Krasnoslobodsk
24K4 Krasnoyarsk
23F5 Krasnyy
22J4 Krasnyye Baki
22H4 Krasnyy Kholm
23J6 Krasnyy Kut
23H6 Krasnyy Luch
23H6 Krasnyy Lyman
23K7 Krasnyy Yar
23E6 Krasyliv
13K5 Krefeld
23G6 Kremenchuk
13O6 Krems an der Donau
22G4 Kresttsy
11L9 Kretinga
32D4 Kribi
11E7 Kristiansand
11I8 Kristianstad
10E5 Kristiansund
11I7 Kristinehamn
20F2 Krk i.
23G6 Krolevets'
11P7 Kronshtadt
37H4 Kroonstad
23I7 Kropotkin
23D6 Krosno
13P5 Krotoszyn
29C8 Krui
21K4 Krumovgrad
23F5 Krupki
21I3 Kruševac
23F5 Krychaw
23H7 Krymsk
21K6 Krytiko Pelagos sea
23G7 Kryvyy Rih
19H6 Ksar Chellala
19H6 Ksar el Boukhari
19D6 Ksar el Kebir
20D7 Ksour Essaf
22J4 Kstovo
29C7 Kuala Lipis
29C7 Kuala Lumpur
29C7 Kuala Terengganu
30B4 Kuandian
29C7 Kuantan
21L3 Kubrat
29D7 Kuching
21H4 Kuçovë
29D7 Kudat
13N7 Kufstein
22J4 Kugesi
10P4 Kuhmo
35B5 Kuito
31B5 Kujang
31F4 Kuji
21I3 Kukës
22K4 Kukmor
21M5 Kula
25O2 Kular
11L8 Kuldīga
23I5 Kulebaki
13M5 Kulmbach
27F3 Kŭlob
26E2 Kul'sary
24I4 Kulunda
31E5 Kumagaya
31C6 Kumamoto
31E6 Kumano
21I3 Kumanovo
32C4 Kumasi
32D4 Kumba
34E1 Kumdah
22K4 Kumeny
24G4 Kumertau
31C5 Kumi
33G4 Kumi
11I7 Kumla
32E3 Kumo
23I6 Kumylzhenskiy
11G8 Kungälv
11H8 Kungsbacka
27G3 Kunlun Shan mts
27J4 Kunming
31B6 Kunsan
10O5 Kuopio
40E2 Kupang
11N9 Kupiškis
23H6 Kup"yans'k
27H2 Kuqa
31D6 Kurashiki
31D6 Kurayoshi
23G6 Kurchatov
21K4 Kŭrdzhali
31D6 Kure
11M7 Kuressaare
24H4 Kurgan
23I7 Kurganinsk
10M5 Kurikka
30H3 Kuril Islands
23H5 Kurkino
33G3 Kurmuk
27G5 Kurnool
31F5 Kuroiso
42E4 Kurri Kurri
23I7 Kursavka
23H6 Kursk
23J7 Kurskaya
23G8 Kurşunlu
36F4 Kuruman
31C6 Kurume
27H6 Kurunegala
21L6 Kuşadası
23H7 Kushchevskaya
30G4 Kushiro
26F1 Kushmurun
31B5 Kusŏng
21M5 Kütahya
23I8 K'ut'aisi
20G2 Kutjevo
13O4 Kutno
34B4 Kutu
48D2 Kutztown
10P4 Kuusamo
11O6 Kuusankoski
22G4 Kuvshinovo
26D4 Kuwait
26D4 Kuwait country
24I4 Kuybyshev
23H7 Kuybysheve
23K5 Kuybyshevskoye Vodokhranilishche resr
27H2 Kuytun
21M6 Kuyucak
23J5 Kuznetsk
23E6 Kuznetsovs'k
23J5 Kuzovatovo
20F2 Kvarnerić sea chan.
32D4 Kwale
37J5 KwaMashu
35D4 Kwa Mtoro
31B6 Kwangju
37G7 Kwanobuhle
37H7 Kwatinidubu
37J5 KwaZulu-Natal prov.
35C5 Kwekwe
36G2 Kweneng admin. dist.
13O4 Kwidzyn
25L4 Kyakhta
27I5 Kyaukpyu
21K5 Kymi
42B6 Kyneton
42F2 Kyogle
31C6 Kyŏngju
31D6 Kyōto
21I6 Kyparissia
27G2 Kyrgyzstan
21J6 Kythira i.
31C7 Kyūshū i.
21J3 Kyustendil
24K4 Kyzyl
26F2 Kyzylkum Desert
24K4 Kyzyl-Mazhalyk
26F2 Kyzylorda

L

11N7 Laagri
32B2 Laâyoune
54D3 La Banda
39H3 Labasa
32B3 Labé
23I7 Labinsk
18D4 Labouheyre
54D4 Laboulaye
45L4 Labrador reg.
45L4 Labrador City
45M3 Labrador Sea
52F5 Lábrea
27J6 Labuhanbilik
29E8 Labuna
24H3 Labytnangi
54D4 La Carlota
27G5 Laccadive Islands
47H1 Lac du Bonnet
51G5 La Ceiba
42A5 Lachlan r.
51I7 La Chorrera
45K5 Lachute
18G5 La Ciotat
44G4 Lac La Biche
48F1 Laconia
47I3 La Crosse
55C2 Ladainha
15E9 La Déroute, Passage de strait
23G8 Ladik
11Q6 Ladoga, Lake
37I5 Ladysmith
38E2 Lae
47I5 Lafayette
47J3 Lafayette
32D4 Lafia
32D4 Lafiagi
18D3 La Flèche
20C6 La Galite, Canal de sea chan.
23J7 Lagan'
17G3 Lagan r.
53K6 Lagarto
11G7 Lågen r.
32D1 Laghouat
55C2 Lagoa Santa
55A5 Lagoa Vermelha
19B5 Lagos
32D4 Lagos
35C4 Lagosa
46D2 La Grande
45K4 La Grande 4, Réservoir
47J5 La Grange
52F2 La Gran Sabana plat.
55A5 Laguna
30B2 Laha
49D4 La Habra
29D7 Lahad Datu
15F9 La Hague, Cap de c.
29C8 Lahat
34E2 Laḥij
11H8 Laholm
27G3 Lahore
11N6 Lahti
33E4 Laï
42F1 Laidley
10M5 Laihia
32D3 L'Aïr, Massif de mts
22K5 Laishevo
11L6 Laitila
28E4 Laiyang
27K3 Laizhou Wan b.
55A5 Lajeado
53K5 Lajes
55A4 Lajes
46G4 La Junta
51H4 La Juventud, Isla de i.
42C4 Lake Cargelligo
47I5 Lake Charles
47K5 Lake City
49E3 Lake Havasu City
48D2 Lakehurst
47K6 Lakeland
47I5 Lake Providence
42D6 Lakes Entrance
48C4 Lakeside
48B1 Lakewood
48D2 Lakewood
10Q6 Lakhdenpokh'ya
32C4 Lakota
10O1 Laksefjorden sea chan.
54B4 La Ligua
19B2 Lalín
19D5 La Línea de la Concepción
27G4 Lalitpur
12J5 La Louvière
46G4 Lamar
44G3 La Martre, Lac l.
34B4 Lambaréné
52C5 Lambayeque
36D7 Lambert's Bay
48A1 Lambeth
19C3 Lamego
52C6 La Merced
54C3 La Merced
46G5 Lamesa
49D4 La Mesa
21J5 Lamia
16G5 Lammermuir Hills
49C3 Lamont
29B6 Lampang
46G6 Lampazos
34E4 Lamu
14E4 Lancaster
47K5 Lancaster
48C2 Lancaster
49C3 Lancaster
45J2 Lancaster Sound strait
13M7 Landeck
46F3 Lander
13M6 Landsberg am Lech
15B8 Land's End pt
13N6 Landshut
11H9 Landskrona
18H3 Langenthal
10□1 Langjökull ice cap
15E7 Langport
18G3 Langres
27I6 Langsa
10J5 Långsele
18C2 Lannion
47K3 Lansing
30B3 Lanxi
32B2 Lanzarote i.
27J3 Lanzhou
29E6 Laoag
27J4 Lao Cai
18F2 Laon
52C6 La Oroya
29C6 Laos
30C4 Laotougou
55A4 Lapa
51I7 La Palma
32B2 La Palma i.
46E7 La Paz
50G6 La Paz
52E7 La Paz
54E4 La Paz
30F3 La Pérouse Strait
54E4 La Plata
54E4 La Plata, Río de sea chan.
11P6 Lappeenranta
10K3 Lappland reg.
21L4 Lâpseki
25N2 Laptev Sea
10M5 Lapua
54C2 La Quiaca
20E3 L'Aquila
49D4 La Quinta
19C6 Larache
46F3 Laramie
55B3 Laranjal Paulista
54F3 Laranjeiras do Sul
19H5 Larba
46H6 Laredo
16E5 Largs
20D6 L'Ariana
54C3 La Rioja
19E2 La Rioja reg.
21J5 Larisa
17G3 Larne
18D3 La Rochelle
18D3 La Roche-sur-Yon
51K5 La Romana
44H4 La Ronge
44H4 La Ronge, Lac l.
11G7 Larvik
46F5 Las Cruces
54B3 La Serena
54E5 Las Flores
54C4 Las Heras
32B2 Las Palmas de Gran Canaria
20C2 La Spezia
51H7 Las Tablas
54D3 Las Termas
51I4 Las Tunas
50C4 Las Varas
54D4 Las Varillas
46F4 Las Vegas
49E2 Las Vegas
52C4 Latacunga
33G1 Latakia
18D4 La Teste
20E4 Latina
47M2 La Tuque
11N8 Latvia
13N5 Lauchhammer
15C8 Launceston
41J8 Launceston
47J5 Laurel
48D2 Laureldale
48B3 Laurel Hill
47L5 Laurinburg
18H3 Lausanne
39H3 Lautoka
18D2 Laval
51J5 La Vega
55B3 Lavras
32C3 Lawra
47H4 Lawrence
48F1 Lawrence
47J4 Lawrenceburg
46H5 Lawton
30F1 Lazarev
21I2 Lazarevac
50D5 Lázaro Cárdenas
11M9 Lazdijai
15F6 Leamington Spa, Royal
15G7 Leatherhead
47I4 Lebanon
48C2 Lebanon
48E1 Lebanon
33G1 Lebanon country
23H5 Lebedyan'
13P3 Lębork
37I3 Lebowakgomo
19C5 Lebrija
54B5 Lebu
20H4 Lecce
20C2 Lecco
21I6 Lechaina
18G3 Le Creusot
15I8 Le Crotoy
19D3 Ledesma
10R4 Ledmozero
14F5 Leeds
15E5 Leek
48C3 Leesburg
47I5 Leesville
13J4 Leeuwarden
40D6 Leeuwin, Cape
51L5 Leeward Islands
21I5 Lefkada
21I5 Lefkada i.
21I5 Lefkimmi
20D2 Legnago
13P5 Legnica
15H9 Le Havre
10P5 Lehmo
13O7 Leibnitz
15F6 Leicester
12J4 Leiden
14E5 Leigh
41H6 Leigh Creek
15G7 Leighton Buzzard
13N5 Leipzig
19B4 Leiria
11D7 Leirvik
27J4 Leizhou Bandao pen.
20C6 Le Kef
11I6 Leksand
12J4 Lelystad
18E2 Le Mans
47H3 Le Mars
55B3 Leme
46G2 Lemmon
49C2 Lemoore
20G4 Le Murge hills
11F8 Lemvig
25N2 Lena r.
15H7 Lenham
23G7 Lenine
23H7 Leningradskaya
11R7 Leningradskaya Oblast' admin. div.
25S3 Leningradskiy
23J6 Leninsk
23H5 Leninskiy
24J4 Leninsk-Kuznetskiy
22J4 Leninskoye
30D3 Leninskoye
18F1 Lens
25M3 Lensk
20G1 Lenti
20F6 Lentini
32C3 Léo
13O7 Leoben
15E6 Leominster
48F1 Leominster
19D2 León
50D4 León
51G6 León
42B7 Leongatha
21J6 Leonidi
30F2 Leonidovo
40E5 Leonora
55C3 Leopoldina
18I3 Lepontine, Alpi mts
18F4 Le Puy-en-Velay
37H2 Lerala
32C3 Léré
19E2 Lerma
48C1 Le Roy
11H8 Lerum
16□ Lerwick
21K5 Lesbos i.
51J5 Les Cayes
27J4 Leshan
22J2 Leshukonskoye
21I3 Leskovac
24K4 Lesosibirsk
37I5 Lesotho
30D3 Lesozavodsk
39I5 L'Espérance Rock i.
18D3 Les Sables-d'Olonne
51K6 Lesser Antilles is
23I8 Lesser Caucasus mts
44G4 Lesser Slave Lake
13P5 Leszno
15G7 Letchworth
44G5 Lethbridge
52E4 Leticia
22G2 Letnerechenskiy
15I8 Le Touquet-Paris-Plage
17E3 Letterkenny
16G4 Leuchars
12J5 Leuven
21J5 Levadeia
10G5 Levanger
23J8 Levashi
46G5 Levelland
14G5 Leven
16F4 Leven, Loch l.
40E3 Lévêque, Cape
13K5 Leverkusen
13Q6 Levice
48D2 Levittown
48E2 Levittown
23H5 Lev Tolstoy
15H8 Lewes
16C2 Lewis, Isle of i.
48C2 Lewisburg
46E2 Lewis Range mts
46D2 Lewiston
46F2 Lewistown
48C2 Lewistown
46H3 Lexington
47K4 Lexington
48B4 Lexington
21H4 Lezhë
23G6 L'gov
27I4 Lhasa
28D4 Lianyungang
27L2 Liaodong Wan b.
30A4 Liaoning prov.
30A4 Liaoyang
30B4 Liaoyuan
30A4 Liaozhong
34B3 Libenge
46G4 Liberal
13O5 Liberec
51G6 Liberia
32C4 Liberia country
18D4 Libourne
34A3 Libreville
33E2 Libya
33F2 Libyan Desert
33F1 Libyan Plateau
20E6 Licata
15F6 Lichfield
35D5 Lichinga
37H4 Lichtenburg
11N10 Lida
11H7 Lidköping
40G4 Liebig, Mount
18I3 Liechtenstein
13J5 Liège
10Q5 Lieksa
13N7 Lienz
11L8 Liepāja
13O7 Liezen
17F4 Liffey r.
17E3 Lifford
42C2 Lightning Ridge
18I5 Ligurian Sea
20F2 Lika reg.
35C5 Likasi
22G4 Likhoslavl'
11H7 Lilla Edet
18F1 Lille
11G6 Lillehammer
11G7 Lillestrøm
35D5 Lilongwe
47K3 Lima
48C1 Lima
52C6 Lima
55C3 Lima Duarte
23J7 Liman
33G1 Limassol
17F2 Limavady
11N8 Limbaži
55B3 Limeira
17D5 Limerick
41H2 Limmen Bight b.
21K5 Limnos i.
53K5 Limoeiro
18E4 Limoges
46G4 Limon
18F5 Limoux
37I2 Limpopo prov.
37K3 Limpopo r.
19E4 Linares
46H7 Linares
54B5 Linares
14G5 Lincoln
47H3 Lincoln
47J3 Lincoln
54D4 Lincoln
13L7 Lindau (Bodensee)
53G2 Linden
35D4 Lindi
30B3 Lindian
6 Line Islands
27K3 Linfen
13K4 Lingen (Ems)
29C8 Lingga, Kepulauan is
55C2 Linhares
27J2 Linhe
30B4 Linjiang
11I7 Linköping
30C3 Linkou
16F5 Linlithgow
16D4 Linnhe, Loch inlet
55A3 Lins
27K2 Linxi
27J3 Linxia
27K3 Linyi
13O6 Linz
18F5 Lion, Golfe du g.
23H5 Lipetsk
21I1 Lipova
34D3 Lira
34C3 Lisala
19B4 Lisbon
17F3 Lisburn
30B4 Lishu
18E2 Lisieux
23H6 Liski
42F2 Lismore
42E4 Lithgow
11M9 Lithuania
13O5 Litoměřice
27I5 Little Andaman i.
11F9 Little Belt sea chan.
51H5 Little Cayman i.
47I2 Little Falls
46G5 Littlefield
15G8 Littlehampton
16B3 Little Minch sea chan.
47I5 Little Rock
30B4 Liuhe
27J4 Liuzhou
49B2 Livermore
14E5 Liverpool
42E4 Liverpool
42E3 Liverpool Plains
42D3 Liverpool Range mts
16F5 Livingston
46E2 Livingston
47I5 Livingston
35C5 Livingstone
20G3 Livno
23H5 Livny
20D3 Livorno
55C1 Livramento do Brumado
15B9 Lizard Point
20F1 Ljubljana
11H8 Ljungby
11J6 Ljusdal
15D7 Llandovery
14D5 Llandudno
15C7 Llanelli
15D6 Llangollen
46G5 Llano Estacado plain
52E2 Llanos plain
15D7 Llantrisant
15D5 Llay
19G3 Lleida
19E2 Llodio
37G3 Lobatse
54E5 Loberia
35B5 Lobito
54E5 Lobos
16E4 Lochy, Loch l.
16F5 Lockerbie
48C2 Lock Haven
48B1 Lockport
22G3 Lodeynoye Pole
20C2 Lodi
49B1 Lodi
34C4 Lodja
13Q5 Łódź
10H2 Lofoten is
23I6 Log
46E3 Logan
44D3 Logan, Mount
20F2 Logatec
19E2 Logroño
11M6 Loimaa
18C3 Loire r.
19D5 Loja
52C4 Loja
10F5 Løkken
22F4 Loknya
32D4 Lokoja
32D4 Lokossa
23G5 Lokot'
11G9 Lolland i.
21J3 Lom
54E4 Lomas de Zamora
40D1 Lombok i.
29D8 Lombok, Selat sea chan.
32D4 Lomé
16E4 Lomond, Loch l.
11P7 Lomonosov
49B3 Lompoc
13S4 Łomża
15G7 London
47K4 London
48A1 London
17E3 Londonderry
40F2 Londonderry, Cape
55A3 Londrina
25S2 Longa, Proliv sea chan.
15E7 Long Ashton
49C4 Long Beach
48E2 Long Branch
15F6 Long Eaton
17E4 Longford
48E2 Long Island
48E2 Long Island Sound sea chan.
30A3 Longjiang
48E1 Longmeadow
15H6 Long Melford
46F3 Longmont
48A1 Long Point Bay
41I4 Longreach
14E3 Longtown
47I5 Longview
29C6 Long Xuyên
28D5 Longyan
24C2 Longyearbyen
11I8 Lönsboda
18G3 Lons-le-Saunier
29C6 Lop Buri
27I2 Lop Nur salt flat
45J5 Lorain
19F5 Lorca
41L6 Lord Howe Island
55B3 Lorena
53I5 Loreto
18C3 Lorient
16D4 Lorn, Firth of est.
18H2 Lorrain, Plateau
46F4 Los Alamos
49C3 Los Angeles
54B5 Los Ángeles
49B2 Los Banos
54A6 Los Chonos, Archipiélago de is
54D3 Los Juríes
46F6 Los Mochis
51H7 Los Mosquitos, Golfo de b.
16F3 Lossiemouth
52E1 Los Teques
15C8 Lostwithiel
54B4 Los Vilos
18E4 Lot r.
54B5 Lota
28C5 Louang Namtha
29C6 Louangphrabang
35B4 Loubomo
32B3 Louga
15F6 Loughborough
17D4 Loughrea
15H7 Loughton
41K2 Louisiade Archipelago is
47I5 Louisiana state
47J4 Louisville
10R3 Loukhi
19B5 Loulé
32D4 Loum
13N5 Louny
18D5 Lourdes
14G5 Louth
21J5 Loutra Aidipsou
21K3 Lovech
11O6 Loviisa
46G5 Lovington
48F1 Lowell
43E5 Lower Hutt
17E3 Lower Lough Erne l.
15I6 Lowestoft
13Q4 Łowicz
41I6 Loxton
39G4 Loyauté, Îles is
23F6 Loyew
21H2 Loznica
23H6 Lozova
35B4 Luanda
35C5 Luanshya
35C5 Luau
32D4 Luba
23D6 Lubaczów
35B5 Lubango
35C4 Lubao
23D6 Lubartów
46G5 Lubbock
13M4 Lübeck
13P5 Lubin
23D6 Lublin
23G6 Lubny
35C5 Lubumbashi
35B4 Lucala
35C4 Lucapa
20D3 Lucca
16E6 Luce Bay
55A3 Lucélia
19D5 Lucena
29E6 Lucena
13Q6 Lučenec
20F4 Lucera
18I3 Lucerne
30D3 Luchegorsk
13N4 Luckenwalde
27H4 Lucknow
13K5 Lüdenscheid
36B4 Lüderitz
27G3 Ludhiana
11I6 Ludvika
13L6 Ludwigsburg
13L6 Ludwigshafen am Rhein
11O8 Ludza
35C4 Luebo
35B5 Luena
47I5 Lufkin
11P7 Luga
18I3 Lugano
19C2 Lugo
20D2 Lugo
21I2 Lugoj
23H6 Luhans'k
23H5 Lukhovitsy
21K3 Lukovit
23D6 Łuków
23J5 Lukoyanov
10M4 Luleå
10M4 Luleälven r.
21L4 Lüleburgaz
47L5 Lumberton
19C3 Lumbrales
20D2 Lumezzane
11H9 Lund
15C7 Lundy Island
14E4 Lune r.
13M4 Lüneburg
18H2 Lunéville
11O10 Luninyets
32B4 Lunsar
30C3 Luobei
27K3 Luohe
27K3 Luoyang
35C5 Lupane
27J4 Lupanshui
21J2 Lupeni
17F3 Lurgan
35C5 Lusaka
35C4 Lusambo
21H4 Lushnjë
26E3 Lut, Dasht-e des.
13N5 Lutherstadt Wittenberg
15G7 Luton
23E6 Luts'k
36D6 Lutzville
34D3 Luwero
29E8 Luwuk
13K6 Luxembourg
13K6 Luxembourg country
33G2 Luxor
22J3 Luza
27J4 Luzhou
55B2 Luziânia
29E6 Luzon i.
29E5 Luzon Strait
23E6 L'viv
11O10 Lyakhavichy
10K4 Lycksele
15H8 Lydd
23F6 Lyel'chytsy
11P9 Lyepyel'
15E8 Lyme Bay
15E8 Lyme Regis
15F8 Lymington
48B4 Lynchburg
48F1 Lynn
18G4 Lyon
23F5 Lyozna
11G7 Lysekil
22J4 Lyskovo
24G4 Lys'va
23H6 Lysychans'k
23J6 Lysyye Gory
14D5 Lytham St Anne's
11P10 Lyuban'
22I4 Lyubim
23G5 Lyudinovo

M

33G1 Ma'ān
13J5 Maastricht
52G2 Mabaruma
14H5 Mablethorpe
37I3 Mabopane
55C3 Macaé
55C1 Macajuba
53H3 Macapá
52C4 Macará
55C1 Macarani
52C4 Macas
27K4 Macau
53K5 Macau
14E5 Macclesfield
40G4 Macdonnell Ranges mts
16G3 Macduff
21I4 Macedonia
53K5 Maceió
32C4 Macenta
20E3 Macerata
52C4 Machachi
34D4 Machakos
52C4 Machala
27H5 Machilipatnam
52D1 Machiques
52D6 Machu Picchu tourist site
15D6 Machynlleth
21M2 Măcin
42E2 Macintyre Brook r.
23H8 Maçka
41J4 Mackay
44E3 Mackenzie r.
44E3 Mackenzie Bay
44E3 Mackenzie Mountains
42F3 Macksville
42F2 Maclean
47I3 Macomb
18G3 Mâcon
47I4 Macon
47K5 Macon
37J4 Madadeni
35E6 Madagascar
21K4 Madan
38E2 Madang
32D3 Madaoua
52G4 Madeira r.
32B1 Madeira terr.
46F6 Madera
27G5 Madgaon
35B4 Madingou
47H3 Madison
47J3 Madison
47J4 Madison
48B4 Madison Heights
47J4 Madisonville
11O8 Madona
21L5 Madra Dağı mts
33G2 Madrakah
47H6 Madre, Laguna lag.
50D5 Madre del Sur, Sierra mts
46F6 Madre Occidental, Sierra mts
46G6 Madre Oriental, Sierra mts
19E3 Madrid
27G6 Madurai
31E5 Maebashi
35E5 Maevatanana
37H5 Mafeteng
42C6 Maffra
35D4 Mafinga
55A4 Mafra
37J6 Magabeni
25Q4 Magadan
52D2 Magangue
32D3 Magaria
23J8 Magas
30B1 Magdagachi
46E5 Magdalena
13M4 Magdeburg
54B8 Magellan, Strait of
20C2 Maggiore, Lake
17F3 Magherafelt
19F6 Maghnia
14E5 Maghull
24G4 Magnitogorsk
47I5 Magnolia
30F1 Mago
32B3 Magṭa' Laḥjar
27I4 Magwe
33H1 Mahābād
35E5 Mahajanga
37H2 Mahalapye
35E5 Mahalevona
35E5 Mahanoro
27J5 Maha Sarakham
34E1 Mahd adh Dhahab
19G6 Mahdia
20D7 Mahdia
53G2 Mahdia
35D4 Mahenge
23F5 Mahilyow
19I4 Mahón
52D1 Maicao
15G7 Maidenhead
15H7 Maidstone
32E3 Maiduguri
47N2 Maine state
45L5 Maine, Gulf of
16F1 Mainland i.
16□ Mainland i.
35E5 Maintirano
13L5 Mainz
42E4 Maitland
31D6 Maizuru
29D8 Majene
19H4 Majorca i.
34B4 Makabana
29D8 Makale
27H2 Makanchi
30F2 Makarov
22I4 Makar'yev
29D8 Makassar
29D8 Makassar, Selat strait
26E2 Makat
32B4 Makeni
35C6 Makgadikgadi depr.
23J8 Makhachkala
27G1 Makinsk
23H6 Makiyivka
21I1 Makó
34B3 Makokou
22G4 Maksatikha
35D5 Makunguwiro
32D4 Makurdi
27G5 Malabar Coast
32D4 Malabo
29B7 Malacca, Strait of
11O9 Maladzyechna
19D5 Málaga
39G2 Malaita i.
33G4 Malakal
29D8 Malang
35B4 Malanje
11J7 Mälaren l.
54C5 Malargüe
26C3 Malatya
35D5 Malawi
22G4 Malaya Vishera
33H1 Malāyer
29C7 Malaysia
13Q3 Malbork
27G6 Maldives
15H7 Maldon
42B6 Maldon
54F4 Maldonado
7 Male
23J8 Malgobek
55C1 Malhada
32C3 Mali
38C2 Malili
34E4 Malindi
17E2 Malin Head
21L4 Malkara
33G2 Mallawī
55A4 Mallét
17D5 Mallow
13K5 Malmédy
15E7 Malmesbury
36D7 Malmesbury
11H9 Malmö
22K4 Malmyzh
22H3 Maloshuyka
23H5 Maloyaroslavets
11O8 Malta
20F7 Malta country
20F6 Malta Channel
14F5 Maltby
29E8 Maluku, Laut sea
11H6 Malung
37I5 Maluti Mountains
47I5 Malvern
23F6 Malyn
23J7 Malyye Derbety
22K5 Mamadysh
37I3 Mamelodi
32D4 Mamfe
52E6 Mamoré r.
32B3 Mamou
38B2 Mamuju
32C4 Man
14C4 Man, Isle of terr.
52F4 Manacapuru
19H4 Manacor
29E7 Manado
51G6 Managua
35E6 Manakara
34F1 Manama
35E5 Mananara Avaratra
35E6 Mananjary
48C3 Manassas
52F4 Manaus
33G1 Manavgat
14E5 Manchester
48C3 Manchester
48E2 Manchester
48F1 Manchester
11E7 Mandal
27I4 Mandalay
27J2 Mandalgovĭ
46G2 Mandan
51I5 Mandeville
35E5 Mandritsara
27G4 Mandsaur
40D6 Mandurah
20G4 Manduria
27G5 Mandya
23E6 Manevychi
20F4 Manfredonia
32C3 Manga
55C1 Manga
34B4 Mangai
21M3 Mangalia
27G5 Mangalore
37H5 Mangaung
15E7 Mangotsfield
19C3 Mangualde
47H4 Manhattan
37K3 Manhica
55C3 Manhuaçu
45L4 Manicouagan, Réservoir resr
45M3 Maniitsoq
29E6 Manila
42E3 Manilla
21L5 Manisa
47J3 Manistee
45I4 Manitoba prov.
45I4 Manitoba, Lake
47J3 Manitowoc
52C2 Manizales
35E6 Manja
47I3 Mankato
32C4 Mankono
27G6 Mannar, Gulf of
13L6 Mannheim
48A3 Mannington
30B4 Manp'o
19G3 Manresa
35C5 Mansa
32B3 Mansa Konko
15F5 Mansfield
42C6 Mansfield
47I5 Mansfield
47K3 Mansfield
52B4 Manta
49B2 Manteca
55C2 Mantena
18E2 Mantes-la-Jolie
55B3 Mantiqueira, Serra da mts
21J5 Mantoudi
11N6 Mäntsälä
10N5 Mänttä
20D2 Mantua
22J4 Manturovo
55A4 Manuel Ribas
55C1 Manuel Vitorino
43E3 Manukau
21L4 Manyas
35D4 Manyoni
50D5 Manzanillo
51I4 Manzanillo
27K2 Manzhouli
37J4 Manzini
33E3 Mao
37H4 Maokeng
46F2 Maple Creek
37K3 Maputo
37K3 Maputo prov.
37H5 Maputsoe
32B2 Maqṭeïr reg.
35B4 Maquela do Zombo
52E4 Maraã
53I5 Marabá
52D1 Maracaibo
52D2 Maracaibo, Lake
54E2 Maracaju
55C1 Maracás
52E1 Maracay
32D3 Maradi
53H4 Marajó, Ilha de i.
26D3 Marand
52D4 Marañón r.
55D1 Maraú
19D5 Marbella
37I3 Marble Hall
37J6 Marburg
13L5 Marburg an der Lahn
20G1 Marcali
15H6 March
52C7 Marcona
27G3 Mardan
54E5 Mar del Plata
33H1 Mardın
16D3 Maree, Loch l.
15I7 Margate
34C3 Margherita Peak
27G2 Margilan
23G7 Marhanets'
55C3 Mariana
47I5 Marianna
47J5 Marianna
34E2 Ma'rib
20F1 Maribor
11K6 Mariehamn
36C3 Mariental
11H7 Mariestad
47K5 Marietta
48A3 Marietta
18G5 Marignane
24J4 Mariinsk
22J4 Mariinskiy Posad
11M9 Marijampolė
55A3 Marília
19B2 Marín
49B2 Marina
11P10 Mar"ina Horka
47J2 Marinette
55A3 Maringá
19B4 Marinha Grande
47J3 Marion
47K3 Marion
47K4 Marion
47L5 Marion
18H4 Maritime Alps mts
23H7 Mariupol'
33H1 Marīvān
34E3 Marka
15G6 Market Deeping
15G6 Market Harborough
14G5 Market Weighton
25S3 Markovo
23J6 Marks
18E4 Marmande
21M4 Marmara, Sea of g.
21M6 Marmaris
18F2 Marne r.
18F2 Marne-la-Vallée
35E5 Maroantsetra
35D5 Marondera
42F1 Maroochydore
33E3 Maroua
35E5 Marovoay
6 Marquesas Islands
55C3 Marquês de Valença
47J2 Marquette
33F3 Marra, Jebel mt.
32C1 Marrakech
33F3 Marra Plateau
33G2 Marsá al 'Alam
34D3 Marsabit
20E6 Marsala
33F1 Marsá Maṭrūh
18G5 Marseille
47H3 Marshall
47I4 Marshall
47I5 Marshall
6 Marshall Islands
47I3 Marshalltown
11J7 Märsta
27I5 Martaban, Gulf of
29D8 Martapura
18H3 Martigny
13Q6 Martin
55B2 Martinho Campos
51L6 Martinique terr.
48C3 Martinsburg
47L4 Martinsville
19E5 Martos
26E1 Martuk
53K6 Maruim
26F3 Mary
41K5 Maryborough
48C3 Maryland state
49B1 Marysville
47I3 Maryville
47K4 Maryville
35D4 Masai Steppe plain
34D4 Masaka
31C6 Masan
35D5 Masasi
19G6 Mascara
55D1 Mascote
37H5 Maseru
26E3 Mashhad
37H5 Masilo
34D3 Masindi
33H1 Masjed Soleymān
17C4 Mask, Lough l.
47I3 Mason City
20D2 Massa
48E1 Massachusetts state
48F1 Massachusetts Bay
20G4 Massafra
35B4 Massango
33G3 Massawa
33E3 Massenya
18F4 Massif Central mts
48A2 Massillon
32C3 Massina
43E5 Masterton
26F4 Mastung
34D1 Mastūrah
11N10 Masty
31C6 Masuda
35D6 Masvingo
37J1 Masvingo prov.
37I1 Matabeleland South prov.
35B4 Matadi
51G6 Matagalpa
32B3 Matam
32D3 Matamey
46G6 Matamoros
47H6 Matamoros
47N2 Matane
47K7 Matanzas
29D8 Mataram
19H3 Mataró
39I3 Matā'utu
50D4 Matehuala
35D5 Matemanga
20G4 Matera
20C6 Mateur
27G4 Mathura
29E7 Mati
55C1 Matias Cardoso
50E5 Matías Romero
15F5 Matlock
55A1 Mato Grosso state
53H7 Mato Grosso, Planalto do plat.
19B3 Matosinhos
55C1 Mato Verde
31D6 Matsue
31E5 Matsumoto
31D6 Matsuyama
18H4 Matterhorn mt.
46D3 Matterhorn mt.
52F2 Maturín
37H5 Matwabeng
16E5 Mauchline
35C5 Maun
37H2 Maunatlala
32B3 Mauritania
7 Mauritius
35C5 Mavinga
33H2 Mawqaq
51K5 Mayagüez
50G5 Maya Mountains
16E5 Maybole
34D2 Maych'ew
18D2 Mayenne
23I7 Maykop
27I4 Maymyo
23J5 Mayna
35E5 Mayotte terr.
23J8 Mayskiy
20E6 Mazara del Vallo
26F3 Mazār-e Sharīf
50C4 Mazatlán
11M8 Mažeikiai
23F5 Mazyr
37J4 Mbabane
32C4 Mbahiakro
34B3 Mbaïki
34D3 Mbale
32E4 Mbalmayo
34B4 Mbandaka
35B4 M'banza Congo
33G5 Mbarara
34C3 Mbari r.
35D4 Mbeya
35D5 Mbinga
32E4 Mbouda
32B3 Mbour
35C4 Mbuji-Mayi
54E3 Mburucuyá
47H5 McAlester
46H6 McAllen
46D3 McCall
46G3 McCook
35D4 Mchinga
44C3 McKinley, Mount
46C2 McMinnville
46H4 McPherson
37H7 Mdantsane
20B6 M'Daourouch
49E2 Mead, Lake resr
48A2 Meadville
18F2 Meaux
34D1 Mecca
48C4 Mechanicsville
12J5 Mechelen
32C1 Mecheria
13M3 Mecklenburger Bucht b.
27I6 Medan
19H5 Médéa
52C2 Medellín
32E1 Medenine
46C3 Medford
48E2 Medford
21M2 Medgidia
48D3 Media
21K1 Mediaș
46F3 Medicine Bow Mountains
44G4 Medicine Hat
34D1 Medina
55C2 Medina
19D3 Medina de Rioseco
20D6 Mediterranean Sea
22J4 Medvedevo
22G3 Medvezh'yegorsk
40D5 Meekatharra
27G4 Meerut
21J6 Megalopoli
33E4 Meiganga
30B4 Meihekou
27I4 Meiktila
13M5 Meiningen
13N5 Meißen
30C3 Meixi
28D5 Meizhou
34D2 Mek'elē
32B3 Mékhé
32C1 Meknès
29C6 Mekong r.
29C7 Melaka
42B6 Melbourne
47K6 Melbourne
23I5 Melenki
19E6 Melilla
23G7 Melitopol'
13O6 Melk
15E7 Melksham
54F4 Melo
16G5 Melrose
42B6 Melton
15G6 Melton Mowbray
18F2 Melun
41H2 Melville Bay
40G2 Melville Island
45H2 Melville Island
13M7 Memmingen
47I4 Memphis
23G6 Mena
47I5 Mena
18F4 Mende
33G3 Mendefera
22L5 Mendeleyevsk
38E2 Mendi
15E7 Mendip Hills
54C4 Mendoza
21L5 Menemen
35B5 Menongue
29B8 Mentawai, Kepulauan is
18H5 Menton
20C6 Menzel Bourguiba
20D6 Menzel Temime
13K4 Meppen
37H5 Meqheleng
20D1 Merano
29G8 Merauke
49B2 Merced
54E3 Mercedes
54E4 Mercedes
55C3 Mercês
15E7 Mere
23H6 Merefa
27I5 Mergui
27I5 Mergui Archipelago is
19C4 Mérida
50G4 Mérida
52D2 Mérida
48E2 Meriden
47J5 Meridian
18D4 Mérignac
42D6 Merimbula
33G3 Merowe
40D6 Merredin
47J2 Merrill
33H3 Mersa Fatma
14E5 Mersey est.
15D7 Merthyr Tydfil
13K6 Merzig
46E5 Mesa
20G4 Mesagne
21I5 Mesolongi
55C2 Mesquita
20F5 Messina
20F5 Messina, Strait of
21J6 Messini
20E2 Mestre
52E2 Meta r.
54C3 Metán
48F1 Methuen
32D1 Metlaoui
34D3 Metu
18H2 Metz
12J5 Meuse r.
15C8 Mevagissey
49E4 Mexicali
50D4 Mexico
47H6 Mexico, Gulf of
50E5 Mexico City
48B3 Meyersdale
26F3 Meymaneh
21J3 Mezdra
22J2 Mezen'
22J2 Mezen' r.
22K3 Mezhdurechensk
24J4 Mezhdurechensk
21I1 Mezőtúr
47I4 Miami
47K6 Miami
47K6 Miami Beach
33H1 Miandowāb
35E5 Miandrivazo
27G3 Mianwali
27J3 Mianyang
35E5 Miarinarivo
24H4 Miass
23D6 Michalovce
47J2 Michigan state
47J3 Michigan, Lake
23I5 Michurinsk
29G7 Micronesia, Federated States of
12I5 Middelburg
37I3 Middelburg
11F9 Middelfart
48C3 Middle River
14F4 Middlesbrough
48D2 Middletown
48E2 Middletown
46G5 Midland
47L3 Midland
17D6 Midleton
10□2 Miðvágur
23D6 Mielec
21K1 Miercurea-Ciuc
19D2 Mieres
46G7 Miguel Auza
31D6 Mihara
23H5 Mikhaylov
23I6 Mikhaylovka
30D4 Mikhaylovka
24I4 Mikhaylovskiy
11O6 Mikkeli
20C2 Milan
21L6 Milas
20F5 Milazzo
15H6 Mildenhall
41I6 Mildura
42E1 Miles
46F2 Miles City
48F1 Milford
15B7 Milford Haven
43A7 Milford Sound inlet
19H5 Miliana
25Q4 Mil'kovo
18F4 Millau
47K5 Milledgeville
45I5 Mille Lacs, Lac des l.
23I6 Millerovo
42E1 Millmerran
48D3 Millville
49B2 Milpitas
15G6 Milton Keynes
47J3 Milwaukee
26E4 Mīnāb
29E7 Minahasa, Semenanjung pen.
27J6 Minas
54E4 Minas
55B2 Minas Gerais state
55C2 Minas Novas
50F5 Minatitlán
29E7 Mindanao i.
32□ Mindelo
13L4 Minden
47I5 Minden
29E6 Mindoro i.
34B4 Mindouli
15D7 Minehead
48E2 Mineola
23I7 Mineral'nyye Vody
46H5 Mineral Wells
48A2 Minerva
23J8 Mingäçevir
19F4 Minglanilla
35D5 Mingoyo
30B3 Mingshui
32D4 Minna
47I3 Minneapolis
47I2 Minnesota state
19H3 Minorca i.
46G2 Minot
11O10 Minsk
13R4 Mińsk Mazowiecki
24K4 Minusinsk
55B2 Mirabela
55C3 Miraí
54E5 Miramar
45L5 Miramichi
54E2 Miranda
19E2 Miranda de Ebro
19C3 Mirandela
20D2 Mirandola
55A3 Mirassol
42C7 Mirboo North
29D7 Miri
54F4 Mirim, Lagoa l.
25M3 Mirnyy
27F4 Mirpur Khas
21J6 Mirtoö Pelagos sea
31C6 Miryang
27H4 Mirzapur
23D6 Miskolc
33E1 Mişrātah
49D4 Mission Viejo
48B1 Mississauga
47J6 Mississippi r.
47J5 Mississippi state
46E2 Missoula
47I4 Missouri r.
47I4 Missouri state
45K4 Mistassini, Lac l.
13P6 Mistelbach
41J5 Mitchell
46H3 Mitchell
41I3 Mitchell r.
17D5 Mitchelstown
31F5 Mito
52D3 Mitú
35C5 Mitumba, Chaîne des mts
31E6 Miura
31F5 Miyako
31C7 Miyakonojō
31C7 Miyazaki
31D6 Miyazu
31D6 Miyoshi
17C6 Mizen Head
23D6 Mizhhir"ya
31F5 Mizusawa
11I7 Mjölby
35D4 Mkata
13O5 Mladá Boleslav
21I2 Mladenovac
13R4 Mława
37H6 Mlungisi
37G3 Mmabatho
34B4 Moanda
47I4 Moberly
47J5 Mobile
47J5 Mobile Bay
35E5 Moçambique
34E2 Mocha
37H3 Mochudi
35E5 Mocimboa da Praia
52C3 Mocoa
55B3 Mococa
35D5 Mocuba
37G5 Modder r.
20D2 Modena
49B2 Modesto
42C7 Moe
11G6 Moelv
16F5 Moffat
34E3 Mogadishu
55B3 Mogi-Mirim
25M4 Mogocha
37G3 Mogoditshane
20H2 Mohács
37H6 Mohale's Hoek
19G6 Mohammadia

35D4 Mohoro
23E6 Mohyliv Podil's'kyy
21L1 Moinești
10I3 Mo i Rana
49D3 Mojave Desert
55B3 Moji das Cruzes
37I5 Mokhotlong
20D7 Moknine
33E3 Mokolo
31B6 Mokp'o
23J6 Mokrous
23J5 Mokshan
10E5 Molde
23F7 Moldova
21M1 Moldovei de Sud, Cîmpia *plain*
37G3 Molepolole
11N9 Molėtai
20G4 Molfetta
19F3 Molina de Aragón
52D7 Mollendo
11H8 Mölnlycke
42D4 Molong
36E5 Molopo *watercourse*
33E4 Moloundou
29E8 Moluccas *is*
53K5 Mombaça
34D4 Mombasa
21K4 Momchilgrad
52D2 Mompós
11H9 Møn *i.*
18H5 Monaco
16E3 Monadhliath Mountains
17F3 Monaghan
20D7 Monastir
23F6 Monastyryshche
30F3 Monbetsu
20B2 Moncalieri
10R3 Monchegorsk
13K5 Mönchengladbach
46G6 Monclova
45L5 Moncton
37J4 Mondlo
20B2 Mondovì
20E4 Mondragone
20E2 Monfalcone
19C2 Monforte
34D3 Mongbwalu
27J4 Mông Cai
33E3 Mongo
27J2 Mongolia
35C5 Mongu
35D5 Monkey Bay
15E7 Monmouth
20G4 Monopoli
19F3 Monreal del Campo
20E5 Monreale
47I5 Monroe
32B4 Monrovia
12I5 Mons
21J3 Montana
46F2 Montana *state*
18F3 Montargis
18E4 Montauban
18G4 Montbrison
18G3 Montceau-les-Mines
18D5 Mont-de-Marsan
53H4 Monte Alegre
55B1 Monte Alegre de Goiás
55A2 Monte Alegre de Minas
55C1 Monte Azul
55A3 Monte Azul Paulista
20E2 Montebelluna
18H5 Monte-Carlo
51J5 Monte Cristi
51I5 Montego Bay
18G4 Montélimar
46H6 Montemorelos
19B4 Montemor-o-Novo
49B2 Monterey
49A2 Monterey Bay
52C2 Montería
54C3 Monteros
46G6 Monterrey
53K6 Monte Santo
55C2 Montes Claros
20F3 Montesilvano
20D3 Montevarchi
54E4 Montevideo
47J5 Montgomery
48A3 Montgomery
18H3 Monthey
48D2 Monticello
19D5 Montilla
18F3 Montluçon
45K5 Montmagny
41K4 Monto
47M3 Montpelier
18F5 Montpellier
45K5 Montréal
16G4 Montrose
46F4 Montrose
51L5 Montserrat *terr.*
15I9 Mont-St-Aignan
27I4 Monywa
20C2 Monza
40D6 Moora
47H2 Moorhead
42B6 Mooroopna
44H4 Moose Jaw
35C6 Mopipi
32C3 Mopti
52D7 Moquegua
11I6 Mora
33E3 Mora
53K5 Morada Nova
35E5 Moramanga
16D4 Morar, Loch *l.*
16E3 Moray Firth *b.*
23I5 Mordovo
14E4 Morecambe
14D4 Morecambe Bay
42D2 Moree
50D5 Morelia
19F3 Morella
19C5 Morena, Sierra *mts*
21K2 Moreni
49D4 Moreno Valley
49B2 Morgan Hill
47K4 Morganton
48B3 Morgantown
18H3 Morges
31F5 Morioka
42E4 Morisset
22K4 Morki
18C2 Morlaix
14F5 Morley
41H3 Mornington Island
32C1 Morocco
35D4 Morogoro
29E7 Moro Gulf
35E6 Morombe
27J2 Mörön
35E6 Morondava
19D5 Morón de la Frontera
35E5 Moroni
34D3 Moroto
23I6 Morozovsk
14F3 Morpeth
55A2 Morrinhos
47K4 Morristown
48D2 Morristown
48D1 Morrisville
53J6 Morro do Chapéu
23I5 Morshanka
20C7 Morsott
54D4 Morteros
42A7 Mortlake
42E5 Moruya
16D4 Morvern *reg.*
42C7 Morwell
13L6 Mosbach
22H5 Moscow
46D2 Moscow
18H2 Moselle *r.*
46D2 Moses Lake
34D4 Moshi
10H4 Mosjøen
13P7 Mosonmagyaróvár
11G7 Moss
36F8 Mossel Bay
41J3 Mossman
53K5 Mossoró
13N5 Most
19G6 Mostaganem
20G3 Mostar
23I7 Mostovskoy
33H1 Mosul
11I7 Motala
16F5 Motherwell
19F4 Motilla del Palancar
19E5 Motril
21J2 Motru
50G4 Motul
34B4 Mouila
18F3 Moulins
27I5 Moulmein
47K5 Moultrie
33E4 Moundou
48A3 Moundsville
46D3 Mountain Home
47I4 Mountain Home
35D5 Mount Darwin
41I7 Mount Gambier
38E2 Mount Hagen
48D3 Mount Holly
41H4 Mount Isa
40D5 Mount Magnet
17E4 Mountmellick
48C1 Mount Morris
47I3 Mount Pleasant
47I5 Mount Pleasant
47K3 Mount Pleasant
15B8 Mount's Bay
46C3 Mount Shasta
46C2 Mount Vernon
47J4 Mount Vernon
19C4 Moura
41J4 Moura
33F3 Mourdi, Dépression du *depr.*
32C3 Mourdiah
17F3 Mourne Mountains *hills*
12I5 Mouscron
32D2 Mouydir, Monts du *plat.*
37H6 Moyeni
52C5 Moyobamba
35D6 Mozambique
35E6 Mozambique Channel
23J8 Mozdok
23H5 Mozhaysk
22L4 Mozhga
35D4 Mpanda
35D5 Mpika
37I4 Mpumalanga *prov.*
35D4 Mpwapwa
20D7 M'Saken
19I6 M'Sila
23F5 Mstsislaw
23H5 Mtsensk
35E5 Mtwara
29C6 Muang Khammouan
34D3 Mubende
32E3 Mubi
35C5 Muconda
55D2 Mucuri
30C3 Mudanjiang
21M4 Mudanya
21N4 Mudurnu
35C5 Mufulira
21M6 Muğla
13M5 Mühlhausen (Thüringen)
29C7 Mui Ca Mau *c.*
17F5 Muine Bheag
16E3 Muir of Ord
31B5 Muju
23D6 Mukacheve
34E2 Mukalla
30C3 Mulan
19E5 Mulhacén *mt.*
18H3 Mulhouse
30C3 Muling
16D4 Mull *i.*
16C4 Mull, Sound of *sea chan.*
48A4 Mullens
17E4 Mullingar
16D5 Mull of Kintyre *hd*
42F2 Mullumbimby
27G3 Multan
27G5 Mumbai
50G4 Muna
15I6 Mundesley
41K5 Mundubbera
27H4 Munger
13M6 Munich
13K5 Münster
13M4 Münster
55C3 Muqui
31E5 Murakami
34C4 Muramvya
22K4 Murashi
21L4 Muratlı
19F5 Murcia
19F5 Murcia *reg.*
21I1 Mureșul *r.*
18E5 Muret
47J4 Murfreesboro
55C3 Muriaé
13N4 Müritz *l.*
10R2 Murmansk
10S2 Murmanskaya Oblast' *admin. div.*
22I5 Murom
30F4 Muroran
31D6 Muroto
47J4 Murray
42A5 Murray *r.*
41H7 Murray Bridge
42A5 Murrumbidgee *r.*
42D5 Murrumburrah
20G1 Murska Sobota
27H4 Murwara
33E2 Murzūq
13O7 Mürzzuschlag
21J3 Musala *mt.*
30C4 Musan
26E4 Muscat
47I3 Muscatine
40G5 Musgrave Ranges *mts*
34B4 Mushie
47H4 Muskogee
34D4 Musoma
16F5 Musselburgh
21M4 Mustafakemalpaşa
42E4 Muswellbrook
33F2 Mūţ
35D5 Mutare
35D5 Mutoko
35E5 Mutsamudu
30F4 Mutsu
55C2 Mutum
34D4 Muyinga
27H4 Muzaffarpur
46G6 Múzquiz
35D5 Mvuma
34D4 Mwanza
35C4 Mwene-Ditu
35C4 Mweru, Lake
11O9 Myadzyel
27I4 Myanmar
27I4 Myingyan
27I4 Myitkyina
21O1 Mykolayiv
21K6 Mykonos *i.*
27I4 Mymensingh
30C4 Myŏnggan
11O9 Myory
10□1 Mýrdalsjökull *ice cap*
23G6 Myrhorod
23F6 Myronivka
47L5 Myrtle Beach
42C6 Myrtleford
13O4 Myślibórz
27G5 Mysore
29C6 My Tho
21L5 Mytilini
21L5 Mytilini Strait
22H5 Mytishchi
35D5 Mzimba
35D5 Mzuzu

N

11M6 Naantali
17F4 Naas
31E6 Nabari
35D4 Naberera
24G4 Naberezhnyye Chelny
20D6 Nabeul
35E5 Nacala
35D5 Nachingwea
47I5 Nacogdoches
19E6 Nador
23E6 Nadvirna
24I3 Nadym
11G9 Næstved
21J6 Nafplio
23J8 Naftalan
34E1 Nafy
29E6 Naga
42B6 Nagambie
31E5 Nagano
31E5 Nagaoka
31C6 Nagasaki
31C6 Nagato
27G6 Nagercoil
31E6 Nagoya
27G4 Nagpur
27I3 Nagqu
20G1 Nagyatád
20G1 Nagykanizsa
33H1 Nahāvand
16F3 Nairn
34D4 Nairobi
30A2 Naji
30C4 Najin
34E2 Najrān
33G4 Nakasongola
31C6 Nakatsu
31E6 Nakatsugawa
33G3 Nakfa
30D4 Nakhodka
29C6 Nakhon Pathom
29C6 Nakhon Ratchasima
29C6 Nakhon Sawan
29B7 Nakhon Si Thammarat
11G9 Nakskov
34D4 Nakuru
23I8 Nal'chik
21N4 Nallıhan
32E1 Nālūt
37I4 Namahadi
27G2 Namangan
42F1 Nambour
42F3 Nambucca Heads
29C5 Nam Đinh
36B3 Namib Desert
35B5 Namibe
35B6 Namibia
46D3 Nampa
32C3 Nampala
31B5 Namp'o
35D5 Nampula
10G4 Namsos
25N3 Namtsy
27I4 Namtu
12J5 Namur
31B6 Namwŏn
29C6 Nan
44F5 Nanaimo
31E5 Nanao
30C3 Nancha
27K4 Nanchang
27J3 Nanchong
18H2 Nancy
27G5 Nanded
32E4 Nanga Eboko
35D4 Nangulangwa
28D4 Nanjing
27K4 Nan Ling *mts*
27J4 Nanning
45N3 Nanortalik
28D5 Nanping
18D3 Nantes
48A1 Nanticoke
48D2 Nanticoke
48F2 Nantucket Sound *g.*
15E5 Nantwich
55C2 Nanuque
27K3 Nanyang
34D4 Nanyuki
49A1 Napa
43F4 Napier
20F4 Naples
47K6 Naples
31D6 Nara
32C3 Nara
11O9 Narach
41I7 Naracoorte
52C4 Naranjal
18F5 Narbonne
20H4 Nardò
45K2 Nares Strait
23J7 Narimanov
27G4 Narmada *r.*
20E3 Narni
24G3 Narodnaya, Gora *mt.*
23H5 Naro-Fominsk
42E6 Narooma
23F6 Narowlya
10L5 Närpes
42C5 Narrandera
42D4 Narromine
45N3 Narsaq
23I8 Nartkala
31D6 Naruto
11P7 Narva
11O7 Narva Bay
10J2 Narvik
22L2 Nar'yan-Mar
27G2 Naryn
27G4 Nashik
48F1 Nashua
47J4 Nashville
47L6 Nassau
33G2 Nasser, Lake *resr*
11I8 Nässjö
35C6 Nata
53K5 Natal
47I5 Natchez
47I5 Natchitoches
49D4 National City
32D3 Natitingou
53I6 Natividade
31F5 Natori
34D4 Natron, Lake *salt l.*
27J6 Natuna Besar *i.*
40D6 Naturaliste, Cape
40C5 Naturaliste Channel
11M8 Naujoji Akmenė
23J8 Naurskaya
39G2 Nauru
11N10 Navahrudak
17F4 Navan
11P9 Navapolatsk
19F2 Navarra *reg.*
22I5 Navashino
51I5 Navassa Island *terr.*
23G5 Navlya
21M2 Năvodari
26F2 Navoi
46F6 Navojoa
46F7 Navolato
26F4 Nawabshah
26D3 Naxçıvan
21K6 Naxos *i.*
30F3 Nayoro
55D1 Nazaré
33G1 Nazareth
55A2 Nazário
52D6 Nazca
21M6 Nazilli
23J8 Nazran'
34D3 Nazrēt
26E4 Nazwá
35B4 N'dalatando
34C3 Ndélé
33E3 Ndjamena
35C5 Ndola
17F3 Neagh, Lough *l.*
21J5 Nea Liosia
21J6 Neapoli
15D7 Neath
34D3 Nebbi
26E3 Nebitdag
22G4 Nebolchi
46G3 Nebraska *state*
47H3 Nebraska City
54E5 Necochea
19F6 Nédroma
23K5 Neftegorsk
30F1 Neftegorsk
24G4 Neftekamsk
23J7 Neftekumsk
24I3 Nefteyugansk
35B4 Negage
34D3 Negēlē
21J4 Negotino
52G4 Negro *r.*
55A4 Negro *r.*
29E7 Negros *i.*
30B2 Nehe
27J4 Neijiang
30A2 Nei Mongol Zizhiqu *aut. reg.*
52C3 Neiva
34D3 Nek'emtē
22I4 Nekrasovskoye
22G4 Nelidovo
27G5 Nellore
14E5 Nelson
43D5 Nelson
44G5 Nelson
45I4 Nelson *r.*
37J3 Nelspruit
32C3 Néma
11M9 Neman
18F2 Nemours
30G4 Nemuro
30G4 Nemuro-kaikyō *sea chan.*
23F6 Nemyriv
17D5 Nenagh
30B2 Nenjiang
47I4 Neosho
27H4 Nepal
42F1 Nerang
25M4 Nerchinsk
22I4 Nerekhta
55A2 Nerópolis
25N4 Neryungri
16E3 Ness, Loch *l.*
21K4 Nestos *r.*
12J4 Netherlands
51K6 Netherlands Antilles *terr.*
13N4 Neubrandenburg
18H3 Neuchâtel
18H3 Neuchâtel, Lac de *l.*
15I8 Neufchâtel-Hardelot
13L3 Neumünster
13K6 Neunkirchen
13P7 Neunkirchen
54C5 Neuquén
13N4 Neuruppin
13P7 Neusiedler See *l.*
13N4 Neustrelitz
13K5 Neuwied
47I4 Nevada
46D4 Nevada *state*
19E5 Nevada, Sierra *mts*
46C3 Nevada, Sierra *mts*
22F4 Nevel'
30F3 Nevel'sk
30B1 Never
18F3 Nevers
20H3 Nevesinje
23I7 Nevinnomyssk
35D5 Newala
47J4 New Albany
53G2 New Amsterdam
48D2 Newark
48D3 Newark
15G5 Newark-on-Trent
48F2 New Bedford
47L4 New Bern
47K5 Newberry
47I5 New Boston
46H6 New Braunfels
48E2 New Britain
38E2 New Britain *i.*
48D2 New Brunswick
45L5 New Brunswick *prov.*
48D2 Newburgh
15F7 Newbury
48F1 Newburyport
39G4 New Caledonia *terr.*
17G3 Newcastle
37I4 Newcastle
42E4 Newcastle
48A2 New Castle
15E5 Newcastle-under-Lyme
14F4 Newcastle upon Tyne
17C5 Newcastle West
48E2 New City
16E5 New Cumnock
27G4 New Delhi
42E3 New England Range *mts*
15E7 Newent
48B1 Newfane
45M5 Newfoundland *i.*
45M4 Newfoundland and Labrador *prov.*
38E2 New Guinea *i.*
33G3 New Halfa
48F1 New Hampshire *state*
48E2 New Haven
47I5 New Iberia
38F2 New Ireland *i.*
48D3 New Jersey *state*
48B2 New Kensington
45K5 New Liskeard
48E2 New London
40D4 Newman
15H6 Newmarket
48A3 New Martinsville
46F5 New Mexico *state*
47I6 New Orleans
48A2 New Philadelphia
43E4 New Plymouth
15D7 Newport
15E6 Newport
15F8 Newport
46C3 Newport
47I4 Newport
48F2 Newport
49D4 Newport Beach
48C4 Newport News
15G6 Newport Pagnell
15B8 Newquay
47I5 New Roads
48E2 New Rochelle
17F5 New Ross
17F3 Newry
25P2 New Siberia Islands
42C4 New South Wales *state*
48B2 New Stanton
47H4 Newton
47I3 Newton
48D2 Newton
48F1 Newton
15D8 Newton Abbot
16E6 Newton Stewart
15D6 Newtown
46G2 New Town
17G3 Newtownabbey
17G3 Newtownards
17F4 Newtownmountkennedy
47I3 New Ulm
48E2 New York
48D1 New York *state*
43D5 New Zealand
22I4 Neya
26E4 Neyrīz
26E3 Neyshābūr
32E4 Ngaoundal
33E4 Ngaoundéré
32E3 Nguigmi
32E3 Nguru
37J5 Ngwelezana
29C6 Nha Trang
41I7 Nhill
37J4 Nhlangano
32C3 Niafounké
48B1 Niagara Falls
48B1 Niagara Falls
32D3 Niamey
30A3 Nianzishan
29B7 Nias *i.*
51G6 Nicaragua
51G6 Nicaragua, Lake
20G5 Nicastro
18H5 Nice
49A1 Nice
27I6 Nicobar Islands
33G1 Nicosia
11L9 Nida
13R4 Nidzica
13L4 Nienburg (Weser)
53G2 Nieuw Nickerie
26C3 Niğde
32D3 Niger
32D4 Niger *r.*
32D4 Nigeria
31E5 Niigata
31D6 Niihama
31D6 Niimi
31E5 Niitsu
13J5 Nijmegen
10Q2 Nikel'
23J5 Nikolayevka
23J6 Nikolayevsk
30F1 Nikolayevsk-na-Amure
22J4 Nikol'sk
23G7 Nikopol'
20H3 Nikšić
33G1 Nile *r.*
48A2 Niles
18G5 Nîmes
30C3 Ning'an
28E5 Ningbo
31F4 Ninohe
32C3 Niono
32C3 Nioro
18D3 Niort
45J5 Nipigon, Lake
45K5 Nipissing, Lake
55A1 Niquelândia
27G5 Nirmal
21I3 Niš
20F6 Niscemi
55C3 Niterói
13Q6 Nitra
39J3 Niue *terr.*
10N5 Nivala
27G5 Nizamabad
22K5 Nizhnekamsk
25K4 Nizhneudinsk
24I3 Nizhnevartovsk
25O2 Nizhneyansk
23I5 Nizhniy Lomov
22I4 Nizhniy Novgorod
22L3 Nizhnyaya Omra
24J3 Nizhnyaya Tunguska *r.*
23F6 Nizhyn
35D4 Njombe
10J5 Njurundabommen
32E4 Nkambe
32C4 Nkawkaw
35D5 Nkhata Bay
35D5 Nkhotakota
32D4 Nkongsamba
31C6 Nobeoka
30F4 Noboribetsu
46E5 Nogales
46E5 Nogales
31C6 Nōgata
18E2 Nogent-le-Rotrou
22H5 Noginsk
30F2 Nogliki
34B3 Nola
22K4 Nolinsk
44B3 Nome
30B3 Nong'an
45K5 Noranda
11I6 Norberg
13K4 Norden
13M4 Norderstedt
13M5 Nordhausen
47H3 Norfolk
48C4 Norfolk
39G4 Norfolk Island *terr.*
24J3 Noril'sk
47H4 Norman
53G3 Normandia
18D2 Normandy *reg.*
41I3 Normanton
10L5 Norra Kvarken *strait*
48D2 Norristown
11J7 Norrköping
11K7 Norrtälje
53G6 Nortelândia
14F4 Northallerton
15G6 Northampton
48E1 Northampton
47O4 North Atlantic Ocean
45K5 North Bay
48A2 North Canton
10N1 North Cape
43D2 North Cape
47L4 North Carolina *state*
47K2 North Channel *lake channel*
17G2 North Channel
46G2 North Dakota *state*
15G7 North Downs *hills*
36D5 Northern Cape *prov.*
17F3 Northern Ireland *prov.*
29G6 Northern Mariana Islands *terr.*
40G3 Northern Territory *admin. div.*
13L3 North Frisian Islands
48E2 North Haven
43D4 North Island
48A2 North Kingsville
31B5 North Korea
49E2 North Las Vegas
46G3 North Platte
46G3 North Platte *r.*
16G1 North Ronaldsay Firth *sea chan.*
44H4 North Saskatchewan *r.*
12H2 North Sea
14F3 North Shields
43E4 North Taranaki Bight *b.*
48B1 North Tonawanda
14E4 North Tyne *r.*
16B3 North Uist *i.*
36G4 North West *prov.*
44H3 Northwest Territories *admin. div.*
14E5 Northwich
14G4 North York Moors
44B3 Norton Sound *sea chan.*
47K3 Norwalk
48E2 Norwalk
10E6 Norway
10E3 Norwegian Sea
15I6 Norwich
48D1 Norwich
48E2 Norwich
31F4 Noshiro
35C6 Nosop *watercourse*
36D2 Nossob *watercourse*
11F7 Notodden
45L5 Notre Dame, Monts *mts*
45M5 Notre Dame Bay
15F6 Nottingham
32B2 Nouâdhibou
32B3 Nouakchott
39G4 Nouméa
32C3 Nouna
39G4 Nouvelle Calédonie *i.*
55C3 Nova Friburgo
55C3 Nova Iguaçu
21O1 Nova Kakhovka
55C2 Nova Lima
23F7 Nova Odesa
53J5 Nova Pilão Arcado
55B2 Nova Ponte
20C2 Novara
45L5 Nova Scotia *prov.*
53J5 Nova Sento Sé
49A1 Novato
55A4 Nova Trento
55C2 Nova Venécia
53H6 Nova Xavantino
25P2 Novaya Sibir', Ostrov *i.*
24G2 Novaya Zemlya *is*
21L3 Nova Zagora
19F4 Novelda
13Q7 Nové Zámky
23G6 Novhorod-Sivers'kyy
20C2 Novi Ligure
21I3 Novi Pazar
21L3 Novi Pazar
21H2 Novi Sad
23I6 Novoanninskiy
52F5 Novo Aripuanã
23H7 Novoazovs'k
22J4 Novocheboksarsk
23I7 Novocherkassk
55C2 Novo Cruzeiro
22I2 Novodvinsk
55A5 Novo Hamburgo
23E6 Novohrad-Volyns'kyy
23I6 Novokhopersk
30C2 Novokiyevskiy Uval
23I7 Novokubansk
23K5 Novokuybyshevsk
24J4 Novokuznetsk
20F2 Novo Mesto
23G6 Novomoskovs'k
23H5 Novomoskovsk
23I6 Novonikolayevskiy
23I7 Novopokrovskaya
23H6 Novopskov
23H7 Novorossiysk
22F4 Novorzhev
23H7 Novoshakhtinsk
24J4 Novosibirsk
22F4 Novosokol'niki
23J5 Novospasskoye
23G7 Novotroyits'ke
23F6 Novoukrayinka
23K6 Novouzensk
23E6 Novovolyns'k
23H6 Novovoronezh
23F5 Novozybkov
13P6 Nový Jičín
23H6 Novyy Oskol
24I3 Novyy Urengoy
22L5 Novyy Zay
42E5 Nowra
13R6 Nowy Sącz
13R6 Nowy Targ
24I3 Noyabr'sk
35D5 Nsanje
32D4 Nsukka
34D4 Ntungamo
33G3 Nuba Mountains
33G2 Nubian Desert
51H4 Nueva Gerona
54B5 Nueva Imperial
52C3 Nueva Loja
46G6 Nueva Rosita
50G6 Nueva San Salvador
51I4 Nuevitas
46F5 Nuevo Casas Grandes
46H6 Nuevo Laredo
39I4 Nuku'alofa
26E2 Nukus
40F6 Nullarbor Plain
34B3 Numan
31E6 Numazu
42B6 Numurkah
45J2 Nunavut *admin. div.*
15F6 Nuneaton
44B4 Nunivak Island
19C3 Nuñomoral
20C4 Nuoro
34E1 Nuqrah
13M6 Nuremberg
23K5 Nurlat
10P5 Nurmes
10M5 Nurmo
45M3 Nuuk
36E7 Nuweveldberge *mts*
24H3 Nyagan'
33F3 Nyala
35D5 Nyamtumbo
22I3 Nyandoma
35D4 Nyasa, Lake
11O10 Nyasvizh
11G9 Nyborg
11I8 Nybro
34D4 Nyeri
23D7 Nyíregyháza
11G9 Nykøbing
11G9 Nykøbing Sjælland
11J7 Nyköping
11J7 Nynäshamn
42C3 Nyngan
18H3 Nyon
13P5 Nysa
35C4 Nyunzu
25M3 Nyurba
35D4 Nzega
32C4 Nzérékoré

O

46□ Oahu *i.*
42E1 Oakey
15G6 Oakham
49A2 Oakland
46C3 Oakridge
48B1 Oakville
43C7 Oamaru
50E5 Oaxaca
24H3 Ob' *r.*
31D6 Obama
16D4 Oban
42D4 Oberon
13N6 Oberpfälzer Wald *mts*
53G4 Óbidos
30F4 Obihiro
23J7 Obil'noye
30C2 Obluch'ye
23H5 Obninsk
34C3 Obo
34E2 Obock
23H6 Oboyan'
21I2 Obrenovac
24I3 Obskaya Guba *sea chan.*
32C4 Obuasi
22K3 Ob''yachevo
47K6 Ocala
19E4 Ocaña
52D2 Ocaña
52C3 Occidental, Cordillera *mts*
52D7 Occidental, Cordillera *mts*
48D3 Ocean City
49D4 Oceanside
21N1 Ochakiv
23I8 Och'amch'ire
16F4 Ochil Hills
15H9 Octeville-sur-Mer
10□1 Ódáðahraun *lava field*
31F4 Ōdate
31E6 Odawara
11E6 Odda
21L5 Ödemiș
11G9 Odense
13O3 Oderbucht *b.*
21N1 Odesa
46G5 Odessa
32C4 Odienné
22H5 Odintsovo
13Q6 Odra *r.*
53J5 Oeiras
23I8 Of
32D4 Offa
13L5 Offenbach am Main
13K6 Offenburg
31E5 Oga
31E6 Ōgaki
46G3 Ogallala
32D4 Ogbomosho
46E3 Ogden
11N8 Ogre
48A3 Ohio *r.*
48A2 Ohio *state*
21I4 Ohrid
21I4 Ohrid, Lake
48B2 Oil City
31C6 Ōita
46G6 Ojinaga
31E5 Ojiya
54C3 Ojos del Salado, Nevado *mt.*
23I4 Oka *r.*
35C5 Okavango Delta *swamp*
31E5 Okaya
31D6 Okayama
31E6 Okazaki
47K6 Okeechobee, Lake
15C8 Okehampton
30F1 Okha
25P4 Okhotsk
30G3 Okhotsk, Sea of
23G6 Okhtyrka
31B8 Okinawa-shotō *is*
46H4 Oklahoma *state*
47H4 Oklahoma City
47H4 Okmulgee
22G5 Okovskiy Les *for.*
22I3 Oktyabr'skiy
23I7 Oktyabr'skiy
24G4 Oktyabr'skiy
25Q4 Oktyabr'skiy
25K2 Oktyabr'skoy Revolyutsii, Ostrov *i.*
22G4 Okulovka
32D4 Okuta
11J8 Öland *i.*
54D5 Olavarría
13P5 Oława
20C4 Olbia
13L4 Oldenburg
14E5 Oldham
17D6 Old Head of Kinsale
48B1 Olean
13S3 Olecko
25N3 Olekminsk
23G6 Oleksandriya
10R2 Olenegorsk
22G4 Olenino
23E6 Olevs'k
19C5 Olhão
36D6 Olifants *r.*
36E7 Olifants *r.*
37J3 Olifants *r.*
53L5 Olinda
19F4 Oliva
54C3 Oliva, Cordillera de *mts*
55C1 Oliveira dos Brejinhos
52C5 Olmos
15G6 Olney
48C3 Olney
11I8 Olofström
13P6 Olomouc
22G3 Olonets
18D5 Oloron-Ste-Marie
19H2 Olot
25M4 Olovyannaya
13R4 Olsztyn
18H3 Olten
21L2 Oltenița
46C2 Olympia
21J4 Olympus, Mount
17E3 Omagh
47H3 Omaha
36D2 Omaheke *admin. reg.*
26E5 Oman
26E4 Oman, Gulf of
33G3 Omdurman
33G3 Om Hajēr
31E6 Ōmiya
24I4 Omsk
25Q3 Omsukchan
31C6 Ōmura
22L4 Omutninsk
54D4 Oncativo
35B5 Ondjiva
32D4 Ondo
27K2 Öndörhaan
22H3 Onega
22H3 Onega *r.*
22G3 Onega, Lake
24E3 Onega, Lake
48D1 Oneida
48D1 Oneonta
21L1 Onești
22G2 Onezhskaya Guba *g.*
31B5 Ongjin
27H5 Ongole
32D4 Onitsha
31D6 Onomichi
49D3 Ontario
48A1 Ontario *prov.*
48C1 Ontario, Lake
53G2 Onverwacht
22K4 Oparino
13P6 Opava
47J5 Opelika
47I5 Opelousas
11P8 Opochka
13P5 Opole
19B3 Oporto
35B5 Opuwo
21I1 Oradea
19F6 Oran
54D2 Orán
30C4 Ŏrang
18G4 Orange
42D4 Orange
47I5 Orange
49D4 Orange
36C5 Orange *r.*
47K5 Orangeburg
50G5 Orange Walk
36C5 Oranjemund
51J6 Oranjestad
21J2 Orăștie
42D6 Orbost
23H8 Ordu
32D4 Ore
11I7 Örebro
46C3 Oregon *state*
46C2 Oregon City
22H5 Orekhovo-Zuyevo
23H5 Orel
24G4 Orenburg
11H9 Öresund *strait*
15I6 Orford Ness *hd*
21M5 Orhaneli
21M4 Orhangazi
22K4 Orichi
52D2 Oriental, Cordillera *mts*
52E6 Oriental, Cordillera *mts*
19F4 Orihuela
23G7 Orikhiv
11N6 Orimattila
52F2 Orinoco *r.*
20C5 Oristano
11N6 Orivesi
53G4 Oriximiná
50E5 Orizaba
55A2 Orizona
37H4 Orkney
16F1 Orkney *is*
55B3 Orlândia
47K6 Orlando
55A5 Orleaes
18E3 Orléans
22K4 Orlov
23I7 Orlovskiy
14E5 Ormskirk
10K5 Örnsköldsvik
32C3 Orodara
29E7 Oroquieta
21I1 Orosháza
46C4 Oroville
30A2 Orqohan
23F5 Orsha
22J4 Orshanka
24G4 Orsk
10E5 Ørsta
18D5 Orthez
20F3 Ortona
52E7 Oruro
20E3 Orvieto
31D6 Ōsaka
11H8 Osby
27G2 Osh
35B5 Oshakati
45K5 Oshawa
47J3 Oshkosh
32D4 Oshogbo
20H2 Osijek
20E3 Osimo
37J4 Osizweni
11J8 Oskarshamn
11G7 Oslo
11G7 Oslofjorden *sea chan.*
23G8 Osmancık
21M4 Osmaneli
13L4 Osnabrück
19D2 Osorno
54B6 Osorno
46D2 Osoyoos
11D6 Osøyri
13J5 Oss
48E2 Ossining
22G4 Ostashkov
12I5 Ostend
10I5 Östersund
13Q6 Ostrava
13Q4 Ostróda
23H6 Ostrogozhsk
11P8 Ostrov
22I4 Ostrovskoye
23D6 Ostrowiec Świętokrzyski
13R4 Ostrów Mazowiecka
13P5 Ostrów Wielkopolski
48C1 Oswego
15D6 Oswestry
43C7 Otago Peninsula
43E5 Otaki
30F4 Otaru
31F5 Ōtawara
11O7 Otepää
35B6 Otjiwarongo
36C1 Otjozondjupa *admin. reg.*
14F5 Otley
23K5 Otradnyy
20H4 Otranto, Strait of
31D6 Ōtsu
45K5 Ottawa
47H4 Ottawa
47J3 Ottawa
47I3 Ottumwa
42A7 Otway, Cape
47I5 Ouachita Mountains
33F3 Ouaddaï *reg.*
32C3 Ouagadougou
32C3 Ouahigouya
32D3 Ouargaye
32D1 Ouargla
32C1 Ouarzazate
36F7 Oudtshoorn
32C1 Oued Zem
20B6 Oued Zénati
34B3 Ouesso
19D6 Ouezzane
19F6 Oujda
10N4 Oulainen
19I6 Ouled Djellal
19G5 Ouled Farès
10N4 Oulu
10O4 Oulujärvi *l.*
10N4 Oulunsalo
20B7 Oum el Bouaghi
15G6 Oundle
19C2 Ourense
53J5 Ouricurí
55A3 Ourinhos
55C3 Ouro Preto
14G5 Ouse *r.*
15H8 Ouse *r.*
16B3 Outer Hebrides *is*
49C4 Outer Santa Barbara Channel
46F1 Outlook
10P5 Outokumpu
41I7 Ouyen
54B4 Ovalle
19B3 Ovar
19D2 Oviedo
23F6 Ovruch
34B4 Owando
31E6 Owase
47I3 Owatonna
48C1 Owego
47J4 Owensboro
49D2 Owens Lake
45J5 Owen Sound
38E2 Owen Stanley Range *mts*
32D4 Owerri
32D4 Owo
10□1 Öxarfjörður *b.*
11J7 Oxelösund
15F7 Oxford
47J5 Oxford
49C3 Oxnard
31E5 Oyama
34B3 Oyem
32D4 Oyo
18G3 Oyonnax
47J5 Ozark
47I4 Ozark Plateau
47I4 Ozarks, Lake of the
25Q4 Ozernovskiy
11M9 Ozersk
30F3 Ozerskiy
23H5 Ozery
23K6 Ozinki

P

45N3 Paamiut
36D7 Paarl
13Q5 Pabianice
27H4 Pabna
52C5 Pacasmayo
20F6 Pachino
50E4 Pachuca
49B2 Pacific Grove
29C8 Padang
22G3 Padany
13L5 Paderborn
15C8 Padstow
20D2 Padua
47J4 Paducah
20F2 Pag
20F2 Pag *i.*
29E7 Pagadian
11N7 Paide
15D8 Paignton
11N6 Päijänne *l.*
11M6 Paimio
48A2 Painesville
16E5 Paisley
52B5 Paita
52F3 Pakaraima Mountains
52G3 Pakaraima Mountains
25R3 Pakhachi
26F3 Pakistan
11M9 Pakruojis
20H1 Paks
29C6 Pakxé
33E4 Pala
18F2 Palaiseau
25Q4 Palana
27G4 Palanpur
37H2 Palapye
25Q3 Palatka
29F7 Palau
29D7 Palawan *i.*
22I4 Palekh
29C8 Palembang
54B6 Palena
19D2 Palencia
20E5 Palermo
47H5 Palestine
27G5 Palghat
55A4 Palhoca
27G4 Pali
7 Palikir
27G6 Palk Strait
23J6 Pallasovka
43E5 Palliser, Cape
19H4 Palma de Mallorca
53K5 Palmares
55A5 Palmares do Sul
55A4 Palmas
32C4 Palmas, Cape
49C3 Palmdale
55A4 Palmeira
54F3 Palmeira das Missões
53K5 Palmeira dos Índios
53J5 Palmeirais
39J3 Palmerston *atoll*
43E5 Palmerston North
20F5 Palmi
52C3 Palmira
49D4 Palm Springs
49A2 Palo Alto
29E8 Palopo
29D8 Palu
18E5 Pamiers
27G3 Pamir *mts*
47L4 Pamlico Sound *sea chan.*
54D5 Pampas *reg.*
19F2 Pamplona
52D2 Pamplona
21N4 Pamukova
21K3 Panagyurishte
27G5 Panaji
51H7 Panama
51I7 Panama, Gulf of
51I7 Panama Canal
47J5 Panama City
51I7 Panama City
29E6 Panay *i.*
21I2 Pančevo
11N9 Panevėžys
29D8 Pangkalanbuun
29C8 Pangkalpinang
45L3 Pangnirtung
10Q5 Pankakoski
55A3 Panorama
30B4 Panshi
50E4 Pánuco
27J4 Panzhihua
34B3 Paoua
20G1 Pápa
43E3 Papakura
50E4 Papantla
16□ Papa Stour *i.*
13K4 Papenburg
33G1 Paphos
38E2 Papua, Gulf of
41J1 Papua New Guinea
15C8 Par
55B2 Pará *r.*
53I4 Pará, Rio do *r.*
40D4 Paraburdoo
55B2 Paracatu
29D6 Paracel Islands
21I3 Paraćin
53K4 Paracuru
55B2 Pará de Minas
46C4 Paradise
53I4 Paragominas
47I4 Paragould
55A3 Paraguaçu Paulista
54E2 Paraguay
54E3 Paraguay *r.*
53I6 Paraíso do Norte
55B3 Paraisópolis
32D4 Parakou
53G2 Paramaribo
55C1 Paramirim
48D2 Paramus
54D4 Paraná
55B1 Paranã
53H8 Paraná *r.*
55A1 Paraná *r.*
55A4 Paraná *state*
55A4 Paranaguá
55A2 Paranaíba
55A4 Paranapiacaba, Serra *mts*
54F2 Paranavaí
55B2 Paraopeba
55C1 Paratinga
55A2 Paraúna
27G5 Parbhani
13M4 Parchim
13O5 Pardubice
52F6 Parecis, Serra dos *hills*
29D8 Parepare
11M6 Pargas
51L6 Paria, Gulf of
53G4 Parintins
18F2 Paris
47H5 Paris
11M5 Parkano
48A3 Parkersburg
42D4 Parkes
20D2 Parma
48A2 Parma
53J4 Parnaíba
11N7 Pärnu
42A3 Paroo *watercourse*
21K6 Paros
21K6 Paros *i.*
54B5 Parral
42E4 Parramatta
46G6 Parras
45G2 Parry Channel
45G2 Parry Islands
47H4 Parsons
18D3 Parthenay
30D4 Partizansk
49C3 Pasadena
47J5 Pascagoula
21L1 Pașcani
23H7 Pashkovskiy
54E4 Paso de los Toros
49B3 Paso Robles
48D2 Passaic
55B3 Passa Tempo
13N6 Passau
54F3 Passo Fundo
55B3 Passos
11O9 Pastavy
52C3 Pasto
53J5 Pastos Bons
11N8 Pasvalys
54B8 Patagonia *reg.*
48D2 Paterson
27H4 Patna
54F3 Pato Branco
53K5 Patos
54F4 Patos, Lagoa dos *l.*
55B2 Patos de Minas
21I5 Patras
55B2 Patrocínio
48B2 Patton
53K5 Patu
18D5 Pau
52E5 Pauini
53K5 Paulo Afonso
55C2 Pavão
20C2 Pavia
21K3 Pavlikeni
27G1 Pavlodar
23G6 Pavlohrad
23J5 Pavlovka
22I5 Pavlovo
23I6 Pavlovsk
23H7 Pavlovskaya
48F2 Pawtucket
29C8 Payakumbuh
46D3 Payette
54E4 Paysandú
23I8 Pazar
21K3 Pazardzhik
20E2 Pazin
48F1 Peabody
44G4 Peace *r.*
46H6 Pearsall
45I2 Peary Channel
21I3 Peć
55C2 Peçanha
10Q2 Pechenga
22M2 Pechora
22L1 Pechora *r.*
22L1 Pechorskaya Guba *b.*
11O8 Pechory
46G5 Pecos
46G6 Pecos *r.*
20H1 Pécs
51J5 Pedernales
55C1 Pedra Azul
55B3 Pedregulho
53J4 Pedreiras
54E2 Pedro Juan Caballero
16F5 Peebles
48E2 Peekskill
43D6 Pegasus Bay
27I5 Pegu
54D5 Pehuajó
11O7 Peipus, Lake
53I6 Peixe
53H6 Peixoto de Azevedo
32D3 Pekinga
21J6 Peloponnese *admin. reg.*
54F4 Pelotas
35E5 Pemba
15C7 Pembroke
45K5 Pembroke
55A3 Penápolis
15D7 Penarth
54A7 Penas, Golfo de *g.*
46D2 Pendleton
55A4 Penha
19B4 Peniche
16F5 Penicuik
29C7 Peninsular Malaysia
48B2 Penn Hills
18H4 Pennine, Alpi *mts*
14E4 Pennines *hills*
48D2 Pennsburg
48D3 Pennsville
48B2 Pennsylvania *state*
48C1 Penn Yan
51H7 Penonomé
14E4 Penrith
42E4 Penrith
47J5 Pensacola
44G5 Penticton
16F2 Pentland Firth *sea chan.*
16F5 Pentland Hills
23J5 Penza
15B8 Penzance
47J3 Peoria
55B2 Perdizes
52C3 Pereira
55A3 Pereira Barreto
23E6 Peremyshlyany
22H4 Pereslavl'-Zalesskiy
30D3 Pereyaslavka
23F6 Pereyaslav-Khmel'nyts'kyy
54D4 Pergamino
54C2 Perico
18E4 Périgueux
24G4 Perm'
21J3 Pernik
18F5 Perpignan
15B8 Perranporth
49D4 Perris
47K5 Perry
46G4 Perryton
47J4 Perryville
16F4 Perth
40D6 Perth
48D2 Perth Amboy
52D6 Peru
20E3 Perugia
23F6 Pervomays'k
23I5 Pervomaysk
23I5 Pervomayskiy
23H6 Pervomays'kyy
20E3 Pesaro
20F3 Pescara
23I7 Peschanokopskoye
27G3 Peshawar
21I4 Peshkopi
21K3 Peshtera
20F1 Pesnica
18D4 Pessac
22G4 Pestovo
23K5 Pestravka
49A1 Petaluma
50D5 Petatlán
15G6 Peterborough
41H6 Peterborough
45K5 Peterborough
48F1 Peterborough
16H3 Peterhead
14F4 Peterlee
48C4 Petersburg
15G7 Petersfield
44C3 Petersville
50G4 Peto
47K2 Petoskey
21J4 Petrich
53J5 Petrolina
55A2 Petrolina de Goiás
27F1 Petropavlovsk
25Q4 Petropavlovsk-Kamchatskiy
55C3 Petrópolis
21J2 Petroșani
23J5 Petrovsk
25L4 Petrovsk-Zabaykal'skiy
22G3 Petrozavodsk
24H4 Petukhovo
22H5 Petushki
25S3 Pevek
13P6 Pezinok
13L6 Pforzheim
37H5 Phahameng
37J2 Phalaborwa
29B7 Phangnga
29C6 Phan Rang
29C6 Phan Thiêt
29C7 Phatthalung
47J5 Phenix City
29B6 Phet Buri
48D3 Philadelphia
29E6 Philippines
29E6 Philippine Sea
37H4 Phiritona
29C6 Phitsanulok
29C6 Phnom Penh
46E5 Phoenix
39I2 Phoenix Islands
28C5 Phôngsali
29C6 Phrae
29B7 Phuket
20C2 Piacenza
21L1 Piatra Neamț
15J9 Picardie *admin. reg.*
18E2 Picardy *reg.*
15F9 Picauville
47J5 Picayune
54D2 Pichanal
54B4 Pichilemu
14G4 Pickering
53J5 Picos
54C7 Pico Truncado
42E5 Picton
55B3 Piedade

46G6 Piedras Negras
10O5 Pieksämäki
10P5 Pielinen *l.*
46G3 Pierre
37J5 Pietermaritzburg
37I2 Pietersburg
37J3 Pigg's Peak
10P6 Pihlajavesi *l.*
22G4 Pikalevo
47K4 Pikeville
13P4 Piła
54E3 Pilar
54E4 Pilar
22J5 Pil'na
52F6 Pimenta Bueno
54E5 Pinamar
51H4 Pinar del Río
21L4 Pinarhisar
52C4 Piñas
13R5 Pińczów
55C1 Pindaí
55B3 Pindamonhangaba
21I5 Pindus Mountains
47I5 Pine Bluff
22I2 Pinega
20B2 Pinerolo
37J5 Pinetown
27K3 Pingdingshan
27J4 Pingxiang
27K4 Pingxiang
55B3 Pinhal
53I4 Pinheiro
40D6 Pinjarra
11O10 Pinsk
13R5 Pionki
13Q5 Piotrków Trybunalski
55A2 Piracanjuba
55B3 Piracicaba
55B3 Piraçununga
53J4 Piracuruca
21J6 Piraeus
55A4 Piraí do Sul
55A3 Piraju
55A3 Pirajuí
53H7 Piranhas
51K5 Piranhas *r.*
55B2 Pirapora
55A1 Pirenópolis
55A2 Pires do Rio
53J4 Piripiri
20D3 Pisa
52C6 Pisco
13O6 Písek
54C3 Pissis, Cerro
50G4 Pisté
20D3 Pistoia
32B3 Pita
55A4 Pitanga
55B2 Pitangui
6 Pitcairn Islands *terr.*
10L4 Piteå
23J6 Piterka
21K2 Pitești
22F3 Pitkyaranta
16F4 Pitlochry
48B2 Pittsburgh
48E1 Pittsfield
42E1 Pittsworth
55B3 Piumhí
52B5 Piura
20F2 Pivka
49C3 Pixley
49B1 Placerville
52E6 Plácido de Castro
48F2 Plainfield
46G5 Plainview
55B1 Planaltina
55A3 Planura
47I5 Plaquemine
19C3 Plasencia
52D2 Plato
46H3 Platte *r.*
47M3 Plattsburgh
13N5 Plauen
23H5 Plavsk
52B4 Playas
48D3 Pleasantville
43I1 Plenty, Bay of *g.*
22I3 Plesetsk
21K3 Pleven
21H3 Pljevlja
13Q4 Płock
21L2 Ploiești
21K3 Plovdiv
11L9 Plungė
15C8 Plymouth
47J3 Plymouth
48F2 Plymouth
51L5 Plymouth
15D6 Plynlimon *hill*
13N6 Plzeň
32C3 Pô
20E2 Po *r.*
46E3 Pocatello
23E6 Pochayiv
23G5 Pochep
23J5 Pochinki
23G5 Pochinok
55C1 Poções
53G7 Poconé
55B3 Poços de Caldas
23H6 Podgorenskiy
21H3 Podgorica
24J4 Podgornoye
23H5 Podol'sk
22G3 Podporozh'ye
36D5 Pofadder
23G5 Pogar
20D3 Poggibonsi
21I4 Pogradec
31C5 P'ohang
51L5 Pointe-à-Pitre
35B4 Pointe-Noire
48D2 Point Pleasant
18E3 Poitiers
27G4 Pokaran
30C4 Pokrovka
25N3 Pokrovsk
23H7 Pokrovskoye
19D2 Pola de Siero
13Q4 Poland
11P9 Polatsk
27F3 Pol-e Khomrī
11L9 Polessk
13O4 Police
23F6 Polis'ke
13P5 Polkowice
23H7 Polohy
23E6 Polonne
23G6 Poltava
11O7 Põlva
10R2 Polyarnyy
25S3 Polyarnyy
10R3 Polyarnyye Zori
21J4 Polygyros
53K5 Pombal
20E4 Pomezia
49D3 Pomona
21L3 Pomorie
13O3 Pomorska, Zatoka *b.*
20F4 Pompei
55A3 Pompéia
22J4 Ponazyrevo
47H4 Ponca City
51K5 Ponce
27G5 Pondicherry
19C2 Ponferrada
55A4 Ponta Grossa
55A3 Pontal
55A2 Pontalina
54E2 Ponta Porã
14F5 Pontefract
55C3 Ponte Nova
53G7 Pontes-e-Lacerda
19B2 Pontevedra
47J3 Pontiac
47K3 Pontiac
29C8 Pontianak
18E2 Pontoise
15D7 Pontypool
15D7 Pontypridd
15F8 Poole
52E7 Poopó, Lago de *l.*
52C3 Popayán
47I4 Poplar Bluff
50E5 Popocatépetl, Volcán *vol.*
35B4 Popokabaka
21L3 Popovo
13R6 Poprad
48C4 Poquoson
55A1 Porangatu
27F4 Porbandar
20E2 Poreč
55A3 Porecatu
23J5 Poretskoye
11L6 Pori
43E5 Porirua
11P8 Porkhov
52F1 Porlamar
21J6 Poros
22G3 Porosozero
10N1 Porsangen *sea chan.*
11F7 Porsgrunn
17F3 Portadown
17G3 Portaferry
47J3 Portage
48B2 Portage
45I5 Portage la Prairie
46C2 Port Alberni
19C4 Portalegre
46G5 Portales
46C2 Port Angeles
51I5 Port Antonio
17E4 Portarlington
47I6 Port Arthur
41H6 Port Augusta
51J5 Port-au-Prince
27I5 Port Blair
19H2 Portbou
43C7 Port Chalmers
47K6 Port Charlotte
51J5 Port-de-Paix
41J3 Port Douglas
55C1 Porteirinha
53H4 Portel
37G7 Port Elizabeth
49C2 Porterville
34A4 Port-Gentil
16E5 Port Glasgow
32D4 Port Harcourt
15D7 Porthcawl
40D4 Port Hedland
15B8 Porthleven
15C6 Porthmadog
49C3 Port Hueneme
47K3 Port Huron
19B5 Portimão
41I7 Portland
42D4 Portland
46C2 Portland
47M3 Portland
18F5 Port-la-Nouvelle
17E4 Portlaoise
47H6 Port Lavaca
41H6 Port Lincoln
32B4 Port Loko
7 Port Louis
42F3 Port Macquarie
41J1 Port Moresby
36C5 Port Nolloth
55A5 Porto Alegre
35B5 Porto Amboim
55A4 Porto Belo
53H4 Porto de Moz
53G7 Porto Esperidião
53I5 Porto Franco
51L6 Port of Spain
20E2 Portogruaro
20D2 Portomaggiore
53I6 Porto Nacional
32D4 Porto-Novo
32□ Porto Novo
55D2 Porto Seguro
20C4 Porto Torres
55A4 Porto União
18I6 Porto-Vecchio
52F5 Porto Velho
52B4 Portoviejo
42B7 Port Phillip Bay
41H6 Port Pirie
16C3 Portree
17F2 Portrush
33G1 Port Said
37J6 Port Shepstone
15F8 Portsmouth
47K4 Portsmouth
48C4 Portsmouth
48F1 Portsmouth
47J6 Port St Joe
33G3 Port Sudan
15D7 Port Talbot
19C4 Portugal
39G3 Port Vila
54B8 Porvenir
11N6 Porvoo
54E3 Posadas
22H4 Poshekhon'ye
29E8 Poso
36F5 Postmasburg
55C2 Poté
20F4 Potenza
37I3 Potgietersrus
23I8 P'ot'i
55D1 Potiragua
32E3 Potiskum
48C3 Potomac *r.*
52E7 Potosí
13N4 Potsdam
15G7 Potters Bar
48D2 Pottstown
48C2 Pottsville
48E2 Poughkeepsie
14E5 Poulton-le-Fylde
55B3 Pouso Alegre
29C6 Poŭthĭsăt
13Q6 Považská Bystrica
22G3 Povenets
19B3 Póvoa de Varzim
23I6 Povorino
49D4 Poway
46E4 Powell, Lake *resr*
44F5 Powell River
53H7 Poxoréu
30C2 Poyarkovo
21I2 Požarevac
50E4 Poza Rica
20G2 Požega
21I3 Požega
13P4 Poznań
54E2 Pozo Colorado
20F4 Pozzuoli
13O6 Prachatice
29B6 Prachuap Khiri Khan
55D2 Prado
13O5 Prague
32□ Praia
53H4 Prainha
47I3 Prairie du Chien
55A2 Prata
55A2 Prata *r.*
20D3 Prato
46H4 Pratt
22I4 Prechistoye
11O8 Preiļi
13N4 Prenzlau
13P6 Přerov
46E5 Prescott
21I3 Preševo
54D3 Presidencia Roque Sáenz Peña
53J5 Presidente Dutra
55B2 Presidente Olegário
55A3 Presidente Prudente
55A3 Presidente Venceslau
23D6 Prešov
21I4 Prespa, Lake
47N2 Presque Isle
14E5 Preston
16E5 Prestwick
37I3 Pretoria
21I5 Preveza
44A4 Pribilof Islands
21H3 Priboj
46E4 Price
11L8 Priekule
11N8 Priekuļi
11M9 Prienai
13Q6 Prievidza
20G2 Prijedor
21H3 Prijepolje
21I4 Prilep
30D3 Primorskiy Kray *admin. div.*
23H7 Primorsko-Akhtarsk
44H4 Prince Albert
45K3 Prince Charles Island
45L5 Prince Edward Island *prov.*
44F4 Prince George
45I2 Prince of Wales Island
44E4 Prince Rupert
41I2 Princess Charlotte Bay
46C2 Princeton
48A4 Princeton
48D2 Princeton
44D3 Prince William Sound *b.*
11Q6 Priozersk
23F6 Pripet *r.*
23E6 Pripet Marshes
21I3 Priština
18G4 Privas
20F2 Privlaka
22I4 Privolzhsk
23J6 Privolzhskiy
23K5 Privolzh'ye
23I7 Priyutnoye
21I3 Prizren
53G3 Professor van Blommestein Meer *resr*
30C2 Progress
23J8 Prokhladnyy
24J4 Prokop'yevsk
21I3 Prokuplje
23I7 Proletarsk
55A3 Promissão
53K6 Propriá
21L3 Provadiya
18G5 Provence *reg.*
48F2 Providence
25T3 Provideniya
46E3 Provo
55A4 Prudentópolis
13R4 Pruszków
23F7 Prut *r.*
23G6 Pryluky
23H7 Prymors'k
23D6 Przemyśl
11P8 Pskov
11O7 Pskov, Lake
11P8 Pskovskaya Oblast' *admin. div.*
21I4 Ptolemaïda
20F1 Ptuj
52D5 Pucallpa
22I4 Puchezh
31B5 Puch'ŏn
22H3 Pudozh
14F5 Pudsey
50E5 Puebla
46G4 Pueblo
19D5 Puente-Genil
50E5 Puerto Ángel
51H7 Puerto Armuelles
52E2 Puerto Ayacucho
52□ Puerto Baquerizo Moreno
50G5 Puerto Barrios
52E1 Puerto Cabello
51H6 Puerto Cabezas
52E2 Puerto Carreño
52C4 Puerto Francisco de Orellana
52E3 Puerto Inírida
51H5 Puerto Lempira
51H6 Puerto Limón
19D4 Puertollano
54C6 Puerto Madryn
52E6 Puerto Maldonado
54B6 Puerto Montt
54B8 Puerto Natales
46E5 Puerto Peñasco
51J5 Puerto Plata
29D7 Puerto Princesa
54E3 Puerto Rico
51K5 Puerto Rico *terr.*
54C8 Puerto Santa Cruz
52C6 Puerto Supe
50C4 Puerto Vallarta
23K5 Pugachev
43C7 Pukaki, Lake
31C4 Pukch'ŏng
20E2 Pula
48A4 Pulaski
46D2 Pullman
27G5 Pune
30C4 P'ungsan
52D7 Puno
54D5 Punta Alta
54B8 Punta Arenas
54E5 Punta del Este
50G5 Punta Gorda
51H6 Puntarenas
27H5 Puri
52F4 Purus *r.*
30C4 Puryŏng
31C6 Pusan
23H5 Pushchino
11Q7 Pushkin
22J3 Pushkinskiye Gory
22F4 Pustoshka
28D5 Putian
29C7 Putrajaya
52D4 Putumayo *r.*
15C6 Pwllheli
10Q4 Pyaozerskiy
23I7 Pyatigorsk
23G6 P"yatykhatky
27I5 Pyè
23F5 Pyetrykaw
27I5 Pyinmana
15D7 Pyle
21I6 Pylos
30B4 Pyŏktong
31B5 P'yŏnggang
31B5 P'yŏngsong
31B5 P'yŏngt'aek
31B5 P'yŏngyang
19H2 Pyrenees *mts*
21I6 Pyrgos
23G6 Pyryatyn
13O4 Pyrzyce
11O8 Pytalovo

Q

37I6 Qacha's Nek
27I3 Qaidam Pendi *basin*
45N3 Qaqortoq
34F1 Qatar
33F2 Qattara Depression
23J8 Qax
23J8 Qazax
33H1 Qazvīn
45M3 Qeqertarsuup Tunua *b.*
33H1 Qeydār
30B3 Qian'an
27I3 Qilian Shan *mts*
33G2 Qinā
30B3 Qing'an
28E4 Qingdao
30B3 Qinggang
30B4 Qingyuan
27K3 Qinhuangdao
27J3 Qin Ling *mts*
27J4 Qinzhou
27K5 Qionghai
30A3 Qiqihar
30C3 Qitaihe
26E3 Qom
33H1 Qorveh
29C6 Quang Ngai
15D7 Quantock Hills
44H4 Qu'Appelle *r.*
20C5 Quartu Sant'Elena
42D5 Queanbeyan
45K5 Québec
45K4 Québec *prov.*
44E4 Queen Charlotte Islands
44F4 Queen Charlotte Sound *sea chan.*
45H2 Queen Elizabeth Islands
56C6 Queen Maud Land *reg.*
42B7 Queenscliff
42B1 Queensland *state*
41J8 Queenstown
43B7 Queenstown
35D5 Quelimane
50D4 Querétaro
26F3 Quetta
50F6 Quetzaltenango
29E6 Quezon City
35B5 Quibala
52C2 Quibdó
52D6 Quillabamba
52E7 Quillacollo
54E4 Quilmes
27G6 Quilon
54B4 Quilpué
35B4 Quimbele
18B3 Quimper
18C3 Quimperlé
47I4 Quincy
48F1 Quincy
29C6 Qui Nhon
19F3 Quinto
42E3 Quirindi
55A2 Quirinópolis
54D3 Quitilipi
52C4 Quito
53K4 Quixadá
53K5 Quixeramobim
27J4 Qujing
41H6 Quorn
27F3 Qŭrghonteppa
28D5 Quzhou

R

10N4 Raahe
16C3 Raasay *i.*
16C3 Raasay, Sound of *sea chan.*
29D8 Raba
32C1 Rabat
38F2 Rabaul
22G2 Rabocheostrovsk
29C7 Rach Gia
13Q5 Racibórz
47J3 Racine
23E7 Rădăuți
47J4 Radcliff
48A4 Radford
21K3 Radnevo
13R5 Radom
21J3 Radomir
13Q5 Radomsko
11N9 Radun'
11M9 Radviliškis
23E6 Radyvyliv
54D4 Rafaela
26E3 Rafsanjān
20F6 Ragusa
29E8 Raha
23F5 Rahachow
27G4 Rahimyar Khan
27G5 Raichur
27H4 Raigarh
46C2 Rainier, Mount *vol.*
27H4 Raipur
11M6 Raisio
27H5 Rajahmundry
27G4 Rajkot
27H4 Rajshahi
23E6 Rakhiv
23G6 Rakitnoye
21K3 Rakovski
11O7 Rakvere
47L4 Raleigh
15C8 Rame Head
21L2 Râmnicu Sărat
21K2 Râmnicu Vâlcea
23H6 Ramon'
49D4 Ramona
37G3 Ramotswa
27G4 Rampur
14C4 Ramsey
48D2 Ramsey
15I7 Ramsgate
11N9 Ramygala
27H4 Ranaghat
54B4 Rancagua
55A3 Rancharia
27H4 Ranchi
17F3 Randalstown
11G8 Randers
10M4 Råneå
27I5 Rangoon
27H4 Rangpur
16E4 Rannoch, L.
29B7 Ranong
29B7 Rantauprapat
20C2 Rapallo
46G3 Rapid City
11N7 Rapla
6 Rarotonga *i.*
34D2 Ras Dejen *mt.*
11M9 Raseiniai
26D3 Rasht
11P9 Rasony
23I5 Rasskazovo
37I4 Ratanda
29B6 Rat Buri
13N4 Rathenow
17F3 Rathfriland
17F2 Rathlin Island
17D5 Rathluirc
27G5 Ratnagiri
23E6 Ratne
46G4 Raton
55C3 Raul Soares
11L6 Rauma
27H4 Raurkela
20E2 Ravenna
48A2 Ravenna
13L7 Ravensburg
27G3 Rawalpindi
13P5 Rawicz
46F3 Rawlins
54C6 Rawson
27H5 Rayagada
30C2 Raychikhinsk
15H7 Rayleigh
42E4 Raymond Terrace
46H6 Raymondville
21L3 Razgrad
21J4 Razlog
15G7 Reading
48D2 Reading
33F2 Rebiana Sand Sea *des.*
40E6 Recherche, Archipelago of the *is*
23F5 Rechytsa
53L5 Recife
37G8 Recife, Cape
13K5 Recklinghausen
54E3 Reconquista
47I5 Red *r.*
48D2 Red Bank
46C3 Red Bluff
14F4 Redcar
41I6 Red Cliffs
44G4 Red Deer
46C3 Redding
15F6 Redditch
53H5 Redenção
49D3 Redlands
47H3 Red Oak
49C4 Redondo Beach
34D1 Red Sea
47I3 Red Wing
49A2 Redwood City
17E4 Ree, Lough *l.*
49C2 Reedley
13N6 Regensburg
32D2 Reggane
20F5 Reggio di Calabria
20D2 Reggio nell'Emilia
21K1 Reghin
44H4 Regina
55B4 Registro
36C2 Rehoboth
48D3 Rehoboth Bay
15G7 Reigate
18G2 Reims
13M4 Reinbek
45H4 Reindeer Lake
19G6 Relizane
13L3 Rendsburg
16E5 Renfrew
54B4 Rengo
21M2 Reni
41I6 Renmark
18D2 Rennes
46D4 Reno
32C3 Réo
17E4 Republic of Ireland
36F5 Republic of South Africa
55A4 Reserva
54E3 Resistencia
21I2 Reșița
55C2 Resplendor
50F6 Retalhuleu
14G5 Retford
21K7 Rethymno
7 Réunion *terr.*
19G3 Reus
13L6 Reutlingen
50B5 Revillagigedo, Islas *is*
27H4 Rewa
46E3 Rexburg
10□1 Reykjavík
46H6 Reynosa
11O8 Rēzekne
13K4 Rheine
13K5 Rhine *r.*
18I2 Rhine *r.*
47J2 Rhinelander
20C2 Rho
48F2 Rhode Island *state*
21M6 Rhodes
21M6 Rhodes *i.*
21J4 Rhodope Mountains
18G5 Rhône *r.*
14D5 Rhyl
53I5 Riachão
55C1 Riacho de Santana
55C1 Riacho dos Machados
55A1 Rialma
49D3 Rialto
27J6 Riau, Kepulauan *is*
54F2 Ribas do Rio Pardo
14E5 Ribble *r.*
11F9 Ribe
55B3 Ribeirão Preto
52E6 Riberalta
23F7 Rîbnița
37K5 Richards Bay
46E4 Richfield
46D2 Richland
42E4 Richmond
47K4 Richmond
47K4 Richmond
48C4 Richmond
49A2 Richmond
47L3 Rideau Lakes
49D3 Ridgecrest
13N5 Riesa
11L9 Rietavas
20E3 Rieti
11N8 Rīga
11M8 Riga, Gulf of
11N6 Riihimäki
32D3 Rijau
20F2 Rijeka
31F5 Rikuzen-takata
21J3 Rila *mts*
18G4 Rillieux-la-Pape
13R6 Rimavská Sobota
20E2 Rimini
45L5 Rimouski
11F8 Ringkøbing
11G9 Ringsted
15F8 Ringwood
42B6 Ringwood
55A4 Rio Azul
52C4 Riobamba
55C3 Rio Bonito
52E6 Rio Branco
54F2 Rio Brilhante
55C3 Rio Casca
55B3 Rio Claro
54D4 Río Cuarto
55C1 Rio de Contas
55C3 Rio de Janeiro
55C3 Rio de Janeiro *state*
55A4 Rio do Sul
54C8 Río Gallegos
50D4 Río Grande
54C8 Río Grande
54F4 Rio Grande
46H6 Rio Grande *r.*
46H6 Rio Grande City
55A5 Rio Grande do Sul *state*
52D1 Ríohacha
52C5 Rioja
50G4 Río Lagartos
53K5 Rio Largo
18F4 Riom
55C3 Rio Novo
55C1 Rio Pardo de Minas
55C3 Rio Preto
46F4 Rio Rancho
55A2 Rio Verde
53H7 Rio Verde de Mato Grosso
23F6 Ripky
15F5 Ripley
14F4 Ripon
15D7 Risca
11F7 Risør
20D2 Riva del Garda
51G6 Rivas
54E4 Rivera
32C4 River Cess
48E2 Riverhead
49D4 Riverside
45L5 Riverview
45L5 Rivière-du-Loup
23E6 Rivne
35C5 Rivungo
34E1 Riyadh
23I8 Rize
15G6 Roade
51L5 Road Town
18G3 Roanne
48B4 Roanoke
47L4 Roanoke Rapids
48B2 Roaring Spring
51G5 Roatán
36D7 Robertson
32B4 Robertsport
45K5 Roberval
40D5 Robinson Range *hills*
41I6 Robinvale
54F4 Rocha
14E5 Rochdale
18D4 Rochefort
22I3 Rochegda
15H7 Rochester
42B6 Rochester
47I3 Rochester
48C1 Rochester
48F1 Rochester
15H7 Rochford
47J3 Rockford
41K4 Rockhampton
40D6 Rockingham
47I3 Rock Island
48F1 Rockland
48C3 Rockville
46F3 Rocky Mountains
55A4 Rodeio
18F4 Rodez
22I4 Rodniki
12I5 Roeselare
49A1 Rohnert Park
13N6 Rohrbach in Oberösterreich
11M8 Roja
54D4 Rojas
11N9 Rokiškis
23E6 Rokytne
55A3 Rolândia
52F6 Rolim de Moura
47I4 Rolla
21L1 Roman
21K2 Romania
18G4 Romans-sur-Isère
29E6 Romblon
20E4 Rome
47J5 Rome
48D1 Rome
15H7 Romford
18F2 Romilly-sur-Seine
23G6 Romny
23J5 Romodanovo
18E3 Romorantin-Lanthenay
15F8 Romsey
19D5 Ronda
54F2 Rondon
53H7 Rondonópolis
11I9 Rønne
11I8 Ronneby
12J5 Roosendaal
18D4 Roquefort
46D5 Rosario
50C4 Rosario
52D1 Rosario
53J4 Rosário
54D4 Rosario
54F4 Rosário do Sul
53G6 Rosário Oeste
18C2 Roscoff
17D4 Roscommon
17E5 Roscrea
51L5 Roseau
46C3 Roseburg
47H6 Rosenberg
13N7 Rosenheim
20F3 Roseto degli Abruzzi
44H4 Rosetown
49B1 Roseville
42F1 Rosewood
36C4 Rosh Pinah
20D3 Rosignano Marittimo
21K2 Roșiori de Vede
11H9 Roskilde
23G5 Roslavl'
20G5 Rossano
32B3 Rosso
15E7 Ross-on-Wye
23H6 Rossosh'
56B4 Ross Sea
13N3 Rostock
22H4 Rostov
23H7 Rostov-na-Donu
10L4 Rosvik
46G5 Roswell
13M6 Roth
14F5 Rotherham
43F4 Rotorua
12J5 Rotterdam
13L6 Rottweil
18F1 Roubaix
15I9 Rouen
16F1 Rousay *i.*
10N3 Rovaniemi
23H6 Roven'ki
20D2 Rovereto
20D2 Rovigo
20E2 Rovinj
23J6 Rovnoye
15G6 Royston
21N1 Rozdil'na
23I5 Rtishchevo
15D6 Ruabon
43F5 Ruahine Range *mts*
34E2 Rub' al Khālī *des.*
24J4 Rubtsovsk
13Q5 Ruda Śląska
23F5 Rudnya
23J6 Rudnya
26F1 Rudnyy
24G1 Rudol'fa, Ostrov *i.*
35D4 Rufiji *r.*
54D4 Rufino
32B3 Rufisque
15F6 Rugby
15F6 Rugeley
13N3 Rügen *i.*
34C4 Ruhengeri
55C1 Rui Barbosa
35D4 Ruipa
50C4 Ruiz
11N8 Rūjiena
35D4 Rukwa, Lake
16C4 Rum *i.*
21H2 Ruma
34E1 Rumāh
33F4 Rumbek
35D5 Rumphi
14E5 Runcorn
35B5 Rundu
35D5 Rusape
21K3 Ruse
15G6 Rushden
42B6 Rushworth
47I4 Russellville
13L5 Rüsselsheim
24I3 Russian Federation
23J5 Russkiy Kameshkir
23J8 Rust'avi
37H3 Rustenburg
47I5 Ruston
42C6 Rutherglen
15D5 Ruthin
48E1 Rutland
22H5 Ruza
23J5 Ruzayevka
13Q6 Ružomberok
34C4 Rwanda
16D5 Ryan, Loch *b.*
23H5 Ryazan'
23I5 Ryazhsk
22H4 Rybinsk
22H4 Rybinskoye Vodokhranilishche *resr*
13Q5 Rybnik
23H5 Rybnoye
15F8 Ryde
15H8 Rye
23G6 Ryl'sk
23K7 Ryn-Peski *des.*
31B8 Ryukyu Islands
23D6 Rzeszów
23I5 Rzhaksa
22G4 Rzhev

S

13M5 Saale *r.*
13M5 Saalfeld
13K6 Saarbrücken
11M7 Saaremaa *i.*
10N3 Saarenkylä
10N5 Saarijärvi
13K6 Saarlouis
21H2 Šabac
19H3 Sabadell
31E6 Sabae
55C2 Sabará
33E2 Sabhā
46G6 Sabinas
46G6 Sabinas Hidalgo
45L5 Sable, Cape
32D3 Sabon Kafi
26E3 Sabzevār
21K2 Săcele
31C6 Sach'on
48F1 Saco
49B1 Sacramento
55B2 Sacramento
49B1 Sacramento *r.*
46F5 Sacramento Mountains
37H7 Sada
19F2 Sádaba
34E2 Şa'dah
32B3 Sadiola
23J7 Sadovoye
11G8 Sæby
11H7 Säffle
46F5 Safford
15H6 Saffron Walden
32C1 Safi
23G5 Safonovo
23G8 Safranbolu
31C6 Saga
31E6 Sagami-nada *g.*
27G4 Sagar
47K3 Saginaw
47K3 Saginaw Bay
19B5 Sagres
47K7 Sagua la Grande
19D2 Sahagún
32D3 Sahara *des.*
32C3 Sahel *reg.*
50D4 Sahuayo
19G6 Saïda
31D6 Saijō
31C6 Saiki
11P6 Saimaa *l.*
15B8 St Agnes
15G7 St Albans
18F3 St-Amand-Montrond
16G4 St Andrews
51I5 St Ann's Bay
45M4 St Anthony
42A6 St Arnaud
47K6 St Augustine
15C8 St Austell
51L5 St-Barthélemy *i.*
14D4 St Bees Head
15B7 St Bride's Bay
18C2 St-Brieuc
48B1 St Catharines
18G4 St-Chamond
47I4 St Charles
48C3 St Charles
47K3 St Clair, Lake
18G3 St-Claude
15C7 St Clears
47I2 St Cloud
15B7 St David's Head
18H2 St-Dié
18G2 St-Dizier
44D3 St Elias Mountains
18D4 Saintes
18G4 St-Étienne
15I9 St-Étienne-du-Rouvray
18E5 St-Gaudens
42D2 St George
49F2 St George
51L6 St George's
17F6 St George's Channel
18I3 St Gotthard Pass
49A1 St Helena
6 St Helena and Dependencies *terr.*
14E5 St Helens
41J8 St Helens
46C2 St Helens, Mount *vol.*
15E9 St Helier
15B8 St Ives
15G6 St Ives
45K5 St-Jean, Lac *l.*
47M2 St-Jérôme
45L5 Saint John
45M5 St John's
51L5 St John's
47M3 St Johnsbury
47I4 St Joseph
15B8 St Just
12C2 St Kilda *is*
51L5 St Kitts and Nevis
53H2 St-Laurent-du-Maroni
45L5 St Lawrence *inlet*
45L5 St Lawrence, Gulf of
44B3 St Lawrence Island
18D2 St-Lô
32B3 St-Louis
47I4 St Louis
51L6 St Lucia
16□ St Magnus Bay
18C2 St-Malo
18C2 St-Malo, Golfe de *g.*
51J5 St-Marc
51L5 St-Martin *i.*
18D4 St-Médard-en-Jalles
18C3 St-Nazaire
15G6 St Neots
18H2 St-Nicolas-de-Port
18F1 St-Omer
47I3 St Paul
15E9 St Peter Port
11Q7 St Petersburg
47K6 St Petersburg
45M5 St-Pierre
45M5 St Pierre and Miquelon *terr.*
18F2 St-Quentin
48A1 St Thomas
18H5 St-Tropez
15F9 St-Vaast-la-Hougue
41H7 St Vincent, Gulf
51L6 St Vincent and the Grenadines
31D6 Sakaide
26D4 Sakākah
21L4 Sakar *mts*
21N4 Sakarya
32C4 Sakassou
31E5 Sakata
31B4 Sakchu
30F2 Sakhalin *i.*
30F2 Sakhalinskaya Oblast' *admin. div.*
30F1 Sakhalinskiy Zaliv *b.*
37I4 Sakhile
23J8 Şäki
11M9 Šakiai
29C6 Sakon Nakhon
31F6 Sakura
23G7 Saky
11J7 Sala
11N8 Salacgrīva
54E3 Saladas
26E5 Şalālah
19D3 Salamanca
50D4 Salamanca
11L8 Salantai
11N8 Salaspils
11N9 Šalčininkai
19D2 Saldaña
36C7 Saldanha
11M8 Saldus
42C7 Sale
24H3 Salekhard
27G5 Salem
46C3 Salem
48A2 Salem
48A4 Salem
48F1 Salem
20F4 Salerno
20F4 Salerno, Golfo di *g.*
14E5 Salford
13Q6 Salgótarján
53K5 Salgueiro
21M5 Salihli
11O10 Salihorsk
35D5 Salima
46H4 Salina
50E5 Salina Cruz
49B2 Salinas
50D4 Salinas
52B4 Salinas
55C2 Salinas
49B2 Salinas *r.*
53I4 Salinópolis
15F7 Salisbury
48D3 Salisbury
15E7 Salisbury Plain
22F3 Salmi
44G4 Salmon Arm
46D3 Salmon River Mountains
11M6 Salo
18G5 Salon-de-Provence
23I7 Sal'sk
54C2 Salta
15C8 Saltash
16E5 Saltcoats
46G6 Saltillo
46E3 Salt Lake City
54E4 Salto
55B3 Salto
49E4 Salton Sea *salt l.*
55D1 Salvador
34F1 Salwah
27I4 Salween *r.*
13N7 Salzburg
13M4 Salzgitter
29E6 Samar *i.*
23K5 Samara
29D8 Samarinda
26F3 Samarkand
33H1 Sāmarrā'
27H4 Sambalpur
35F5 Sambava
23D6 Sambir
54E5 Samborombón, Bahía *b.*
31C5 Samch'ŏk
34D4 Same
34E1 Samīrah
23J8 Şämkir
39I3 Samoa
20F2 Samobor
22I3 Samoded
21J3 Samokov
21L6 Samos *i.*
23I6 Samoylovka
29D8 Sampit
23H8 Samsun
32C3 San
34E2 San'ā'
33H1 Sanandaj
46G5 San Angelo
46H6 San Antonio
54B4 San Antonio
54D6 San Antonio Oeste
20E3 San Benedetto del Tronto
49D3 San Bernardino
54B4 San Bernardo
46G6 San Buenaventura
52E2 San Carlos
54B5 San Carlos
54B6 San Carlos de Bariloche
54D5 San Carlos de Bolívar
49D4 San Clemente
52D2 San Cristóbal
54D4 San Cristóbal
50F5 San Cristóbal de las Casas
51I4 Sancti Spíritus
29D7 Sandakan
21J4 Sandanski
16G1 Sanday *i.*
15E5 Sandbach
11G7 Sandefjord
49D4 San Diego
21N5 Sandıklı
11D7 Sandnes
10H3 Sandnessjøen
23D6 Sandomierz
20E2 San Donà di Piave
27I5 Sandoway
46D2 Sandpoint
10□2 Sandur
47K3 Sandusky
11G7 Sandvika
11J6 Sandviken
46E5 San Felipe
52E1 San Felipe
54B4 San Felipe
19C5 San Fernando
29E6 San Fernando
46H7 San Fernando
49C3 San Fernando
51L6 San Fernando
54B4 San Fernando
52E2 San Fernando de Apure
47K6 Sanford
47L4 Sanford
48F1 Sanford
49A2 San Francisco
54D4 San Francisco
49A2 San Francisco Bay *inlet*
19G4 San Francisco Javier
49C3 San Gabriel Mountains
25N3 Sangar
49C2 Sanger
20G5 San Giovanni in Fiore
29D7 Sangkulirang
27G5 Sangli
32E4 Sangmélima
46F4 Sangre de Cristo Range *mts*
52E6 San Ignacio
52F7 San Ignacio
49D4 San Jacinto
31E5 Sanjō
49B1 San Joaquin *r.*
49B2 San Joaquin Valley
54C7 San Jorge, Golfo de *g.*
29E6 San Jose
49B2 San Jose
51H7 San José
29E6 San Jose de Buenavista
46E6 San José de Comondú
52D3 San José del Guaviare
54E4 San José de Mayo
51K5 San Juan
54C4 San Juan
54E3 San Juan Bautista
52E2 San Juan de los Morros
46F4 San Juan Mountains
54D4 San Justo
18I3 Sankt Gallen
13O6 Sankt Pölten
13O7 Sankt Veit an der Glan
33G1 Şanlıurfa
52C3 San Lorenzo
54D4 San Lorenzo
19C5 Sanlúcar de Barrameda
50C4 San Lucas
49E4 San Luis
54C4 San Luis
49B3 San Luis Obispo
50D4 San Luis Potosí
46H6 San Marcos
20E3 San Marino
20E3 San Marino *country*
54C4 San Martín
54B6 San Martín de los Andes
49A2 San Mateo
54D6 San Matías, Golfo *g.*
50G6 San Miguel
54C3 San Miguel de Tucumán
55A1 San Miguel do Araguaia
32C4 Sanniquellie
23D6 Sanok
32C4 San-Pédro
54D2 San Pedro
49C4 San Pedro
46G6 San Pedro de las Colonias
51K5 San Pedro de Macorís
54E2 San Pedro de Ycuamandyyú
50G5 San Pedro Sula
16F5 Sanquhar
49A2 San Rafael
54C4 San Rafael
20B3 San Remo
50G6 San Salvador
54C2 San Salvador de Jujuy
32D3 Sansanné-Mango
19E3 San Sebastián de los Reyes
20F4 San Severo
49D4 Santa Ana
50G6 Santa Ana
46F6 Santa Bárbara
49C3 Santa Barbara
55C2 Santa Bárbara
49B3 Santa Barbara Channel
55B3 Santa Bárbara d'Oeste
49D4 Santa Catalina, Gulf of
55A4 Santa Catarina *state*
49B2 Santa Clara
51I4 Santa Clara
49C3 Santa Clarita
49A2 Santa Cruz
52F7 Santa Cruz
53K5 Santa Cruz
55D2 Santa Cruz Cabrália
51I4 Santa Cruz del Sur
32B2 Santa Cruz de Tenerife
54F3 Santa Cruz do Sul
46F4 Santa Fe
54D4 Santa Fé
55A3 Santa Fé do Sul
53I4 Santa Helena
55A2 Santa Helena de Goiás
53I4 Santa Inês
32□ Santa Maria
49B3 Santa Maria
53H4 Santa Maria
54F3 Santa Maria
55B1 Santa Maria da Vitória
55C2 Santa Maria do Suaçuí
55C3 Santa Maria Madalena
52D1 Santa Marta
49C3 Santa Monica
49C4 Santa Monica Bay
55C1 Santana
19E2 Santander
20C5 Sant'Antioco
53J4 Santa Quitéria
19B4 Santarém
53H4 Santarém
49A1 Santa Rosa
54D5 Santa Rosa
54F3 Santa Rosa
50G6 Santa Rosa de Copán
46E6 Santa Rosalía
55A2 Santa Vitória
49D4 Santee
51H7 Santiago
51J5 Santiago
54B4 Santiago
54F3 Santiago
19B2 Santiago de Compostela
51I4 Santiago de Cuba
54D3 Santiago del Estero
19G3 Sant Jordi, Golf de *g.*
55D1 Santo Amaro
55C3 Santo Amaro de Campos
55A3 Santo Anastácio
55B3 Santo André
54F3 Santo Angelo
32D4 Santo António
55A3 Santo Antônio da Platina
55D1 Santo Antônio de Jesus
52E4 Santo Antônio do Içá
51K5 Santo Domingo
55B3 Santos
55C3 Santos Dumont
54E3 Santo Tomé
50G6 San Vicente
52C6 San Vicente de Cañete
29C6 Sanya
55B3 São Bernardo do Campo
54E3 São Borja
55B3 São Carlos
55B1 São Domingos
53H6 São Félix
55D1 São Félix
55C3 São Fidélis
55B1 São Francisco
55C1 São Francisco *r.*
55A5 São Francisco de Paula
55A4 São Francisco do Sul
54F4 São Gabriel
55C3 São Gonçalo
55B2 São Gonçalo do Abaeté
55B2 São Gonçalo do Sapucaí
55B2 São Gotardo
55C3 São João da Barra
55B3 São João da Boa Vista
19B3 São João da Madeira
55B1 São João da Ponte
55B3 São João del Rei
55C1 São João do Paraíso
55A5 São Joaquim
55B3 São Joaquim da Barra
55A4 São José
55A3 São José do Rio Preto
55B3 São José dos Campos
55A4 São José dos Pinhais
55A5 São Leopoldo
55B3 São Lourenço
53J4 São Luís
55A2 São Luís de Montes Belos
55A3 São Manuel
55D2 São Mateus
55A4 São Mateus do Sul
53J5 São Miguel do Tapuio
18G4 Saône *r.*
55B3 São Paulo
55A3 São Paulo *state*
52E4 São Paulo de Olivença
55C3 São Pedro da Aldeia
53J5 São Raimundo Nonato
55B2 São Romão
55B3 São Roque
55B3 São Sebastião
55B2 São Sebastião do Paraíso
53H7 São Simão
55B3 São Simão
32D4 São Tomé
32D4 São Tomé and Príncipe
55B3 São Vicente
21N4 Sapanca
32C3 Sapouy
23I5 Sapozhok
30F4 Sapporo
33H1 Saqqez
29C6 Sara Buri
20H3 Sarajevo
24G4 Saraktash
23J5 Saransk
24G4 Sarapul
47K6 Sarasota
21M1 Sarata
46F3 Saratoga
49A2 Saratoga
23J6 Saratov
23J5 Saratovskoye Vodokhranilishche *resr*
26F4 Saravan
21L4 Saray
21M6 Sarayköy
20C4 Sardinia *i.*
26F3 Sar-e Pol
27G3 Sargodha
33E4 Sarh
26E3 Sārī
21M5 Sarıgöl
41J4 Sarina
33E2 Sarīr Tibesti *des.*
31B5 Sariwŏn
21M4 Sarıyer
27G2 Sarkand
21N5 Şarkikaraağaç
21L4 Şarköy
18I3 Sarnen
47K3 Sarnia
23E6 Sarny
21L4 Saros Körfezi *b.*
23I5 Sarova
11G7 Sarpsborg
18H2 Sarrebourg
20G1 Sárvár
31C6 Sasebo
44H4 Saskatchewan *prov.*
44H4 Saskatchewan *r.*
44H4 Saskatoon
37H4 Sasolburg
23I5 Sasovo
32C4 Sassandra
20C4 Sassari
13N3 Sassnitz
27G4 Satpura Range *mts*
23D7 Satu Mare
46F6 Saucillo
11E7 Sauðárkrókur
26D4 Saudi Arabia
45J5 Sault Sainte Marie
47K2 Sault Sainte Marie
26F1 Saumalkol'
18D3 Saumur
35C4 Saurimo
20I2 Sava *r.*
32D4 Savalou
47K5 Savannah
47K5 Savannah *r.*
29C6 Savannakhét
51I5 Savanna-la-Mar
10L5 Sävar
21L5 Savaştepe
20C2 Savona
10P6 Savonlinna
11I8 Sävsjö
33G2 Sawhāj
42F3 Sawtell
40E1 Sawu, Laut *sea*
14G5 Saxilby
15I6 Saxmundham
32D3 Say
34F2 Sayhūt
27K2 Saynshand
48D2 Sayreville
16F2 Scapa Flow *inlet*
14G4 Scarborough
45K5 Scarborough
51L6 Scarborough
18I3 Schaffhausen
13N6 Schärding
48E1 Schenectady
20D2 Schio
13L3 Schleswig
13M4 Schönebeck (Elbe)
13L7 Schwäbische Alb *mts*
13L6 Schwäbisch Hall
13N6 Schwandorf
13N5 Schwarzenberg
13M7 Schwaz
13O4 Schwedt an der Oder
13M5 Schweinfurt
13M4 Schwerin
18I3 Schwyz
20E6 Sciacca
20F6 Scicli
16F4 Scone
42E4 Scone
16F3 Scotland *admin. div.*
46G3 Scottsbluff
47J5 Scottsboro
48D2 Scranton
14G5 Scunthorpe
21H3 Scutari, Lake
15H8 Seaford
14G4 Seamer
47I4 Searcy
46C2 Seattle
32D3 Sebba
21J2 Sebeş
11P8 Sebezh
47K6 Sebring
44F5 Sechelt
52B5 Sechura
37I4 Secunda
27G5 Secunderabad
47I4 Sedalia
18G2 Sedan
20B6 Sedrata
11M9 Šeduva
32B4 Sefadu
37H2 Sefare
21L5 Seferihisar
27I6 Segamat
22G3 Segezha
32C3 Ségou
19D3 Segovia
32C4 Séguéla
46H6 Seguin
10M5 Seinäjoki
15H9 Seine *r.*
15G9 Seine, Baie de *b.*
18F2 Seine, Val de *valley*
11M9 Sejny
29C8 Sekayu
32C4 Sekondi
34D2 Sek'ot'a
14F5 Selby
35C6 Selebi-Phikwe
21M5 Selendi
32B3 Sélibabi
22G4 Selizharovo
16G5 Selkirk
45I4 Selkirk
44G4 Selkirk Mountains
47J5 Selma
49C2 Selma
23G5 Sel'tso
22L4 Selty
52D5 Selvas *reg.*
44E3 Selwyn Mountains
29D8 Semarang

23G5 Semenivka
22J4 Semenov
23I7 Semikarakorsk
23H6 Semiluki
46G5 Seminole
27H1 Semipalatinsk
26I3 Semnān
52E5 Sena Madureira
31C7 Sendai
31F5 Sendai
32B3 Senegal
13D5 Senftenberg
34D4 Sengerema
23K5 Sengiley
53J6 Senhor do Bonfim
20E3 Senigallia
18F2 Senlis
37H6 Senqu r.
18F2 Sens
50G6 Sensuntepeque
27I2 Senta
31B5 Seoul
31B5 Sep'o
45L4 Sept-Îles
23I6 Serafimovich
29E8 Seram i.
29F8 Seram, Laut sea
21I2 Serbia and Montenegro
23J5 Serdobsk
29C7 Seremban
35D5 Serenje
22J5 Sergach
22H4 Sergiyev Posad
33G1 Serik
22K4 Sernur
24H4 Serov
37H2 Serowe
23H5 Serpukhov
55C3 Serra
53K5 Serra Talhada
21J4 Serres
53K6 Serrinha
55C2 Sèrro
55A3 Sertanópolis
55B3 Sertãozinho
11Q6 Sertolovo
35C6 Serule
20C2 Sestri Levante
11P6 Sestroretsk
18F5 Sète
55B2 Sete Lagoas
32D1 Sétif
31C6 Seto
32C1 Settat
14E4 Settle
19B4 Setúbal
19B4 Setúbal, Baía de b.
23J8 Sevan
23J8 Sevan, Lake
23G7 Sevastopol'
15H7 Sevenoaks
15E7 Severn r.
22I2 Severnaya Dvina r.
25L1 Severnaya Zemlya is
24H3 Severnyy
22H2 Severodvinsk
10R2 Severomorsk
24K3 Severo-Yeniseyskiy
23H7 Severskaya
23I7 Severskiy Donets r.
52C3 Sevilla
19D5 Seville
44D3 Seward
7 Seychelles
25Q3 Seymchan
47J4 Seymour
21K2 Sfântu Gheorghe
20D7 Sfax
15E7 Shaftesbury
27H4 Shahdol
26E3 Shahr-e Kord
22G4 Shakhovskaya
26F3 Shakhrisabz
23I7 Shakhty
22J4 Shakhun'ya
32D4 Shaki
22I3 Shalakusha
23J8 Shali
26E2 Shalkar
46G4 Shamrock
28E4 Shandong Bandao pen.
28E4 Shanghai
30B3 Shangzhi
30B3 Shanhetun
17D5 Shannon est.
17D5 Shannon r.
17C5 Shannon, Mouth of the
28D5 Shantou
27K4 Shaoyang
16G1 Shapinsay i.
33H2 Shaqrā'
27I4 Sharjah
11Q9 Sharkawshchyna
40C5 Shark Bay
48A2 Sharon
22J4 Shar'ya
34D3 Shashemenē
23J5 Shatki
23I5 Shatsk
23H5 Shatura
47J3 Shawano
47H4 Shawnee
23H5 Shchekino
22L2 Shchel'yayur
23H6 Shchigry
23F6 Shchors
11N10 Shchuchyn
23H6 Shebekino
26F3 Sheberghān
47J3 Sheboygan
37J3 Shebunino
15H7 Sheerness
14F5 Sheffield
22H4 Sheksna
41I2 Shelburne Bay
47J4 Shelbyville
48B3 Shenandoah Mountains
32D4 Shendam
22I3 Shenkursk
30C3 Shenshu
23I5 Shentala
30A4 Shenyang
23E6 Shepetivka
42B6 Shepparton
15H7 Sheppey, Isle of
45K5 Sherbrooke
46F3 Sheridan
47H5 Sherman
12J5 's-Hertogenbosch
15F5 Sherwood Forest reg.
30C2 Sheryshevo
16☐ Shetland i.
46H2 Sheyenne
16D4 Shiel, Loch l.
27K3 Shijiazhuang
31C6 Shikoku i.
14F4 Shildon
27I4 Shilka
23I5 Shilovo
31E6 Shimada
30B1 Shimanovsk
31C6 Shimonoseki

16E2 Shin, Loch l.
48A3 Shinnston
34D4 Shinyanga
31F5 Shiogama
26E4 Shīrāz
27K3 Shiyan
27J3 Shizunai
31E6 Shizuoka
21H3 Shkodër
31D6 Shōbara
37H2 Shoshong
23G6 Shostka
23I7 Shpakovskoye
23F6 Shpola
47I5 Shreveport
15E6 Shrewsbury
30A1 Shuangcheng
30I2 Shuangliao
47N3 Shukowegan
30B3 Shulan
21L3 Shumen
11K5 Shumilina
23G5 Shumyachi
22G3 Shuya
22I4 Shuya
27F2 Shymkent
23G7 Shyroke
11M9 Šiauliai
37I2 Sibasa
20F3 Šibenik
25M3 Siberia reg.
26F4 Sibi
34B4 Sibiti
21K2 Sibiu
27I6 Sibolga
16D3 Sibsagar
27J4 Sichuan Pendi basin
20E6 Sicilian Channel
20F5 Sicily i.
52D6 Sicuani
19H6 Sidi Aïssa
19G5 Sidi Ali
19F6 Sidi Bel Abbès
20C7 Sidi Bouzid
32B2 Sidi Ifni
32C1 Sidi Kacem
15H6 Sidlaw Hills
15D8 Sidmouth
46G2 Sidney
46G3 Sidney
47K3 Sidney
33G1 Sidon
11M10 Siedlce
13L5 Siegen
13Q5 Sieradz
10O5 Siilinjärvi
27G4 Sikar
32C3 Sikasso
47J4 Sikeston
11M9 Šilalė
27I4 Silchar
21M4 Šile
20C6 Šiliana
33G1 Silifke
21L2 Silistra
21M4 Silivri
11I6 Siljan l.
11F8 Silkeborg
11O7 Sillamäe
11L9 Šilutė
55A2 Silvânia
46F5 Silver City
48C3 Silver Spring
21M5 Simav
48A1 Simcoe
45K5 Simcoe, Lake
23H7 Simferopol'
49B1 Simi Valley
34D3 Simi?
21J1 Şimleu Silvaniei
53J5 Simplício Mendes
41H4 Simpson Desert
11J9 Simrishamn
52C2 Sincelejo
13L6 Sindelfingen
21M5 Sîndirgi
32D3 Sindor
32C3 Sines
22I4 Sinfra
33G3 Singa
32C3 Singapore
32D3 Singapore country
35D4 Singida
29C7 Singkawang
42E4 Singleton
20C4 Siniscola
29E8 Sinjai
15F6 Sinnamary
23B8 Sinop
53G6 Sinop
30B4 Sinp'a
31B5 Sinp'o
26F3 Sheberghān
47J3 Sheberghān

11H7 Skara
13R5 Skarżysko-Kamienna
13Q6 Skawina
14H5 Skegness
10L4 Skelleftå
10L4 Skelleftehamn
14E5 Skelmersdale
11G7 Ski
11F7 Skien
13R5 Skierniewice
20B6 Skikda
14E5 Skipton
11F8 Skive
11F9 Skjern
23H5 Skopin
21I4 Skopje
11H7 Skövde
30A1 Skovorodino
12I4 Skuodas
11H9 Skurup
11J6 Skutskär
16C3 Skye i.
21K5 Skyros
11G9 Slagelse
11P7 Slantsy
21K2 Slatina
18D4 Slave Coast
32D4 Slave Coast
24I4 Slavgorod
20I2 Slavonski Brod
23E6 Slavuta
23F6 Slavutych
30C4 Slavyanka
23H7 Slavyansk-na-Kubani
21L3 Slawno
15G5 Sleaford
16D3 Sleat, Sound of sea chan.
17E5 Slieve Bloom Mts hills
17G3 Slieve Donard hill
17D3 Sligo
17D3 Sligo Bay
20D7 Slippery Rock
48A2 Slippery Rock
21L3 Sliven
23I8 Slobodskoy
21L2 Slobozia
11N10 Slonim
15G7 Slough
13Q6 Slovakia
20I1 Slovenia
23H6 Slovenj Gradec
23H6 Slov"yans'k
13P3 Slupsk
11Q10 Slutsk
27J1 Slyudyanka
45L4 Smallwood Reservoir
11P9 Smalyavichy
11O9 Smarhon'
21I2 Smederevo
21I2 Smederevska Palanka
30D2 Smidovich
23F6 Smila
41J8 Smithton
42F3 Smithtown
23G5 Smolensk
21K4 Smolyan
21K4 Smolyan
21K1 Smyadovo
46D2 Snake r.
46E3 Snake River Plain
39G6 Snares Islands
13I4 Sneek
15H6 Snettisham
14E3 Snizort, Loch b.
43E4 Snowdon mt.
42D6 Snowy r.
42C6 Snowy Mountains
46G5 Snyder
35E5 Soanierana-Ivongo
33G1 Silistra (?)
21L2 Sobinka
53I4 Sobral
22K4 Sochi
30F2 Sochi
31B5 Söch'ŏn
1107 Society Islands
24H3 Socorro
52D2 Socorro
55B3 Socorro
26E5 Socotra i.
19E3 Spain
15G6 Sodankylä
11J6 Söderhamn
11J7 Söderköping
46D4 Södertälje
21H6 Sodo
21I3 Sofia
11D6 Sofiyivka
41H4 Simpson Desert
1119 Šimonys
52C2 Sindal (?)
13L6 Sindelfingen
21M5 Sindirgi
31C5 Sindor
32C4 Sines
32G3 Sinfra
30A4 Singa
2113 Singapore
53J5 Simplício Mendes
35D4 Singida
35D5 Singkawang
42E4 Singleton
23I7 Siniscola
29E8 Sinjai
15I6 Sinnamary
26I4 Sinop
26I4 Sinop
10J5 Sinsang
13M5 Sinsang
3084 Songhua Hu resr
26I3 Songjianghe
29C7 Songkhla
31B5 Sŏngnam
31B5 Sŏngnam
13I6 Songo
30A3 Songyuan
3082 Songo
37I5 Son La
31C6 Sonmiani
31B5 Sŏnch'ŏn
32G5 Sonneberg
26E4 Sonora r.
46C5 Sonoran Desert
50G6 Sonsonate
13Q3 Sopot

21K3 Sopot
20G1 Sopron
20E4 Sora
10J5 Söråker
47M2 Sorel
19E3 Soria
23F6 Soroca
29E6 Sorong
34D3 Soroti
20F4 Sorrento
29E6 Sorsogon
10O6 Sortavala
31B5 Sōsan
37I3 Soshanguve
22L3 Sosnogorsk
23I5 Sosnovka
11P7 Sosnovyy Bor
13Q5 Sosnowiec
15I9 Sotteville-lès-Rouen
32C4 Soubré
51L6 Soufrière
51L6 Soufrière vol.
19G6 Sougueur
20B6 Souk Ahras
32C1 Souk el Arbaâ du Rharb
18D4 Soulac-sur-Mer
46F3 Soure
19H5 Sour el Ghozlane
53K5 Sousa
20D7 Sousse
20D7 Sousse
15F8 Southam
14F5 Southampton
14F5 South Anston
37I5 South Australia state
46G3 South Bend
47J3 South Bend
47K5 South Carolina state
29D6 South China Sea
46G3 South Dakota state
15G8 South Downs hills
37G3 South-East admin. dist.
15H7 Southend-on-Sea
36G3 Southern admin. dist.
43C6 Southern Alps mts
40C7 Southern Ocean
16E5 Southern Uplands hills
54I8 South Georgia i.
54I8 South Georgia and South Sandwich Islands terr.
16B3 South Harris pen.
43D7 South Island
31B5 South Korea
49B1 South Lake Tahoe
15F8 Southminster
48C3 South Mountains hills
41L5 South Pacific Ocean
14D5 Southport
16G2 South Ronaldsay i.
49A2 South San Francisco
14F3 South Shields
43E4 South Taranaki Bight b.
16B3 South Uist i.
43A8 South West Cape
48A1 Southwold
15I6 Stratford
15F6 Stratford-upon-Avon
16F3 Strathspey valley
15C8 Stratton
13N6 Straubing
40G6 Streaky Bay
15E7 Street
21J2 Strehaia
11N8 Strenči
20F5 Stromboli, Isola i.
16G1 Stornoway
11G7 Strömstad
16G1 Stronsay i.
15E7 Stroud
11F8 Strugi-Krasnyye
22I4 Struma r.
21J4 Strumica
48A2 Struthers
36F5 Strydenburg
13R4 Stryy
13R4 Stupino
29E9 Sturt Creek watercourse
20H1 Sturt Plain
20G1 Sturt Stony Desert
21K3 Stutterheim
20G1 Stuttgart
23J8 Stuttgart
23J8 Tashir

25N4 Stanovoy Khrebet mts
42E2 Stanthorpe
47K5 Sumter
13R5 Starachowice
22F4 Staraya Russa
21K3 Stara Zagora
13O4 Stargard
13O4 Starogard Gdański
22G4 Staritsa
47J5 Starkville
23H6 Starobil's'k
23E6 Starokostyantyniv
23H7 Starominskaya
23H7 Staroshcher-binovskaya
23F5 Staryya Darohi
13O5 Stary Oskol
23I5 Stavropol'
23I7 Stavropol'skaya Vozvyshennost' hills
46F3 Steamboat Springs
10G4 Steinkjer
36C5 Steinkopf
36D7 Stellenbosch
13M4 Stendal
11G7 Stenungsund
46H5 Stephenville
23J6 Stepnoye
37I5 Sterkfontein Dam resr
46G3 Sterling
24G4 Sterlitamak
48A2 Steubenville
15G7 Stevenage
36E7 Steytlerville
13N6 Steyr
44E4 Stikine Plateau
15G8 Stillwater
46G4 Stillwater
15G6 Stilton
21J4 Štip
16F4 Stirling
10G5 Stjørdalshalsen
11K7 Stockholm
48A2 Stockport
49B2 Stockton
14F4 Stockton-on-Tees
14F4 Stokesley
14F4 Stoke-on-Trent
20G3 Stolac
11O11 Stolin
15E6 Stone
16G4 Stonehaven
16B2 Stornoway
23E6 Storozhynets'
46H3 Storm Lake
47H3 Storm Lake
15H6 Stowmarket
17E3 Strabane
13N3 Strakonice
49A2 South San Francisco (?)
36D8 Strand
43E4 Strangford Lough inlet
16D6 Stranraer
18H2 Strasbourg
42C6 Stratford
48A1 Stratford
15F6 Stratford-upon-Avon
16F3 Strathspey valley
15C8 Stratton
13N6 Straubing
40G6 Streaky Bay
15E7 Street
21J2 Strehaia
11N8 Strenči
20F5 Stromboli, Isola i.
16G1 Strömstad
16G1 Stronsay i.
15E7 Stroud
11F8 Strugi-Krasnyye
22I4 Struma r.
21J4 Strumica
48A2 Struthers
36F5 Strydenburg
13R4 Stryy
13R4 Stupino
21I1 Sturgis
29E9 Sturt Creek watercourse
20H1 Sturt Plain
20G1 Sturt Stony Desert
21K3 Stutterheim
13L6 Stuttgart
20G1 Szombathely

13P6 Šumperk
29M3 Sumqayıt
42B6 Sunbury
14F4 Sunderland
10J5 Sundsvall
10F5 Sunndalsøra
49A2 Sunnyvale
10O5 Suoyarvi
32C4 Sunyani
29D8 Surabaya
29D8 Surakarta
27G4 Surat
29B7 Surat Thani
23G5 Surazh
24I3 Surgut
21J3 Surdulica
24I3 Surgut
29C6 Surin
53G3 Suriname
21I4 Sürmene
23I6 Surovikino
23I5 Surskoye
10J1 Surtsey i.
29E8 Susaki
46C3 Susanville
25P3 Susuman
21M5 Susurluk
36E5 Sutherland
42E2 Sutherland
49B1 Sutter
15F6 Sutton Coldfield
15G7 Sutton in Ashfield
39I3 Suva
31E5 Suwa
21L2 Suwałki
31B5 Suwŏn
31E5 Suzaka
28E4 Suzhou
31E6 Suzuka
22I4 Suzdal'
24C2 Svalbard terr.
23H6 Svatove
22J3 Svecha
11O9 Svendborg
11G9 Svendborg
11F9 Svendborg
23I6 Sveti Nikole
11O11 Svetlaya
24J3 Svetlogorsk
29D7 Svetlograd
11L9 Svetlyy
23J6 Svetlyy Yar
21L4 Svilengrad
21K3 Svishtov
13P6 Svitavy
23F6 Svobodnyy
30C2 Svyatahorsk
23H5 Svyetlahorsk
39I3 Swains Island atoll
36B2 Swakopmund
15H6 Swale r.
15F8 Swanage
42A5 Swan Hill
15G7 Swanley
15D7 Swansea
15D7 Swansea Bay
37J4 Swaziland
1015 Sweden
46G5 Sweetwater
36E8 Swellendam
13P5 Świdnica
13O4 Świdwin
13O4 Świebodzin
13O4 Świecie
15D7 Swindon
13O4 Świnoujście
18I3 Switzerland
22G5 Sychevka
21J2 Sýyan (?)
11N8 Syeverodonets'k
22K3 Syktyvkar
27H4 Sylhet
34F1 Syltheim (?)
52F8 Tarija
27H3 Tarim Basin
21K2 Târgu Neamţ
21K2 Târgu Secuiesc
34F1 Tarif
27H3 Tarim Basin
21J3 Tarko-Sale
32C4 Tarkwa state
19E3 Tarragona
19G2 Tarrafal
21J3 Târnăveni
23D6 Tarnobrzeg
22J3 Tarnogskiy Gorodok
13P5 Tarnów
13R6 Tarnowskie Góry
13R6 Tarnowskie Góry
33G1 Tarsus
23D8 Tartăr
11N7 Tartu
23J8 Tashir

13P6 Šumperk (Tajikistan section)
27G3 Tajikistan
29B6 Tak
33H1 Takāb
31D6 Takahashi
31E5 Takaoka
43E3 Takapuna
31E5 Takasaki
31E6 Takefu
19G6 Takhemaret
27H3 Taklimakan Desert
30D4 Takum
23I6 Talachyn
19C4 Talavera de la Reina
54B5 Talca
54B5 Talcahuano
22H4 Taldom
27G2 Taldykorgan
47K5 Tallahassee
11N7 Tallinn
23F6 Tal'ne
23I6 Talovaya
11M8 Talsi
52C7 Taltal
32C3 Tamale
31D6 Tamano
32D2 Tamanrasset
32B3 Tambacounda
23I5 Tambov
23I6 Tamsweg
54B5 Tamel Aike (?)
50E5 Tampico
13N7 Tamsweg
11M9 Telšiai
21L6 Tilos i.
21L6 Tilos i.
41K5 Tin Can Bay
21K6 Tinos i.
21K6 Tinos i.
21L6 Tiranë (?)
19D3 Tiétar, Valle de valley
23G8 Tosya
47K5 Totness
32C4 Tot'ma
53G2 Totton
22I4 Tottori
21M2 Tigheciului, Dealurile hills
15F8 Tiptree
32E4 Tira

32C1 Taza
20B5 Tazmalt
23I8 T'bilisi
32D4 Tchamba
34B4 Tchibanga
33D4 Tcholliré
43A7 Te Anau, Lake
50F5 Teapa
27H3 Tébessa
32C3 Tébourba
49D4 Tecate
32C4 Techiman
54B6 Tecka
50D5 Tecomán
50D5 Tecpan
50D5 Tecuala
21L2 Tecuci
26F3 Tedzhen
50G4 Tekax
21L4 Tekirdağ
33G1 Tel Aviv-Yafo
54B5 Telêmaco Borba
12I5 Telšiai
32C3 Télimélé
32D3 Tillabéri
21L6 Tilos i.
11M9 Telšiai
21L3 Telavi
50O5 Telsen
13N7 Tamsweg
25N2 Tiksi
18G5 Tilburg
15H7 Tilbury
32C4 Tillabéri
27H3 Temirtau
23I5 Temnikov
22I2 Temora
45I5 Timmins
31E6 Temryuk
54B5 Temuco
52C4 Tena
29D7 Tenby Wells
15E6 Tenbury Wells
32C4 Ténéré reg.
32C2 Ténéré du Tafassâsset des.
32B2 Tenerife i.
32B2 Ténès
27K3 Tangshan
25P2 Tenkeli
31E6 Tenkodogo
29D7 Tanjay
29D7 Tanjungredeb
40G3 Tennant Creek
47J4 Tennessee r.
47J4 Tennessee state
50F5 Tenosique
47K5 Teotepeque (?)
29D7 Tanjungselor
32D3 Tanout
50F5 Teplice
23H5 Teploye
50G4 Tequila
32D3 Teramo
20E3 Teramo
19E6 Terebovlya
52C5 Teresópolis
32C3 Terekli-Mekteb
24H4 Teresina

27K3 Tianjin
30C4 Tianqiaoling
27J3 Tianshui
19G6 Tiaret
32C4 Tiassalé
32E4 Tibati
33D4 Tibesti mts
19D3 Tibet, Plateau of
15H7 Ticehurst
50G4 Ticul
11H7 Tidaholm
32B3 Tidjikja
30A4 Tieling
27G2 Tien Shan mts
11I6 Tierp
54C8 Tierra del Fuego, Isla Grande de i.
54C8 Tierra del Fuego, Arcipelago is
22F4 Tikhoretsk
22G3 Tikhvin
33H1 Tikrit
25N2 Tiksi
18G5 Tilburg
15H7 Tilbury
32C4 Tillabéri
21L6 Tilos i.
41K5 Tin Can Bay
21K6 Tinos i.
21K6 Tinos i.
26F3 Tin Can Bay
47K6 Titusville
21J4 Tisza r.
23H7 Titao
52E7 Titicaca, Lake
47J3 Traverse City
20F1 Tivoli
15D8 Tiverton
30H3 Tivoli (?)
50E4 Tizimín
19I5 Tizi Ouzou
30F2 Titao
38D2 Tlaxcala
19F6 Tlemcen
37G3 Tlokweng
46E3 Tremonton
20C4 Tobermory
52C5 Tobol r.
24H4 Tobol'sk
52D4 Tocantins state
50D4 Tocuyo (?)
55A1 Tocantins r.
47K5 Tocopilla
48D2 Toconao
15D7 Tocuwal
54D5 Togo
32D4 Togo
32D4 Toktogul
30E4 Tōkamachi
32D4 Tokat
30A4 Tokoname
11M9 Toksook Bay (?)
23H7 Tokushima
15H8 Tokuyama
32C4 Toyohashi
33G1 Tolbukhin
23I5 Tol'yatti
52F6 Tomakomai
50G4 Tomar
46G4 Tomaszów Lubelski
23D6 Tomaszów Mazowiecki
21M7 Tombigbee r.
21I5 Tombouctou
23J8 Tomelloso

27K3 Tianjin
19F4 Torrent
30C4 Torreón
27J3 Tianshui
19G6 Torres
32C4 Torres Novas
19B4 Torres Vedras
38E2 Torres Strait
32E4 Tibati
19F5 Torrevieja
10D7 Torridge r.
16D3 Torridon, Loch l.
50C2 Tortona
19G3 Tortosa
13O4 Toruń
17D2 Tory Island
17D2 Tory Sound sea chan.
22G4 Torzhok
31D6 Tosa
20C3 Toscano, Arcipelago is
23H5 Tosno
23G8 Tosya
47K5 Totness
32C4 Tot'ma
53G2 Totton
22I4 Tottori
50E4 Toluca
11H7 Tidaholm
32E4 Toumodi
23H7 Toul
18G5 Toulon
18E5 Toulouse
32C4 Toumodi
32D3 Tournai
12I5 Tournai
18G4 Tournon-sur-Rhône
43C7 Timaru
18E3 Tours
23H7 Timashevsk
32C3 Timbedgha
32C3 Timbédra
30F4 Towada
23D2 Timimoun
21I2 Timișoara
45I5 Timmins
31E6 Toyohashi
31E6 Toyonaka
31E6 Toyo-gawa
31E6 Toyooka
41K6 Tumby Bay
30C4 Tumen
32C3 Tumu
53G3 Tumucumaque, Serra hills
42D5 Tumut
15H7 Tunbridge Wells, Royal
42F4 Tuncurry
32D3 Tundun-Wada
35D5 Tungor
30F1 Tungor
20D6 Tunis
20D6 Tunis, Golfe de g.
32D1 Tunisia
32D1 Tunja
47J5 Tupelo
52E8 Tupiza
54C4 Tupungato, Cerro mt.
13P7 Turda
11J1 Turda
26F2 Turgay
21L3 Türgovishte
21L5 Turgutlu
34D3 Turkana, Lake salt l.
26F2 Turkestan
26E3 Turki
23I6 Turki
26F3 Turkmenabat
26E2 Turkmenbashi
26E2 Turkmenistan
51J4 Turks and Caicos Islands terr.
11M6 Turku
34D3 Turkwel watercourse

U
53K5 Ubá
55B2 Ubaitaba
55B1 Ubaté
34B4 Ubangi r.
31C6 Ube
19E4 Ubeda
55B2 Uberaba
29C6 Ubon Ratchathani
23I8 Ucar
52C4 Ucayali r.
13G4 Uckfield
15H8 Uckfield
30A4 Uda r.
11G7 Uddevalla
22I3 Udine
11G7 Uddevalla
29C6 Udon Thani
31E5 Udupi
31E5 Ueda
31C6 Ueno
13M4 Uelzen
34B4 Uíge
32B4 Ugab watercourse
34D3 Ugab
30F2 Uglegorsk
22H4 Uglich
22H4 Uglich
30F3 Uglovka (?)
12I5 Uherské Hradiště
34D3 Uijeongbu
11G7 Ujjain
12I5 Ujungpandang
25I2 Ukholovo
30G2 Ukhrul
10O5 Ukhta
30H2 Ukiah
30B4 Ukmergė
30A4 Ukraine
31E5 Ukraïins'k
11N10 Ukholovo
23I5 Ukholovo